Boston
Hartford
Providence
West Point
New Haven
Philadelphia
New York City
Flint
Detroit
Cleveland
Youngstown
Princeton
Toledo
Vermilion
Pittsburgh
Annapolis
Trenton
Chicago
Wilmington
Indianapolis
Morgantown
Baltimore
from Greece
Washington,
D.C.
Kansas City
St. Louis
Louisville
Frankfort
Warrensburg
Knoxville
Tulsa
Cherokee
Murphy
West Memphis
Tupelo
Dallas
Birmingham
Atlanta

THE FLAME

The Flame

---✳---

AN UNLIKELY PATRIOT
FINDS A COUNTRY
TO LOVE

STEVE BARR with **JOHN POPPY**

WILLIAM MORROW AND COMPANY, INC.

NEW YORK

Libary of Congress Cataloging-in-Publication Data

Barr, Steve.
   The flame: an unlikely patriot finds a country to love.
   1. Olympic torch relay—United States. 2. Olympic Games (23rd: 1984: Los Angeles, Calif.) I. Poppy, John. II. Title.
GV721.92.B37   1987   796.4'8   87-14152
ISBN 0-688-06557-0

Printed in the United States of America

First Edition

1 2 3 4 5 6 7 8 9 10

BOOK DESIGN BY ABE LERNER

To
the truest American I know,

MY MOM

ACKNOWLEDGMENTS

Our book itself stands as our thanks to the people who really brought it about—the many, many Americans who reminded us, at every turn, what our country is made of. You make us proud to be your neighbors.

It became a book because the people closest to us shared our desire to tell a true story about a rebirth of hope and purpose. Inadequate though our thanks will be, we still want to offer them.

Fred Hill loves writers and writing, and that may partly explain why he is an artist among literary agents; he brought us together, disciplined us through half a dozen early drafts, saw what we wanted to say, and made sure we never forgot it.

Pat Golbitz, our editor at William Morrow and Company, gave us something priceless: not only her firm, astute guidance, but also the patience to let us work out the results.

Julia Poppy is really the other author of every book John touches. She heard every story, then read every story, then re-read every story, until you'd think she'd have cut off our sandwiches and told us to come see her when we were done; instead, she not only kept us around, she kept responding, offering us the gift of her support and intelligence.

Diane Pierno: best friend for life. Walter Capps and Marie Cantlon: Thank you for your guidance. Rich Leib: for your constant encouragement. And the Hotel Wurzel.

Bill Mattman, who delivered the flame safely to Los Angeles, and Mr. Patience, Joel Fishman. The amazing Wally McGuire. And all of Steve's fellow torch rats: Bruce Berrol, Jeff Black, David Halliburton, Suzanne Lipps, Luanne Morikawa, Lynn Sadler, Kelly Sarber, Maris Segal, Larry Silman, Joyce Tate, Dan Triest, Jan Williams, Trish Wisner, and Mark Zangrando.

Finally, Peter Ueberroth, whose idea the torch run was, and AT&T and the Telephone Pioneers, without whose support the whole thing could not have happened.

To all our friends and allies, thank you. We will always be grateful.

CONTENTS

All the Best

"Look at that boy sweat. How far you suppose he's been running like that? Hot as it is . . ."

And how many hours had the people been waiting in this steaming sunshine on the shoulder of Highway 6? The glare was so bright by midmorning that you could barely see the flame of the torch. Sitting in the open car ahead of the runner, we heard the man in the short-sleeved white shirt and Purina Feeds cap talk to his friend as we passed. Along country roads where families came out to the end of a lane and smiled, and people stood scattered in twos and threes, you could sometimes pick out whole sentences like that. When the crowds got big, like the one we knew was going to meet us in the evening in Memphis, all you could hear in the overall uproar were fragments of words.

A lot of the comments we'd heard in the last few weeks were full of surprise. Someone would lean out for a better view and say, "Oh, look! It's a woman!" or, "Hey! It's a kid." I guess they had expectations about who was strong enough to carry the Olympic torch for a kilometer. The voice usually floated on a background of noise, the sounds of people up and down the line anticipating a great event. No national news organization had caught on yet to what was happening as the torch passed. Yet everywhere we took it, the local people knew.

Here, an uncommon hush seemed to have settled on the roadside. Maybe it was my imagination. I'd had expectations, too, about what would show up as we got ready to run across America. As I left California five months before, much of what I knew about my own country had been hearsay. I had approached the South warily, filled with prejudices that may or may not have been born of some truth. New friends and generous teamwork over the last few months had set many of those notions straight; still, violent things had happened in the past, some unexpected things had already happened elsewhere in our travels, and we never knew what would happen next.

Maybe we really had run into a stunned silence. Nobody actually said, "Look at the black guy." But the runner was Stan Harris, an AT&T man from Georgia, and Stan is black. This was Mississippi. The heat pressed down. An overpass stood up ahead. People had stopped their cars on it and climbed out to line the railing above Stan's path.

As the overpass loomed overhead, the hush seemed to deepen. If someone was going to do something, it could be now. Stan had the torch at shoulder height as he approached the shadow of the overpass. Then we heard something—a sharp "pop" that cut through the other sounds. Eyes searched for its source. Only it was no explosion. It was a single pair of hands, clapping. Other hands joined in. The solitary claps gathered into a patter of applause, like cool raindrops on the baking pavement. Then they grew to a roar, swelled by whistles and people shouting.

"Here it comes!"

"Go, U.S.A.! Go, U.S.A.!"

A guy on the overpass flailed a big American flag in figure-eights. Smaller flags fluttered as people waved them overhead and at arm's length in front. Stan Harris looked up and hefted the torch as high over his head as his arm would reach, acknowledging the people with thrusts to right and left.

"Way to go, man!" people yelled. "Looking good!"

"We're with you!"

People at ground level started breaking away from their places and running along in the heat, some clapping their hands over their heads as they kept pace.

"God bless America," a young woman called from the roadside, ten feet from Stan. "God bless you." Beside her, clutching the shoulder of a fourth- or fifth-grader, a young man stood absolutely still except for the hand waving his flag, tears streaming into his smile.

It was happening again. All the small feelings, mine included, were washing away in a surge of something none of us had expected and none of us, yet, could name. It was like seeing people you thought you knew, but hadn't really known, falling in love.

THE FLAME

1

High Hopes and Low Doubts

The sun warmed us for most of the morning. Around eleven, the roof of the student center slid a shadow across the ROTC sergeant's table; then the Iranian Students Against Khomeini's; then my table and its REGISTER TO VOTE sign.

"Think it's time to move?" I asked the sergeant.

"Where to?" he said, friendly enough, but looking as if he wondered what parts of our anatomy we were talking about moving—our feet, our minds, or what.

"Over there a couple of yards," I said. "So we can stay in the sun." We all nodded at each other, got up, and hauled our stuff a bit to the left.

Now we could go on being serious and comfortable at the same time. There is much to be said for seriousness. There is also something in the mind of a college sophomore that lets him figure he can do his best to save the world and his conscience and work on his tan at the same time.

Our move narrowed the corridor our fellow students had been using to dodge our offerings as they headed for the student store to buy blue books, magazines, and yogurt-covered nuts. Moments before, my roommate Kurt and two girls from our dorm had come by on their way to the beach to see if I wanted to go. Sometimes I wondered why I stayed at my table when so few seemed to care. Not that you could blame anyone. Santa Barbara sometimes looked too pretty and contented to be connected to the real world, and on this day a cheery sun and light, warm breeze off the Pacific made it extra doubtful that many of us would be much interested in considering whether we were doing all we could to make the real world—our own country, particularly—work as well as we assumed it should.

The sergeant was a confident, reliable-looking guy, alert to anyone who looked curious about the ROTC. He had been getting the fewest visitors. The anti-Khomeini students had pictures of forlorn children that stopped people for a moment; then most walked by, looking perplexed by Iranians denouncing not only the Shah but also the Ayatollah who was currently holding fifty-two American hostages. I was a sort of public utility: Your voter's franchise updated, free, no salesman will call. Once in a while Norman, the local student Communist, came by and shouted at the sergeant until a crowd gathered: "The tyrant training corps, that's what you are! Oppressors! Hired guns of imperialism!" Nobody yelled much at me. There was little communication between the three tables, except occasionally when a puff of wind blew our papers around and we all scurried to help each other.

Classes broke at ten to noon, and the action picked up.

"Are you registered to vote?"

"Yeah, at home."

"Got your absentee ballot?"

"Ah, it's too much of a hassle to send away for it."

"Are you registered to vote?"

"Don't wanna do jury duty."

"Jury duty comes from your driver's license."

"Aha. Okay, see ya."

"Are you registered to vote? If you've moved or missed the last election you have to re-register."

Some said yes, they were, and may actually have been planning to vote. Others were just getting me out of their face. Now and then, a couple would stop and pick up a clipboard with the registration cards on it; that seemed to attract others. Several times, people actually had to wait because all five of my clipboards were circulating through the crowd. That was a big smile.

The lunch crowd thinned back to a trickle. There was no escaping the shadows now, and even pulling on a sweatshirt didn't keep me from shivering. Along came a woman, probably a graduate student, if looking better defined than the rest of us meant anything. She stepped along, looking past our tables to the student center door.

"Are you registered to vote?"

She slowed, but kept going. She turned her head. She had been frowning; now she also looked puzzled.

"Vote?" she asked. I nodded. She said, "No. Thanks."

"All you have to do is fill this in," I told her hopefully, holding out a clipboard.

She stopped and came back. "Do you really think that's going to do any good? Do you really?"

Usually, I'd have been ready with an answer (as teachers and friends had pointed out for years), but something in the way she engaged the question took me by surprise. All I managed was a shrug.

"Let me tell you something," she said. "There's nobody out there." She saw I still hadn't got into gear. "Have you noticed what happens to people who stick their heads up too high?" Still no reply. "They get removed. Start making something really happen, and you get blown away."

Her fierceness jarred a little of my voice back to life. "Well . . . not every time. A lot of people . . ."

She stared me down. "What happened to John Kennedy?"

"Killed."

"And his brother?"

"Okay, I get your point, but . . ."

"What about Martin Luther King?"

"Look . . ."

"That canceled *their* vote, didn't it?"

"Look," I finally managed to say, "you can't just dwell on the worst moments. You can't give up and say that's *America* a hundred percent. People keep trying to make up for creeps like Oswald and Sirhan and what's his name . . ."

"By doing what? Voting?"

"Well, yeah, among other things. If the good people don't vote, you get what you deserve. A crappy government. The good candidates won't come forward."

"Oh, terrific," she said. "When did I get to vote on Vietnam? Where were all your good people in the government then? Okay, a lot of people did go around asking, 'Does this war make any sense?' And they had a war on their hands right here at home. A lot of so-called *patriots* thought up a neat slogan—'America, Love It or Leave It.'"

I remembered the bumper stickers.

"You know what that kind of *patriot* is saying?" She answered herself. "He's saying the job's done. No more improvements necessary. There's no room for you or me to say, 'Hey, wait a minute—we got something great, got it as a gift, and now we're screwing it up.' Forget that. They say shut up or leave."

What kept me off balance was that she wasn't acting particularly angry. She was not shouting; she was not on the attack; she was not, from what I could see, full of passionate intensity. She was more—what?—disappointed. A rejected lover.

"C'mon," I pleaded. She waited politely. "You know it goes bad when you don't *use* your vote. You gotta keep pushing."

She wasn't buying. "So," she said suddenly, "tell me. Who's making such a big difference now?"

With a little time to reflect, I might have said . . . oh, people on school boards; Gloria Steinem; the last guy in your district who got elected, with or without your vote. But I was so rattled that I resorted to talking about myself. "I haven't seen much of the world, but I'm glad I was born here. At least this country doesn't keep you stuck where you started. My mother was a dental assistant when we were growing up. My stepfather repairs vending machines. The family is blue collar all the way, all right? Nobody ever thought about college. But here I am, and here you are. If it weren't for good legislation, the University of California wouldn't even exist."

"That's just the last of the leftovers," she said. "Look around. Carter doesn't know what he's doing. Reagan thinks if you're poor there's something wrong with your morals. The whole government is full of people who don't give a damn about anything but hanging on to their jobs. And to hell with the rest of us. While the power play is on, those guys get everybody looking the other way with speeches about this land of opportunity and loving the Founders' ideals. And all the way up, they salute the flag. Oh, you better salute the flag. Or you better leave."

If this was a debate, my side of it wasn't doing well enough to keep on. So much in her abandoned hopes had a familiar tone. She was no solitary voice; you had only to look around to see people, whether or not they agreed with her specifics, drifting toward her course of action—or, rather, inaction. I think that, mainly, I was stunned by recognition. Unwillingly, uncomfortably, some time before she showed up, I'd felt the touch of the feelings she expressed.

But what do you do? Quit? There was still that clipboard in my hand, and I offered it to her one more time. Palm down, she pushed it away. Then her eyes softened and her frown smoothed out, and she smiled a little.

"Look, nothing personal," she said. "I didn't mean to jump you, but I don't have a lot of confidence left in the American dream. Okay?"

Maybe I read too much into her tone, but it was almost intimate. She might have been saying, "You've been there, too, haven't you?"

I thought I had. But I hadn't been anywhere yet.

2

McGuire's Gift

The old Chevy Caprice came through like a champion. If that car were a person, you'd admire how gallantly it performed in the face of disdain and outright insult. People approaching it for the first time were often so struck by the mottled gray paint and scuffed black seats that they would slow down, or just stop, to get the full effect; then I would put on devil-may-care airs and toss off remarks like, "It may be ugly, but it gets six miles to the gallon."

For all that, this morning the car chugged smoothly through the rivers of traffic and rolled into the parking lot half an hour early. Along with thirty-nine other applicants, I wanted with all my heart to be on time today.

A few spaces away, a young woman sat looking straight ahead through the windshield of a road-stained brown Toyota with Minnesota license plates. She glanced over at the squeak of the Chevy's brakes. I raised my hand in greeting. She raised hers. Her expression, hopeful and apprehensive and something else, said she was probably here for the same job interview. Maybe when the excitement started inside, she wouldn't look so tired. Was it from driving so far? The back of her car was piled to the roof with boxes, clothes on wire hangers, domestic stuff like a toaster oven, an iron, and a lamp shade or two. Or was it from tension? I wondered how many of the rest of us were trying to hide our nerves.

"Hi," she said.

"Hi, how's it going?" I called back.

She smiled, and that look stayed in her eyes: big, brown, doubting eyes.

Behind us, Washington Boulevard ran through Marina del Rey. Ahead, in the early light of a cool overcast, stood a former helicop-

20

ter assembly plant full of people working for the Los Angeles Olympic Organizing Committee. Inside, Wally McGuire probably had a telephone in his hand.

Until that summer I had known next to nothing about McGuire, except that he was some kind of famous campaign consultant. Then, one day, a friend named Bill Schultz called up at the law firm that was patiently giving me shelter in Los Angeles—a junior clerk's job, running errands and copying documents—while I figured out what to do next. By the time you were through college it seemed reasonable to expect that you'd know your calling, or at least have enough clues about it to get started on your mission in life. The job helped immensely in erasing an early notion of applying to law school. So far, though, it had not replaced the notion with a new one. I hadn't found my niche yet.

"Listen," Bill said, "try the Olympic Committee. They're talking about staging a torch relay all the way across the country."

It was nice of him to keep me in mind. But I didn't care all that much about the Los Angeles Olympics. There had been all sorts of stories about politicians and business people squabbling over them for the last four years. "Thanks, Bill," I said, "but it sounds like too much office politics."

"Well, if that's your problem, you got no problem," Bill said. "You don't have to be in an office. They're going to need a bunch of people out on the road to do the advance work."

I hadn't thought of that. Bill heard the silence and kept talking.

"I hear they're hiring Wally McGuire to run the thing. You know who he is. Did Midwestern advance work for McGovern in '72. Did advance for Jerry Brown's campaigns for governor and president. Advanced international trips for President Carter—Saudi Arabia, Jerusalem when Carter was doing the shuttle between Israel and Egypt, West Berlin, Hill 49 in South Korea, Brasilia. He runs training seminars for advance people, too. He's the best."

Bill had the hook set. He went on and sank it deeper.

"How are they going to schedule ten thousand runners, or whatever, across the whole country and get it right every day? They must be looking for a hundred advance people to make it even halfway possible. Why not take a shot?"

A few days later McGuire was looking at me levelly across his desk and saying with a hint of a grin, "There's only one problem with all this. The LAOOC announced the torch relay before they figured out how to do it. Here's everything I know so far: The torch is going to leave New York next year on May 8. It's going to arrive at the Memorial Coliseum here in time for the opening ceremonies on July 28. In between, several hundred million people are going to see it, one way or another, and they're never going to forget seeing it." He stopped. That was apparently the end of that category.

"Here's what I don't know: Anything that's going to happen in between. I don't know how many states the flame will go through. They announced fifty; we can't do that in the time we have. I don't know how many runners we'll have. I don't know how many advance people we can afford. Nobody has ever done anything this big before. So we'll see. Stay in touch."

At quarter to nine, I took a deep breath, locked the door of the Chevy, and started toward the building. The young woman pulled herself out of the Minnesota car at the same time. You could almost hear her sigh. We both said "Hi" again, and I asked, "Are you really from Minnesota?"

She nodded. "I drove out here from St. Cloud with all my stuff. They said I had a chance?" The question mark hung there. "Hope I find a place to live soon. . . ."

We came to the door and I was reaching for it when a different woman, about our age but done up in a sharp business outfit, cut in front of us. She strode up to the building and yanked the door open. The smile she threw at us said, "This is my door, come on through," as if she'd had a bowl of nails for breakfast.

An LAOOC volunteer in a blue blazer checked us against a list and sent us to Security. A guard in a holding room looked at identification—"Driver's license with a picture, that's fine"—and issued visitor's badges. The antiterrorist screening cranked up the tension. You'd think we were in the Pentagon or State Department. Not that I knew what those places felt like. I hadn't been out of California since I was eleven.

An escort in the official crisp blazer and freshly pressed pants arrived to lead us across the work area. The outside of this place looked like just another Los Angeles factory, yet it had a touch of one of those James Bond movies in which an innocent-looking mountainside rumbles open to reveal a city. Two hundred thousand square feet, fifteen hundred people. Carpeting everywhere. Hundreds of desks in a huge bullpen, like the world's biggest newspaper city room, flanking the walkway that took us diagonally across the building toward an enclosed meeting room. Sleek posters and framed pictures of Olympic athletes on the walls in the distance. Cascading down from the ceiling two stories overhead, banners of hot magenta, vermilion, chrome yellow, green, and aqua—the "Festive Federalism" colors of the Los Angeles Olympics. High in one corner, some glassed-in offices and a walkway from which LAOOC Chairman Peter Ueberroth could survey his empire.

In the meeting room, tables and chairs were neatly arranged in a hollow square. People stood around, not sure it would be cool to claim a seat and sit in it.

I was leaning half-possessively on a chair when a face at the door made me almost sigh in relief. The woman just coming in looked familiar. But where had we known each other? . . . College. We'd both been at the University of California, Santa Barbara (UCSB). Even in a room full of strivers, she stood out: black hair, strong dark eyes with a flash of humor, an athlete's body, five feet seven or so. Her green pants suit was fashionable, but how would it impress a judge looking for conservative costumes? You might dismiss a regard for appearance as amusing or irritating, depending on your point of view. Let's just say that a number of the people in that room didn't care to have appearances work against them. I had scrounged together a blue blazer and gray slacks. No matter how hot it got, I would be keeping the blazer on to hide a hole in the elbow of an ancient button-down shirt.

Our eyes met and the woman from U.C. took the seat next to me. "I'm Suzanne Lipps," she said before I got my own name out. A memory made me smile so broadly that she put on a guarded look.

"What's so funny?" she asked.

"You had a car at college, didn't you? With personalized license plates? Are you MS. LIPPS?"

"Still am," she said, and now we were both smiling. Having a friend to sit with gave us an unexpected, and very welcome, bit of security.

Wally McGuire started the meeting. Whatever the rigors of the

23

work he'd done, he looked fresh and young—in his early thirties, most likely—and there didn't seem to be any gray in his dark brown hair. Standing at six feet one, he looked a bit like Alan Alda, calm and confident and in control. He gave an impression of knowing his craft so thoroughly that he could be serious and relaxed at the same time. McGuire took charge of us immediately and permanently.

He introduced the half-dozen executives flanking him at the head table. Some were from AT&T, the corporate sponsor of the torch relay. AT&T was going to put up ten million dollars for vehicles, maintenance, and people; also, they would provide a cadre of experienced runners to carry the torch in places where local runners were scarce. "Some of these other poobahs," he added, were from Burson Marsteller, AT&T's public relations company.

"We're here because of Peter Ueberroth's vision," McGuire said. "He's been looking for ways to share the Olympics with the whole country, beyond just putting it on TV. Also, you know by now, he wants to do something that'll live on after the games are over. So he and the organizing committee came up with a way to provide a legacy for young people. A torch relay can do both jobs—help share the Olympics, and provide the legacy for youth.

"The sharing: That's going to be done by runners who carry the Olympic flame, right out in the open, across the United States, step by step, where as many people as we can pull out there will see it for themselves.

"The legacy for young people: That'll come from individual Americans. Anyone who raises three thousand dollars—from another person, from organizations, businesses, or wherever—earns the right to carry the torch for a kilometer. A Youth Legacy Kilometer, we're calling it, a YLK. Or they can designate someone else to carry it. Three thousand bucks is a lot of money, and that's exactly the point. It represents a real commitment. I guess you all know where the money goes."

He looked around as if he had asked a question. Silence. Then a brave one across the room from him raised a hand and said, "The Olympic Committee?"

"That wouldn't sound too inspiring on the six o'clock news, would it?" McGuire answered, not quite smiling. "Nope. Local community charities get it. Boys Clubs. Girls Clubs. YMCAs and YWCAs. The Special Olympics for handicapped kids."

24

The guy who had raised his hand winced and blushed. "Don't worry," McGuire told him. "That doesn't count against you. Those details aren't what this meeting is about." He looked around at the rest of us. "The point is, there's only one way this idea is going to work—it has to catch the attention of the whole country. The flame has to do more than just get seen. It has to *touch* people, somehow. Very, very seldom does that just happen by itself. Someone has to make it happen. Making it flawless, famous, inspiring, is the job that some of you are going to get to do."

His "some of" put the needle to nerves that had almost relaxed.

Torch relays have been a part of the modern Olympics since 1936, when runners hand-carried a flame from Olympia, Greece, to the opening ceremonies of the games in Berlin. What was new about this one was its grand scale.

"We've got a hell of a lot of ground to cover and practically no time to do it in," McGuire said. "Ueberroth didn't say how to do it. All he said was: When you set the route for this torch relay, be an artist. Paint a picture across this country."

He stopped. He waited. We waited. No one even coughed. Presently he said, "We're going to pull this off by putting people—people we *trust*—on the roads across America and blazing a trail for the runners. Most of you have done some sort of advance work, right? For candidates or concerts or something?"

Hands went up around the room.

"Well, you know that a good crowd doesn't just happen. Almost never. You build it. All you have to do this time is guarantee that every kilometer of the route goes where it paints the best picture. AT&T has already drawn maps of the routes they want. For each day, you'll get a start point and an end point. Everything in between is up to you. You approve AT&T's route, or you decide where it has to change. Either way, it becomes yours. You're going to test every foot of it personally. You're going to organize people in every community along the way, and on stretches of highway that don't even have communities. You're going to make sure that people don't miss their chance to get close to this thing."

What McGuire had put together was more than a training session. It was also the end of a long elimination contest for the Torch Relay Advance Team. I don't know how many names he started with. He had weeded the applications down to several hundred, now to forty. By tomorrow night, he would know which of the forty he was going to keep.

"As you know," he said, "there are fifteen places on the team."

He repeated some warnings he had given, apparently to test our resolve, in earlier meetings. "You people who make it on to the Torch Relay Advance Team are going to be on the road for eight months, seven days a week, at least twelve hours a day. The life will be lonely. You won't see your friends for a long time. You'll have three weeks from today to quit whatever job you have now, get your life together, and leave. You're going to say no a hundred times for every yes, to poobahs who aren't used to having anybody contradict them, least of all a stranger from out of town. You'll be out there with very little protection."

He paused. When he resumed talking it was more slowly, in a different tone. A sudden depth in his voice made me sit up and lean forward.

"I remember one night in 1972," he said. "In the middle of Chicago, for McGovern. Sitting in a bar, lonely and depressed—I wasn't stupid, we all knew there was no chance we'd win—wondering, 'What am I doing here? Why ain't I in law school where my parents want me?' All of a sudden somebody punched up 'Knights in White Satin,' the old Moody Blues song, on the jukebox, and I got even sorrier for myself.

"Next morning, though, McGovern came and we actually had a lot of people out there for him. He talked about how we shouldn't let Vietnam make us forget the strong heart that has kept this country alive. He said we'd endured as a nation because all of us ordinary people take ideas like justice and equality and liberty seriously. I really don't think the people who cheered were too interested, just then, about whether the guy was a Democrat or a Republican, or a winning candidate or a losing one, or a politician at all. They were cheering him for reminding them that they really are good people. That set me up again."

Then he looked up as if he had been caught drifting off the point, and switched back to being tough.

"*You* are going to be where the buck stops. Just about everybody you meet is going to have a different agenda from yours, and you're going to have to figure out what to do about it. You'll be making decisions on the spot, with no place to hide and nobody to tell you whether you did it right or wrong. You'd better have an awful good reason for wanting this job, or you won't make it to the finish line."

Wally had a great gift for us—an adventure. It offered generous opportunities for failure; a step into the unknown; a reasonably serious purpose, since all things Olympic have their effects on national prestige; and even an element of danger, what with assorted terrorists no doubt already thinking hard about ways to plant bombs under manhole covers and get off some shots from a hillside. For anyone lucky enough to take part in it, this could be a lift out of the ordinary life.

It seemed that Wally had surprised himself. His burst of passion and commitment surprised me, too; and it stirred me. I wanted to take part in something so worthwhile that when I spoke about it someday, it would stir other people. I wanted a purpose. That was an old desire. It had a way of showing up like an unexpected visitor.

The instant people my age start to talk even semi-passionately about material stuff, you can see us checking our defenses. "So what are you doing now?" you'd ask when you ran into somebody from college. The embarrassing temptation was to measure each other by money. Now and then I would lie, just to break the rhythm: "I'm leaving next week for Burma with the Peace Corps." That would usually draw a look so blank that you could practically read the thought scrolling across the other person's forehead ("So he didn't take any business courses . . ."). A lot of us probably wished we had the guts to join the Peace Corps. Instead, we buried ourselves in safer goals and resigned ourselves to flinching at the usual accusations: Too damn many young people care first and last about their own comforts. They keep their distance from any kind of commitment so they can drive BMWs and drink imported diet beer.

I wouldn't deny wanting some comforts. Yet knowing that possessions were a short comfort in the long run was, in a rasping sort of way, a consolation. If you're capable of being bored by property, you still have a chance to open up and feel something in you stir at the sight of passion and devotion.

So that was Wally McGuire's gift at the beginning: Permission to be inspired.

27

Not that I knew it at the time. For two days, the world outside that room was about as real as a dream. Reality, for each of the forty candidates for fifteen jobs, was this: Put some good moves on those guys at the head table, or get cut.

Every time a candidate spoke, five others usually jumped up to show off how much smarter they were. The atmosphere of one-upmanship kept me on edge, and it had the same effect on Suzanne. She noticed me making notes on a yellow pad and wrote one of her own: "Did I make total ass of self with last answer, or what?"

"No," I scribbled back, "AT&T poker faces almost smiled."

To blow off some of the pressure, Suzanne and I started trying to top each other in razzing the competition. We made notes as solemnly as if they were the official minutes, then looked around the room to divert attention from the hand that pushed them over.

Suzanne: "One more time for that campaign speech, pls." (After what must have been the fifteenth assertion that these Olympics are not just a sporting event—they are a challenge for American Democracy.)

Once in a while, we forgot to scoff. Suzanne: "Poor girl across the room—giving up? Wish one of the poobahs would ask her to talk." That was the woman from Minnesota. Through the first day, she sat with her hands tightly folded while the more articulate people around her worked to make their impression on the examiners, and she said nothing. Not a word. By midmorning of the second day we could tell she wasn't going to make it, and so could she. Her face was pale; she looked as if she had almost given up breathing. She was almost whispering the despairing thoughts aloud. She had taken the big chance, even when everybody at home was saying it was crazy. She had packed up and driven all the way from St. Cloud, and now she'd have to look for some drone job in L.A.—or, worse, drive back home and face her friends and family with that car full of stuff that had looked so hopeful when she set off for her new life.

As we broke for lunch, I said to Suzanne, "It's just too sad. If I get the job, I'm going to give it to her."

Suzanne flashed me a look that said, "Sure you are."

At nine o'clock on the second night, three hours past the scheduled end of the seminar, Wally McGuire looked around and said the time had come to sum up. Suzanne and I sat back. When he called on people, he always started on the other side of the room. This time, to my shock, he pointed at me.

Only one thought came to mind as I pushed back my chair and stood up. "What excites me about this project is that it could be *the* story of 1984." I said it and sat down, as surprised as anyone in the room. I was actually getting wrapped up in this thing.

Going first turned out to be lucky. The later a candidate spoke, the more he or she had to struggle to make a speech that hadn't already been made. For some, the last spiel was a last chance to deliver a wake-up call to the judges. Through no fault of the speakers, we started hearing variation after variation on the same points:

"These Olympics will be a test of American character."

"We will show the rest of the world what makes America great."

"We're a can-do people, and once again we're going to do what the rest of the world says is impossible."

Even this late in the game, some candidates wiped away tears as they spoke. A note from Suzanne summed up the effect: "Emotional volleyball." One minute, you sympathized with the search for new things to say. The next, you wondered how genuine the tears were. How many more "challenges" and "Americas" were we fated to hear?

Forty-five minutes later the summing up was halfway around the room. For some time I had been sliding up and down in my chair, praying for the scene to fast-forward. The nineteenth or twentieth candidate began:

"This whole wonderful opportunity makes me feel good to be an American. This is the greatest country on Earth, and the Olympics *always* give me a reason to feel a special, special pride in my country. . . ." Her chin quivered, her eyes filled, and her voice shut down to a squeak. One hand went up to her eyes, and the other waved gently in a signal that she was overcome.

To me, standing up in this room and spilling tears while you waved the flag to sell yourself went too far. We were in there competing for a job. And one thing the poobahs had made very clear in those two days was that this was going to be a job for realists, not weepy patriots.

The Torch Relay Advance Team was supposed to marshal effective tactics in support of an event that had problems. The Mexico City Olympics in 1968 had black-power demonstrations. Munich in 1972 had a massacre of Israeli athletes. Moscow in 1980 had a U.S. boycott. Now Los Angeles in 1984 had talk of the Soviets retaliating with their own boycott, plus indications that practically nobody across the United States cared much what happened to the games. The mood around Los Angeles ranged from indifference to opposition. Columnists kept suggesting that the Olympics were falling apart.

Presumably, a big part of the job would be to exercise control. When the rules of presidential delegate selection changed in 1972, Wally McGuire and a few other influential operatives transformed the methods of political advance work. Before, you scheduled a candidate by constituencies, studying who the supporters were, where they were, and when they would see you. Now, you schedule your candidate by media market. The advance man, not the supporters, takes the initiative.

In the era of television, you don't just hope for a crowd. You build it. You don't just expect enthusiasm. You stage it. You set up interviews and speeches on flights of steps and other handsome backdrops. You bring in people whose job is to cheer loudly. You wedge spectators into the smallest available area and suggest angles for the TV crews that cut off the edges of the crowd, so it looks endless. Whether or not your candidate is a leader, you manipulate arrangements to make him or her look like one.

The name of the game is, in a word, manipulation. We would be practicing politics as usual.

Once upon a time, a job had presented itself that looked like a match between my dreams of *Mr. Smith Goes to Washington* and the real world: LOCAL CIVICS TEACHER RUNS FOR LEGISLATURE.

It was 1982. I was finishing my senior year of college. Jack O'Connell had taught civics until he went to work in the Santa Barbara district office of State Senator Omer Rains. He was in his late twenties, a friendly guy you could have fun with at a baseball game. Jack's idea of a good time was going to Bob's Big Boy and getting a Coke with real cherry syrup. He cared about schools, putting drunk drivers in jail, and the environment.

"I know it's not proper to write on the back of formal stationery," he said in one note that I kept, "but I'm saving my stationery while saving a tree." That was no joke. He really believed it.

His sincerity would probably have looked hokey on anyone else, but it fitted Jack. The district assembly seat came open and Jack decided to run for it because, he'd say as we drank his homemade milk shakes, "We've got to put education back as one of our high priorities. I think we can stop the oil rip-off on our beaches. And we have a lot more unfinished business."

I couldn't believe my good luck. "Here's this friend of mine," I thought, "a good guy with ideals. He could possibly be elected to the state legislature. And he isn't even a millionaire."

Other people asked us, "Why are you guys even bothering? Brooks Firestone has it sewed up." They had a point. Firestone was a nice guy, too. In addition, he was a Republican, but moderate; on good terms with the popular local rancher and president, Ronald Reagan; was forty-five and looked like a United States senator; had a famous name and the money that came with it; and owned a winery, so no matter how rich he was he could also say he was a small businessman. He could afford to be affable and call out, "Brother Steve!" whenever we ran across each other around town.

By comparison, Jack was just an ex-teacher, and looked it. No money, no business, no connections. Just Jack, his wife Doree, and me. We were so out of it in the beginning that when we called Sacramento, lobbyists wouldn't even talk to us. For campaign literature we had a black-and-white photo of Jack with some school-children, and a few little flyers listing the things he cared about.

"What the hell," Jack said when we saw what a complete under-dog he was, "we can give it to 'em straight and not worry about losing votes."

You can be an idealist and still want to win, though. As we drove up and down the coast between Santa Barbara and Oxnard, and it looked as if he could actually attract some votes, we'd look at each other and Jack would say, "We gotta find a way to get the Party's money in the campaign. No money, no chance."

One day Brooks Firestone visited a UCSB political science class and offhandedly answered a student's double-barreled question: Where did he stand on the Equal Rights Amendment and abortion rights? Well, he said, he had a woman running his winery and a woman running his campaign, and that ought to prove he had nothing against women, but of course, his position was clear on both the ERA and abortions; he opposed them.

Firestone was a nice guy and O'Connell was a nice guy. What we did in the name of politics after we heard about Firestone's offhand comment was not so nice. I spent a day on the phone tracking down five students who would sign affidavits that they had heard it. Then we printed up a message from O'Connell to the effect that "My opponent, Brooks Firestone, has said he opposes the Equal Rights Amendment. If you believe as I do in the ERA, sign this petition and I'll take it to Sacramento for you after you elect me."

Firestone denied making the comment. We sprang our affidavits. Jack O'Connell had the voters' attention—and, as night follows day, the party's attention.

Consultants stepped in and suddenly we had a quarter-million-dollar campaign budget. Suddenly this was no longer my friend Jack and Doree and me putting together a homegrown little campaign. Suddenly it was a targeted race. We had fancy four-color brochures that unfolded into posters, a privately printed magazine devoted entirely to Jack O'Connell, a TV blitz, and heavyweight managers from headquarters handling everything. The earnest local teacher became a thoroughly coached politician for whom many positions relied on a poll, every speech aimed for a calculated impact area. For the rest of the campaign, the O'Connell people kept pushing Firestone as far to the right as they could, then painting him as a reactionary.

Before things started speeding up, Jack looked at me and said, seriously, "If I ever turn into a whatever-it-takes-to-get-a-vote manipulator instead of somebody who votes for his convictions, kick me." By the time I was tempted to do it, my friend was gone and I could tell that his request was withdrawn. O'Connell won the assembly seat in an upset, and settled in as a smooth office-holder who works hard for his district. He does vote for education, he does vote to jail drunk drivers, and he does work for the environment. But whenever we see each other, we both feel a little uneasy—as if we both felt a tug at our idealistic past and a memory of what can happen to ideals. Anyway, I moved to Los Angeles to finish my thesis, and our paths diverged.

My disappointment showed me up as naïve, I guess. It really had seemed that we would make some changes. For a while I had let myself imagine: Maybe, I had thought, we'll dissolve some of the doubts that have been forming a crust over my hopes.

Well, that was just one campaign—not the biggest event in a life that, with any luck, should be fairly long. But it was not so easy to disregard the patriotic speeches. They kept coming from every direction. The finer their sentiments—love your country, respect the Founders' ideals—the more I wondered how many of us really lived up to them.

I had looked to local politics for proof that my disillusionments were illusions themselves. Now I put my hopes on a journey into my own country.

LOS ANGELES, JANUARY 3, 1984

Driving into the LAOOC parking lot on the first Tuesday of the year was much easier than it had been three weeks before. Wally McGuire was gathering the fifteen members of his Torch Relay Advance Team—whom he called, because of the initials, "torch rats"—to brief us and give us our starting assignments.

The camaraderie of the road had already converted McGuire's own name. To the members of his team from here on, he was Wally.

He took us through the mechanics of renting cars, filing expense reports, and using AT&T calling cards. *"Use* those cards," he said. "I want you to stay in touch with me. Call in every day, you hear?"

The United States was, most of it, a country I had heard about but had not visited. Outside of a few spots—Cupertino, in Silicon Valley forty miles south of San Francisco, where my mother and stepfather lived; Fort Leonard Wood, Missouri, when I was seven going on eight and my mother found work there; Santa Barbara for college; a little bit of L.A.—I had a limited sense of America and the Americans who live out there. Now this man was talking, with a casualness I couldn't even begin to pretend to feel, about sending us out there on a mission.

Wally was saying, ". . . your food allowance is twenty-five dollars a day." I made a sound: "Oof!" He looked over and said, reassuringly, "Take it easy. That'll be enough."

Oh, I said, I guess so: "That's what I've been spending in a *week."*

Finally, the assignments. Some people got faraway, exotic places like New York, Boston, and Washington. I drew San Diego and a bit of advice: "Be there tonight." My first contact would be an AT&T regional manager.

Later, after marking some ideas for routes that the torch runners could take between the start time and end time for San Diego, I showed my map to Wally and asked what he thought. He ran his finger along the penciled lines, and after a few minutes he looked up. "Fine," he said. "Now go and see what it feels like on the ground."

"Wally," I said, "do you do requests?"

"Depends," he said. "What song do you want?"

"I'd love to see the East Coast, if you could find a way to send me there."

"Don't worry," he said. "You'll get to see it all."

3

Initiation Day

The Budget Rent-A-Car was an American mini-van, I think a Plymouth. It shined, its odometer showed three miles, and it smelled brand-new. My first new car; my first day on the road. The window crank turned as smooth as milk to let in some soft air. The afternoon was bright, warm, and fragrant, the sort of day people in the frozen parts of the country must think of when they say "Sunny California" in January.

The stereo was already set to 91X, the powerful station in Tijuana. Out came an old English Beat song with a traveling lilt. "I'm on my way, won't be back for many a day." I hummed with them.

"Good-bye, everybody, good-bye, everybody."

San Diego is like the good-natured little brother who gets less than his share of attention because big, famous Los Angeles is always showing off its muscles and gold chains. It's such a pleasant place, with its mild weather and gardens full of flowers, that the good nature fits it easily.

Breakfast the next morning was a comfortable way to get acquainted with Joyce Tate, the other torch rat on this trip. By eleven o'clock, we were riding an elevator to the heights of a midtown office building, eager for our first meeting: with the AT&T executive who had drawn a route for the runners through San Diego.

Waiting outside his door gave us some happy minutes. It was like waiting for a gate to open on a new world. My brand-new suit felt crisp and smooth, we had just expensed a breakfast for the first time, we had begun an enterprise that rolled up our expectations and desires into one neat package. A receptionist even asked cheerfully, as if the wait were really for our convenience, "Would you like a donut? Some coffee?"

There is something exhilarating about having work you regard as important. The day before, in bringing us up to date on what details anyone knew of the torch relay, Wally had repeated that it would succeed or fail on the quality of our efforts.

We had exactly eighteen weeks from this morning to prepare a relay run that was going to cover at least nine thousand miles across the United States. The flame would arrive from Greece by air; as we already knew, it would leave New York City on May 8. Runners would pass it from hand to hand for eighty-two days, showing it (the Olympic Committee hoped) to all of America along the way. The last runner would carry it into the Los Angeles Memorial Coliseum for the opening ceremonies of the Twenty-third Olympiad on July 28.

Wally had persuaded Ueberroth that there was no hope of making competent arrangements for all fifty states. But he had cut out just seventeen. The torch route still passed through thirty-three states and the District of Columbia, and touched every region of the country except Alaska and Hawaii. The run was to be no tidy little zip across the continent; it would be a tremendous voyage, swooping up and down the United States in great loops. Down through the crowded Northeast to the nation's capital. A swing past the Great Lakes. A plunge into the South, another swing across to Arkansas, then a turn up into Missouri. Another plunge to Texas, another swing across to New Mexico, and a turn up to Colorado. Then a long, nearly straight ascent to the northwest corner of Washington State, and the final plunge down the Pacific Coast.

But precisely which roads it would travel and who would greet it each day, no one could say. Planners at AT&T had used computers to lay out a general route that didn't specify highways and streets. Local people, AT&T and otherwise, had plotted some more specific routes. Nobody knew how long a run the local routes composed— "As close as I can figure, the torch'll be in Montana on opening day," Wally declared. We would re-draw the routes. More than that, though:

"The line you set for the runners through each community has to represent the community *truly*," Wally told us. "Not just its best, not just its worst."

Our procedure would be to drive over every possible route, measure it on the car odometer, and time it. Eight miles an hour was the average runner's speed. That's twelve and four-fifths kilometers. Hills, altitude, heat, or other local conditions would change the calculation. A number of AT&T people might feel, since they had done a lot of preliminary work and their company was paying, that they owned the torch run, and possibly us. "Well," Wally said, "life ain't fair. They don't." Torch rats were to study each local proposal, when one was available, to see if it was practical. Where it wasn't, we were to use our common sense to fix it. We would solicit advice from the officials, elected or hired, who controlled permits and such, and act as a bridge between AT&T and other local people. Once we decided on a route, we were to report it to Wally and move on to the next place. Later, we would come back, looking for local color and ways to stage events that would draw attention to the torch and make its passage a moment people would remember.

In any event, Wally held us fully responsible. If one of us said Stacy Velman would hand the torch to Cindy Ley at Seventh and Ohio streets at 2:42 P.M. on the eighth of June in Mission, Kansas, he expected that, and precisely that, to happen. "Your job is to translate lines on a map into footsteps on the pavement," he had said, and then shut his mouth and stared at us until he saw that we took his point.

Our wait was over. The AT&T executive opened his door with a big, friendly smile and beckoned us in. Photographs on the walls of his office showed him with Senator Pete Wilson, the former mayor of San Diego; Ronald Reagan; and other famous faces frozen in the smile of a photo opportunity. He had a big desk in front of a broad window that looked over pastel buildings and the deep blue of San Diego Bay. A couple of his assistants sat off to one side during the settling-in pleasantries.

"Boy, oh boy, did your guys put us through a workout to get the torch down here," he said, adding a head shake to his smile.

"It looks as if they plan to make us all work," I said, cautiously.

"I got to be a regular lobbyist," he said with a wink. "Thought I had it made with Ueberroth, and then guess what? I had to do it all over again with Fishman." Joel Fishman was chairman of the Torch Relay Foundation.

"Do you know, we haven't spent much time with either of them," I said. "Have we, Joyce?" Joyce shook her head.

"Well, we pulled it off. We really did it," the executive said. "Fishman said if we wanted the torch we'd have to sell two hundred kilometers. So we went out and we did it. Raised six hundred thousand dollars. You don't want to hear how many meetings and lunches and presentations that took."

"I can imagine," I said.

"And I'm not even talking about the people we wore out getting the route squared away."

We knew nothing of his route. Joyce kept pretty quiet, so it was up to me to say, "Yes, the route. We're really interested in that. Can we look at your map?"

"Oh, yes indeed," he said. "We've got the whole town excited about our little route here. Take a look at this."

Instead of pulling out a little Rand McNally map like mine, he stood up and walked across the room with his two assistants. "Where are they going?" Joyce murmured.

They stopped at a huge board propped against a wall. The assistants turned it around, and there, dwarfing the three of them, was a blown-up map of the San Diego area. Joyce and I stared at it a moment, then risked a sideways glance at each other. A line of red paint snaked out to the desert, through La Mesa to the east of San Diego proper and practically every other outlying town, curved down to Chula Vista near the Mexican border, dipped into downtown San Diego, and finally straightened up to head north. We were looking at an intricate disaster.

"Well," the executive said, raising a hand to the board. "There she is." He stepped back to his desk. "Here." He handed me a half-inch stack of papers. On top was a miniature of the wall display. The rest were photocopies of one newspaper article after another. Pictures in many of them showed him standing in front of the map. He had already announced the route. To the people of San Diego, it was a fact.

Why all those little towns? Something in a frame behind his desk caught my eye. It said he was a city councilman in La Mesa. That made sense of his motives. Taking care of the home folks. I'd have done the same. Only . . . we had to tell him there would have to be another plan.

"That certainly is impressive," I said. "You must have done a huge amount of work on it." Everyone gazed at it for a moment. "You know, there's one problem. We've got exactly one point eight days in San Diego, and it looks to me as if the map there has . . . let's see, five minutes per kilometer and a kilometer is what, six inches on your map: at least three days, maybe more."

He gave me a sharp look, and said nothing. I pulled out my map and spread it on his desk. We leaned over it and I ran my finger along the route, as Wally had done. "This is essentially the same as yours," I said, not sure it sounded convincing, "just streamlined a bit to fit the time we have. Come in State Route 15, see, go through Balboa Park, over to Coronado Island. Come back over the high bridge at dusk, with the sun setting behind the runner. Have a big event at Seaport Village, and bed down for the night near Sea World."

"Hold it," he said. "You say do all of that in one day?"

"We pretty much have to," I said. "It leaves us four-fifths of the next day to get to the Orange County border—through La Jolla, Oceanside, San Juan Capistrano, all that beautiful scenery along the coast."

"And to hell with the beautiful scenery around here, I suppose," he said. The way he jerked himself back from our map and straightened up was alarming.

"It is beautiful, and I think we touch a lot of it," I said. And, it probably wouldn't be smart to add right now, the Chamber of Commerce ought to love it. "It would be great if we could go to all the suburbs. I wish we could. But the torch has to be up past San Clemente by the second night."

"You people from Los Angeles!" He put his hands flat on the desk and leaned forward. "You never did understand! San Diego is not just one place! It's a collection of places! People out in the towns are San Diego, too! Do *you* think you know this place better than I do?"

"No, sir," I said. "I just . . . The torch has to be at the opening ceremonies on the twenty-eighth of July. It has eighty-two days to get there from New York. We can't change it to eighty-three days. We've just got to work things out within the limits."

"Your limits!" he said, with a challenging glare. "I've already

39

announced . . ." He took a deep breath and blew it out so hard that his lips fluttered.

For all that this was serious business, an element of the preposterous seemed to have crept in. Here it wasn't even lunchtime, and we already had the makings of slapstick—runners dashing this way and that, bouncing first off the executive as he pointed to one street, then off me as I pointed to another. I can't say I felt detached enough to be amused just then. But I did catch myself wondering, "What if we ruffle everyone we meet like this?" We'd have a comedy instead of a torch run. The country wouldn't cheer; it would spend eighty-two days laughing.

I hiked up my sleeve to pretend to look at my watch. "Oops. Better let our next meeting know we're going to be late. We can work this out if we all just stay with it, don't you think? If you'll excuse me for a minute—is there a place where I can use the phone?"

The cheerful receptionist put me in an empty office, and I called Wally. "It's not just that the man looks important. He's starting to yell. He sounds as if he's going to dig in his heels for his route. What do I do?"

"I don't hear anything to get sweaty about," Wally said. "You don't have to work with the guy. Your route looked fine to me. If he likes his own so much better, tell him to get his map framed and hang it on the wall." So. Wally wasn't leaving us out here completely unprotected, after all. The boss would back us up. That felt good.

Back in the meeting, things stayed tense all the way through the handshakes and good-byes. "Let me drive over the route and do some figuring," I said from the doorway, "and I'll get back to you."

"I'll be right here," he said from behind his desk.

Joyce and I went off to meet a policeman. A captain in the California Highway Patrol had generously arranged for one of his troopers to show us around. The trooper put the charm back in the day. He wore his immaculate uniform like an ex-football player, which he was, with an air of relaxed, friendly confidence. He made things so easy and friendly that I forgot to write down his name, which was as all-American as his looks. I hope he won't mind if I call him Ken.

"What do you think of this route?" I asked him, unfolding my map. He scanned it.

"Looks like it'll give San Diego a good chance to show off," he said. "Want to see what that yellow line you drew looks like through the windshield?"

I had never been on this side of a cop before. By the time we headed up toward Sea World at about eighty miles an hour, we'd had a couple of hours of looking out at the world from another angle—the way a movie camera takes a character's point of view to show other characters reacting to it. Civilians on the road kept doing what I had always done: seeing the CHP car, suddenly slowing down, peeking nervously at it.

Ken could have arrested almost anybody we passed. "See that blue Fairlane? His registration just expired. That Dodge has a loose muffler. This guy here is doing sixty-three. Ordinarily, I won't stop him if he stays under sixty-five."

"So it's true? You give us ten miles an hour? Sometimes?"

"Sometimes," he said, laughing. "There's not enough of us to get every speeder. If you're endangering people, doing a lot of lane changing, really speeding, acting drunk, we'll go after you. On a slow day, well, we might enforce the letter of the law. You never know which day that's going to be, do you?"

To our thanks as we got out, he said, "My pleasure. If there's ever anything I can do for you, let me know." No other policeman had ever let me go like that.

4

Innocent in Oregon

Sheets of rain beat on the fuselage during our approach. Cinching the seat belt a little tighter, I let my mind's eye see us hydroplaning off the end of the runway. No wonder the University of Oregon teams are the Ducks. When the captain let the engines wind down, a steady drumming on the skin of the airplane took over as background music.

The view through a taxi window on the way to the motel was diffused softly through the wet. A glowing fan of raindrops spread under every streetlight. The most striking detail of Portland so far was the posture of the evening walkers. Far from hunching over and squinting and acting drenched and miserable, most strolled along looking comfortable, even jaunty, under their slickers and umbrellas.

Maris Segal could not be finding this weather as cozy as the Oregonians did. She was from Winter Haven, Florida. The youngest torch rat and the most confident—it had been Maris who swept by the girl from Minnesota and me that first morning in Los Angeles—she had been in Portland for a day.

"So. Here's tomorrow's schedule," she said at dinner. "Nine A.M., meet three Pioneers outside the AT&T building. It's not far. See the route they suggest."

The Telephone Pioneers of America turned out over the next few months to be a priceless gift to all of us. The Pioneers are a service organization with half a million members, and at times it seemed as if we had them all on our side. The only requirement for membership is eighteen years with a telephone company (plus, apparently, an inclination to help other people). Some are retired, some still on the job. Pioneers contribute more than five million dollars a year to community projects. For the torch relay, Pioneers in each state had taken on logistics in their home areas—they volunteered to drive vehicles, act as marshals and pathfinders, set up rest stops, arrange permits, get uniforms, operate ham radios, and above all, suggest the path the torch should take. They were our prime resource. Most of them worked on their own time, without pay. Up to this time, though, I hadn't met one.

"The head man wondered if you and I would come over and let him and his wife fix us a home-cooked meal," Maris said. "The Pioneers here are really friendly."

"That's a relief," I said.

"Why? Are you surprised?" she asked.

"No, no," I said, regretting the slip. "There was a guy in San Diego who didn't see eye to eye with us. No problem."

The truth was, I hadn't expected her to say it. Many Pioneers had been in their jobs as long as we had been alive. They worked for a quasi-military company with a reputation for doing things by the book. They fitted my idea of middle-aged, conventional people with a distaste for winging it. But of course, I was starting to make a habit of being surprised.

Next morning, the Pioneers showed us a route that expertly showed off the timberland, rivers, and city neighborhoods of a piece of the country they clearly loved. Then Maris headed for Seattle. I got into a white Dodge and started ducking log trucks on Route 99E, heading for Salem, forty-five miles to the south. Reaching for something in the glove compartment, I wrenched my neck, and by the time I got to a motel, everything above the right shoulder blade had seized up with pain.

"Do you have a room with a bathtub?" I asked the woman behind the counter.

"Sure, honey, have yourself a float," she said.

I wanted to hug her. If a hotel room is arranged so I can sit in a tub to soak my nervous back while I watch television and have a telephone next to me, I'm in heaven. In this one I could angle the bathroom mirror to reflect the bedroom TV. So what if the phone by the bed wouldn't reach the tub? Two out of three was great.

The first thing was to start the hot water. The next was to call Wally. No matter how late we did it, he wanted to hear what we had accomplished. I could hear the keys of his computer clicking

43

as he put in my name, location, and telephone number. He asked, "Is it getting any easier?"

I laughed, relieved that he could be so casual about the San Diego problem. Getting off to such a combative start hadn't been much of a present for the boss. "It sure is," I said. "I haven't managed to make any enemies yet. People here have big hearts."

"Keep moving," he said.

The tub had a few more minutes to run, so I called Evelyn Barham, the Pioneer responsible for the segment from Oregon City just below Portland to Eugene, sixty-five miles farther down the road. Her husband answered.

"Mr. Barr? Evelyn just stepped out, but she won't be long." He sounded as if he had been waiting all evening for the call from the man from the Olympic Committee. "She asked me to apologize if you called. She should be right back. She wants to call you the minute she comes in."

Mr. Barr? No, I'm just Steve. I wasn't used to making anyone nervous. "Mr. Barham? It's my fault, really. If this is too late, we can talk in the morning."

"Oh, no, it's no trouble. Just give me your number."

So I did, and eased into the steaming water, letting the heat start its job. The phone rang. Heaving myself out of the tub, trying to hold on without using the right side, I slipped and flailed that arm, the other, legs, feet, everything, like all the Three Stooges at once, and barely avoided crashing. By the time I reached the phone, naked, dripping, and amazed I'd made it, I must have sounded a little goofy. "Hello? Mrs. Barham? Don't hang up. Sorry it took me so long to answer. I was soaking a sore back."

"Oh, my," she said, like a sweet grandmother.

"I'm sorry I called so late," I said. "We should get together in the morning, if that's okay with you."

She interrupted, all concern: "How did you hurt your back? At least you've got a bath going. Do you have some aspirin? We can bring you a heating pad."

"Oh, no, it's nice of you to offer"—I certainly couldn't ask a complete stranger to drive God knows how many miles at eleven o'clock at night with a heating pad—"the hot water will probably take care of it. Would nine tomorrow in the coffee shop downstairs be okay for you?"

44

The next morning, Evelyn and Paul Barham were already in a booth when I arrived. They looked exactly as she sounded, smiling people who were probably ideal grandparents. Following LAOOC protocol, I was in my blazer and tie and slacks, looking—I hoped—older and more official than I felt.

The backache was a minor annoyance, but I must have favored the shoulder, for Evelyn glanced at it and looked concerned. "How's your back? Oh, that does look painful." Actually, the tie that had me around the throat was more to blame—that, and my natural awkwardness. "Here, we brought you some Ben-Gay, and here are some aspirins. You probably have your own, but we wanted to be sure. Are you certain that you wouldn't like to have our heating pad? It's in the car."

I hadn't been mothered like that in a long time. With an affectionate fuss like that coming at you, you'd have to be spectacularly pompous not to just smile and relax. So that's what all of us did. Instead of starting our business meeting with sports chat or the weather, the usual ice-breakers, we were doing what we did best—Evelyn being maternal, and I being someone who could use a little help.

All we had to do, really, was touch base. The route through here was straightforward: Get on Route 99 and drive. When the check came, Paul reached for it, shooing away my AT&T expense account.

"You're our guest and we want to treat you," he said, seriously. I really must have been an innocent if I'd thought people did that only when they wanted something. Maybe the people in this corner of the country really were just plain kind to visitors.

Eugene is the home of the University of Oregon. It is also the center of a major wood products region that makes much of the nation's plywood. Eugene and Springfield, the city next door, are the head of a series of flood control dams that have turned the Willamette River Basin to the southeast into a series of handsome reservoirs and spots for fishing, boating, and looking. All that, plus Eugene's rose and rhododendron gardens and the nearby forests, made for a straightforward torch route. The runners would come in one end, hit the high spots, and go out the other end.

"Not that I want to hurry you away," the Pioneer there said at noon, "but you better get moving if you want to make Klamath Falls by tonight." He looked concerned. "Be sure you get over the Willamette Pass by nightfall. Route 58 ices up, and you don't want to slide off or get hit by a logging truck."

In a Sherlock Holmes movie, he'd have been saying, "Beware of the moors."

He knew what he was talking about. An hour up the grade of Route 58, past the Lane County Sheriff's Station at Dexter, patches of snow appeared in the woods that flanked the road. Within another hour, banks of snow humped up higher than the car roof. Toward the summit, the pavement started getting slick with ice.

Even driving through what amounted to a tunnel of snow, it was easy to see that the road was thoughtfully planned, with plenty of pullouts for passing and a number of exits for camping and picnicking in the forests on both sides. I got over the Willamette Pass all right, and descended until Route 58 turned south onto Route 97 toward Klamath Falls. Crater Lake was somewhere off to the right, and the road started climbing again. It was lonely, with few houses in view under an overcast sky.

Toward four, I started wondering how far the next pass was and worrying about being stuck there. According to the map, I should be just about at a 4,591-foot summit and Klamath Falls should be only another thirty-five or forty miles, but was it? To the left, a homemade sign said LAST FOOD AND GAS FOR 35 MILES. Time to pull in and ask.

There was a gas pump and a little cluster of buildings consisting of what looked like a rustic lodge, a bait and tackle shop, and a modest diner with another sign: HOME MADE SOUP. Inside the diner, seven or eight men sat in the light that poured in through big windows, looking comfortably permanent.

The countryside showed no sign of any place for them to have come from; if they worked nearby, you'd think they'd have been out doing it, and they didn't seem to be skiers. They did, however, have an eerie sort of likeness. They were all ages, mostly from thirty to sixty. They all wore plaid blanketing jackets and they all had caps, either stocking caps or peaked caps with furry ear flaps, and they all had either full beards or long sideburns and mustaches. If they had shaved, each would probably have looked different from the others, but at a flash impression, they looked like brothers. The waitress, a woman about forty, gave me a smile.

"Chicken noodle soup, to go," I said. While she went for it, I approached the man nearest the door. "I'm headed for Klamath Falls. Could you tell me, is it more than thirty or forty miles?"

He turned his head slowly and looked at me. After a few seconds, he said, "Huh. Klamath Falls. I don't think I've been there for fifteen, sixteen years."

In L.A., you'd drive a car forty miles for a hamburger, without thinking twice.

He seemed to have ended the conversation. "I just came from Eugene," I said, hoping to prolong it a bit. "Have you been there?"

"Nope."

From down the line came an opinion: "Klamath Falls can't be more than an hour away. Two at the most. Just don't rush it."

I nodded my thanks, paid for my soup, and went outside. It was hard to figure. This was not a town. No movie theaters. No baseball stadiums. Apparently a short day's work, or none at all, in the snow season. Yet this was where the man had been in his life. What was there for him to do here? The soup was warm and good. Maybe he stayed for the soup.

5

Paydirt: the East

The Torch and News bullpen at the LAOOC had a huge Xerox copier that was about a dozen feet long and did everything but write your name for you, except when I went near it. Then it would break. Wally had the same effect on it. When I spotted him, it was already on "Tilt," with Wally squinting at it in exasperation—the all-knowing, all-powerful McGuire, who could get an American president through the Middle East with every day's detail in place, at that moment looking just like me.

He turned away from the machine. "Ah, Barr. You're going to get your wish. We're going to send you east."

Paydirt! At last! The great cities my friends and I had longed to get to, the immense, intricate settings for the history and myths we had heard all our lives: family politics in the Kennedys' Boston. Energy and power in Manhattan. Government City, D.C. The Northeast had been my fantasy. Now it was almost a reality.

"I want you and Silman to start in New York," he said. "You're going to trouble-shoot the route up through New England and back down to Washington."

"Who's Silman?" I asked. In the shock of happiness, I couldn't match the name with a face.

"He's a lanky fool like you," Wally said, absently, staring at the buttons on the machine as if he hoped he'd find one he remembered. Except for moments when he looked straight at you to drill in a point, he gave an impression of being eternally preoccupied with a million details, and he said that sort of thing in an offhand voice that provided no clue to how he meant it. This time it sounded like affection, but who could tell?

"I'm already finding mistakes in the schedule that shouldn't be

48

there," he said, just as absently. Then he turned his attention from the buttons to me, and the preoccupation disappeared. "If we don't put a stop to them right now, you guys won't believe the mess we'll have on our hands this summer. The schedule's gotta be sound."

Larry Silman and I got acquainted a couple of mornings later, at breakfast on our way to the airport. We were about the same height, at six feet two, and different in other ways. His hair is red-blond, mine is dark; he wore a mustache, I didn't; he came across so sure of himself that he never seemed to ask questions.

The temperature outside the Café Casino in Santa Monica was eighty-two and the Pacific sparkled under the warm sun—the last California day we would see for a while. Larry had no doubts about what we were going to do when we arrived in the promised land across the continent. He had a list of restaurants we should try: Gallagher's Steak House in New York, Locke-Ober's and Jimmy's in Boston. . . .

NEW YORK, JANUARY 19

The sky was dark by the time the United jet descended toward La Guardia Airport. Still, I strained toward the window for a glimpse of the lights of Manhattan. Nothing. Just the rattle of snow on the window. The airplane touched down in a blizzard, temperatures in the twenties, and a wind like knife blades. The ground was white.

"Steve! Steve!" There was our welcoming committee.

"Whoa whoa whoa," Larry said. "Which one is your friend, my friend? Introduce me, fast."

Stephanie Dournbos and I have known each other since junior high school in Cupertino. We had shared a special bond, a fascination with New York—more precisely, with life outside a California suburb. She got away first, thanks to the modeling jobs that her sunny blond girl-next-door looks helped her get, and moved to Manhattan with her sister Dee. And there they were, waving excited hellos.

Larry could have our room at the Sheraton Centre Hotel to himself for tonight. Steph and Dee and their three roommates were going to let me crash at their place so we could talk for a few hours before Steph left in the morning for a three-week job in Japan.

Larry kept winking at me as if he thought I were going to an orgy. "Be good," he said.

"Go hose off, Silman," I said. "They're my *friends*."

"Yeah, right, right," he said, waving good-bye, winking, and heading out to find the Renault Alliance we had rented.

Stephanie and Dee took me in a borrowed car to the East Twenties. Getting out near Lexington Avenue, I stopped just to savor the sight and smell of the big-city street. Peaceful at midnight, with snow falling past the glow of street lamps, it was hushed and pretty, not at all the way I'd imagined Manhattan.

Upstairs, we met the roommates, two other girls and a dancer named Nick. Five people in a two-bedroom place. A real New York starving artist setup. They had to have a house meeting before we could go out for some food. I parked on a mattress on the floor. Soon, they were squabbling:

"That's *your* call, you pay for it."

"No, I wasn't even here when it was made—look, nine-thirty A.M., not P.M. . . ."

"Full rent? But I was only here three weeks of that month. . . ."

Steph looked my way every few minutes with a nervous smile. I figured everyone would notice me less if I got on the phone, so I called my mom.

"Where are you?" she wanted to know. "What time is it there? What show are you watching? Or is that an argument in the background?"

The meeting was better than television. To me, the scene had a certain romance. Even though the five friends were arguing at the moment, they had all made a leap away from home, they were making it on their own in the big city as artists or whatever, they were together and helping each other.

After an hour they finished up their discussion and we all found a table at The Burger Spot nearby. In contrast to the quiet of the street outside, the place was packed with noisy diners—at almost 2:00 A.M. in the middle of the week. Don't people in New York ever sleep? The roommates looked warily at the menu, and I recognized the calculations going through their minds. "Hmm, two-fifty for the plain burger; wonder if I've got enough for the salad, too."

I said, "By the way, this is on me, for letting me stay at your place tonight." There was obvious relief all around.

At seven o'clock (four in the morning for me, California time), we were all up to say good-bye to Stephanie. The people who had bickered the night before hugged their roommate, some of them in tears, kissing her.

Over and over they said, "We'll miss you, Steph, take care of yourself." Then she left for Japan, everyone else left for work, and it was quiet again.

Now the way to see the East Side was to go for a run. I pulled on some Nikes and old yellow sweats and jogged toward the East River. It took about as far as the first street crossing to realize what an odd sight I made in a teeming, tough part of town where most people work for survival, not their aerobic conditioning.

Last night's ideal city looked different by daylight. Gray overcast, gray slush, some homeless people pushing baskets, puddles of ice water to step in. But the bubbling life of the city was anything but gray. Trucks crammed into every available space, blocking parts of the street. Two men in peacoats and knit caps unloading food from a big van onto an elevator that came right out of the sidewalk, yelling to each other in Spanish. Oriental women piling vegetables on a sidewalk stand. Black children and teenagers, walking, looking in store windows. Just about every color, except for the pink skins and yellow hair that had been everywhere I looked twenty-four hours before. I was so busy looking that I stepped in one puddle after another.

At the East River I stopped to sniff some deep breaths. The river smelled of oil, and the air was so cold that it felt like bites in my nose. But it also smelled of the ocean beyond the limits. All I could think of was how fortunate I was. The day before yesterday I had been jogging on the beach in Santa Monica. The day before that, on the Marina in San Francisco. Here, by magic, I was on the other side of an entire continent—the continent, the country, that most of the people in the world probably wish they could get into. Who knew where I'd be tomorrow? This was great. I was out of the coop, seeing things, feeling free.

By midday, Larry had his map open in the passenger seat and I was driving over the route, kilometer by kilometer, through Manhattan and the Bronx. Or trying to.

"So this is gridlock," Larry said, glancing up at the trucks loom-ing over both sides of us and the kamikaze cabbie banging his horn behind us. "How are your nerves holding up?"

"Oh . . . just . . . fine," I growled through clenched teeth, exag-gerating for a laugh. "I'm sure I have at least another two minutes in me. Maybe even three."

The car ahead of us moved four feet. Immediately, kamikaze cabbie jabbed his head out of his window. "Ey! Ey!" he shouted up at us. "C'mon, for Chrissake! Ya through witcher beauty rest or *what*? Move up or move off!"

A few hours of that and we had worked our way as far north as Central Park. In the dark, halfway up Manhattan, cold and groggy and beat, we quit for the day.

Wally couldn't believe it. Larry called him, and most of his end of the conversation went, "That's right, but . . . one-way streets . . . traffic . . . footbridges . . . I know, but . . ." He held the phone away from his ear so I could hear the response.

"I thought you guys would be in *Connecticut* by now." Wally wasn't shouting, exactly, but he was coming through loud enough. "What the hell have you been *doing*?"

Clearly, the thing to do was to blaze out of New York tomorrow and get at least as far as Connecticut. Neither of us wanted to tell him a second time that we were still in the city.

By midmorning the next day I was riding shotgun somewhere north of Yankee Stadium, my eyes bouncing from the map to the blank streets outside and back again, trying to spot a landmark that would give Larry some clue to which way he should turn.

"Look," he said. He pointed to a stout lady towing a shopping basket, muffled up to the eyes against the cold. I rolled down the window.

"Excuse me," I called. "We're lost. Are we anywhere near For-dham University? Is this the Bronx?"

She cocked her head as if she hadn't quite heard. Again: "Where are we? The Bronx? Mt. Vernon?" Still no response. Again: "Can you tell us where we are?"

Suddenly, four feet from our hood, a car door burst open and a man I hadn't noticed—a huge man—leaped out and took two strides that put him a few inches from my face. All I could see was a stocking cap, a stubble of beard, a cigar stub, and lots and lots of teeth.

"You're in the fuckin' *Bronx*!!!" the giant bellowed. In a Loony Tunes cartoon, my hair would have been blown straight back by the blast. Maybe he had been trying to sleep; whatever, he wasn't looking for a response. Larry pulled us away as I rolled up the window, and we were a couple of blocks along by the time I managed to say in a tiny Jerry Lewis voice, "Thanks, man."

6

Two Cheers for Tradition

NEW HAVEN, JANUARY 20

It was in New Haven that we noticed that people and scenery don't always match.

When Larry pushed open the door of Malone's, the sight that greeted us made him stop and say, "Hey, all right!" Thanks to his little black book, we were stepping into the traditional pub you'd want to find in a New England town.

Cruising around looking for it, we had seen the outlines of Yale University roofs against the night sky. "This is great, this is great," I babbled while Larry parked. "People who fought in the American Revolution had *grandfathers* who graduated from Yale. Meanwhile, back home in California—Indian villages. We think the Spanish missions are old, ha! This college was fifty or sixty years old by the time they planted the first cross out there." And so on, to Larry's visible boredom.

Inside, Malone's had all the comforts of a good bar. The light jazz drifting from the speakers was just soft enough that you could hear the person next to you, and just loud enough that if you wanted to sip your beer and listen to the music, you could. The lighting was just subdued enough to relax you without making you squint. The walls and furniture were dark walnut. A warm fire added a touch of light in the back. The whole place seemed hand-rubbed with tradition, a perfect resting spot for Larry and me to take the edge off after two long days in our tiny, cramped rent-a-car.

Looking around after the bartender drew our beers, I started feeling that there was something . . . off . . . about Malone's. I stared at a wall filled with Yale sports pictures and pennants, and thought it was odd that the football schedule poster had been updated with black Magik Marker only to the first game. The season was over.

54

We strolled over to the jukebox. It had some great old bar standards like Tony Bennett, Nat King Cole, even a Billie Holiday.

"Let's see," Larry said, "'Current Rock Hits'—uh, oh. Foreigner. Boston. Peter Frampton. We're in the seventies here."

"Yeah. This box needs some serious updating," I concluded, with the finality of a twenty-three-year-old who knows precisely what's hot and what's not. Pressing keys A-4, A-6, and C-28 got us all Sinatra. Sinatra seemed appropriate.

By the time we got back to the bar, Larry had pulled out his LAOOC card and told everyone we worked for the Olympics. I felt more like listening than talking, but what the hell. We each had our own ways. Larry's announcement interested the bartender, a clean-shaven guy a year or two older than us, only briefly. The bartender didn't look like a man in charge of a lively pub; either he was bored or he really didn't want to be there. The only time that look left him was when he'd glance down, with concern, toward the end of the bar at a gray-haired guy drinking alone who looked as if he were about to fall off his stool. The older man had turned his head when Larry flashed the card, but after a few mutters he had gone back to looking into his glass.

The bartender, the gray-haired man, and everyone else in the place shared two distinguishing marks: A certain button-down look, and a strong impression of dissatisfaction. Malone's was full of blue Oxford-cloth shirts, tweed, and wrinkled foreheads. It just didn't seem right. Maybe I'd watched too many episodes of *Cheers*. It must be nice to get away from the troubles of the day to a place where everybody knows your name and they're always glad you came. Sitcoms aside, there must be real taverns where you can always find a friend, where the neighborhood keeps its continuity from year to year, and the wood practically glows with the sense of fraternity. So what was it with Malone's? I mean, this was Friday night. That doesn't mean the place had to have one guy after another buying the house drinks, or loud off-key versions of "Irish Eyes Are Smiling," but I was really tempted to ask the bartender, "What's the story here?"

Larry and I had finished our drafts. It was my turn to call Wally, and as I got up I realized we hadn't eaten all day and that the beer was making me a little top-heavy. The bar seemed noisier by the pay phone. Sinatra was singing "You Make Me Feel So Young"

55

behind me. I didn't think I slurred any words in telling Wally everything was fine in Connecticut, but it was one of those times when you couldn't be sure the other person wasn't wondering about the way you talked.

Just as we started, two guys next to me escalated an argument they had been building. One of them yelled, "Hey, man, why don't you keep your big nose outta my life?" I put one hand over my open ear so I could hear Wally ask, "Where are you, anyway?"

"Oh, some restaurant we found on the road," I lied. "First place we came across." Just then the argument turned into a fistfight. One of the guys knocked the other into me, jarring the phone loose. The handset dangled and bounced off the wall as I grabbed for it, and Wally's voice kept coming faintly out of it.

"*What* the hell is going on there?" The fact that I could hear him at all meant that the usually calm tone had an annoyed edge. At that moment, someone started playing "Knights in White Satin" on the jukebox.

"Wally, you won't believe it, but do you hear the song? Remember the story you told us about being on the road? . . . Oops, look out, the little guy's down. Now he's up. They're still swinging. Now they're leaving." By the time Wally hung up, who knows what he thought?

The gray-haired man from down the bar had moved up near Larry and demanded a refill. "Come on, Eddie," the bartender was saying, "you don't need any more." Eddie glared and jabbed a finger toward his glass. The bartender sighed and poured another whisky. It was odd. A man behind a bar can shut you off at his discretion. What made him so obedient to Eddie?

In the Commons at college, I'd learned to amuse myself by wadding up napkins and pitching them into empty glasses. Now I hit Larry's glass from four or five feet away. That got Eddie's attention. He wadded up his own napkin, threw it at my glass, missed. I replied with a clean shot into his, and the contest was on. Eddie kept shooting and missing while I put four in a row into his glass. Well, maybe the soggy paper would keep him from drinking any more for a while. The next thing we knew, half the people in the place had caught the basketball fever. Balled-up napkins were flying everywhere. The bartender did nothing about it.

About then, a delivery man brought in a couple of kegs of beer.

He didn't hand the clipboard to the bartender to sign. He handed it to Eddie. Aha. Eddie owned the place. When he swayed off to the men's room I finally did ask the bartender, "What's the story?"

"Eddie's wife died six months ago," he said. "And then his son died. He was a nice guy. Fun, you know? But he went bitter. Before, he would take a drink with his friends. Now he drinks all the time. It's like he wants to hurt himself."

Eddie came back. "You there, big guy," he said. "I bet you like to arm wrestle."

"No, no thanks, I don't."

"Come on, let's see how strong you are, Mr. Olympics."

I really didn't want to compete. I had forty pounds on him and a lot less to drink. But his challenges got increasingly loud, and we finally put our elbows on a table and started. I wondered, How am I going to get out of this gracefully? If I lose, it'll look so stupid that he'll probably be more insulted than if I win. After a first fierce push, there was no strength in his arm, but I held him up and we went back and forth while I tried to decide what to do. Finally it just got too ridiculous and I had to put his arm down. Eddie withdrew to his stool around the corner to talk to himself.

Through it all, Larry had been the real star of the bar, talking to one and all about the Olympics. Even if he was doing a good job of building interest in the torch run, by now I just wanted to get out, and I started saying, "Hey, Larry, let's go." The young beer-truck driver came back in, evidently finished with his route and ready for some refreshment, and Eddie's mutters got loud.

"You guys are gonna run me out of business," he announced to the driver, who did his best to pretend he didn't hear. "I give you free drinks and whatta you do, you raise your prices on me." The driver was concentrating on not looking at him. Eddie got off his stool, swayed over behind him, and before anyone realized what was happening, hooked his hand in the man's collar and hauled back on it. They both hit the floor and started rolling around. To get Eddie off, the driver finally had to pop him over the eye. As we left, there was Eddie, on his feet, weaving, now with a dab of blood on his forehead. So much for *Cheers.*

Outside Malone's, we spotted another bar several doors away. It was so full that you could hear sounds of celebration from the street. We were tired, we'd really had enough to drink, we should be finding a place to stay—but we had come all this way to discover places and meet people, and where could a stranger in town meet people if not in a bar? Against all reason, Larry and I wanted to keep going a little longer. So we stepped through the next set of doors, into a place so completely packed with people that it looked like layers of them, wall to wall. The noise was deafening. What conversation we could hear was louder and lighter than in Malone's. The lights were brighter. The place looked sharper-edged and somehow less comfortable. It didn't have the brush of warmth, along with the tragedy and drama, that you felt at Malone's. This could have been any bar in Los Angeles.

Before I could pull off my coat and catch my breath, two customers who had been at Malone's spotted Larry and raised a cry, "Hey! Hey! It's the Olympic guys! These guys are running in the Olympics!"

No, no, we tried to insist, we're not running, we're just driving around. Larry disappeared into the mob, and one of the hue-and-criers pushed me over to the bar. "Give this man a beer!" he shouted. "He's from Los Angeles and he's running in the Olympics!"

No, I started to say again. He was looking at me. Other people were looking at me. But nobody seemed to be making eye contact. Maybe they'd been in there too long. "No, we're just working out a route for—"

"That's great, that's great! What distance do you run? Hey, this guy is running in the Olympics!" Where was Larry? We've had enough of the bar scene. There was something cold about this loud crowd. I wondered if a lot of them were Malone's regulars who drifted down here when Eddie went sour. His place had a reputation once; that's why Larry had heard of it. Had they left him just when he needed them? Where was their loyalty? It was time to find a meal and a bed.

Yale was still out there when I opened my eyes the next morning. Time to put on my sweats and Nikes for a run. The sun was bright—a good thing, considering the mean wind that hit you the instant you stepped outside. The temperature must have been five below zero. It was too cold to run, and too exciting not to.

That first daylight view of Yale had it all. Here was an upper-class Ivy League university right in the middle of a town that had seen some hard times, from the look of it. New Haven had at least a couple of slummy looking blocks within easy running distance of the Gothic dormitories on Memorial Quadrangle. A nice balance. Going to college on the beach in California had left me yearning for the mystique of two-hundred-year-old buildings with ivy, not bougainvillea, growing on them, the tradition of football rivalries in frosty weather, and Nathan Hale and Noah Webster on the list of graduates. On top of that, Yale was in the middle of the city, involved.

Running and looking, marveling at my luck in being there, I forgot the cold for almost too long, and clumped back to my room just short of frostbite.

7

Car Thieves

The Super Bowl was less than sixteen hours away, so we hustled toward Boston, intent on settling down for a little time-out in front of a television set on Sunday afternoon. But the real magnet for both of us was across the Charles River, in Cambridge. We got rooms near Harvard Square.

Now we were at *the* university, the one the other traditional schools got their traditions from. You always heard, growing up, that Harvard was the best. That alone had stoked my curiosity about what such a place looked like and felt like. And there was even more: It was part of the territory where the Kennedys lived and campaigned, walking the wards, seeing the people and being seen. Love him or hate him, John F. Kennedy pulled young people into public life in a way that few professional politicians ever had. It was hard to imagine him coming from any place but here. He used television, sure, but that didn't make him special; there were people here, up behind those windows with the warm yellow light coming out, who had heard him up close, touched his arm, who knew his family. Who still feel like family. With all their crowds and worn old pavements and people bumping up against each other so casually, these Northeastern cities had a feel of community that never occurred to me in the suburbs on the Pacific rim.

We wandered out to look for a burger and soak up the sights. Hearing about Harvard Yard, I'd always thought they might have a gate they closed at night, but you can walk through it any time. We got out of the car and admired the old buildings. Old was right. Beautiful Colonial brick, like Massachusetts Hall. The ivy would be perfect when it sprouted leaves in the spring. But old wasn't everything. Huge was the word for the columns and the sweep of

60

steps up to Widener Library, and modern was what you'd have to call the Le Corbusier style of the Carpenter Center near the Fogg Museum.

On Massachusetts Avenue we heard some New Wave music coming from a club. The three-dollar cover charge almost stopped us, but it was ten o'clock at night by now, the place was warm, and from inside the band sounded great, so Larry went to park the car while I found us a couple of seats. The people inside dealt a final blow to my stereotype of eastern college crowds. Among the button-downs, chinos, and Weejuns, they sported a mix of semi-punk dyed hair in spikes, T-shirts, and thrift-shop outfits.

The band started playing, and soon they were cooking. It was so loud that conversation was impossible. Some people pushed back tables to make a little place to dance; some just listened. The band apparently had a following; people around us lip-synced words to songs I'd never heard. The beat cut through any differences there might have been between townies and students. People in preppy getups bobbed their heads next to people who looked as if they slept on the streets. We were in familiar territory, among our peers for the first time in several days, and got nicely relaxed. It was well past midnight when fatigue set in and we headed for the door.

The cold smacked us as we emerged, and we hustled a couple of blocks down to Larry's parking spot and looked across the street to . . . no car. Barely peeping out from a snow bank where he had parked was the tip of a fire hydrant. I would never have seen it, either. We had been towed. Damn. We wanted to rest tomorrow, not stumble around a tow yard—if the tow yards around here were even open on Sundays. And we'd certainly need the car first thing on Monday. Better try for it now.

Larry called the police from a phone booth on the corner while the cold chewed through my Topsiders and three pairs of socks and started working on my toes. They told him the location of the tow yard, way off in some mysterious corner of Cambridge. We didn't know one end of this city from another. Son of a . . . How were we going to get there, or back to the hotel, before we froze solid? Just then a cab cruised by, and with some frantic yells and waves we got it to stop.

Across town, the driver let us out in front of a chain-link fence topped by barbed wire that surrounded a massive collection of automobiles, some topped by a foot of snow. There was no sign of human life in there. The only thing missing was the dog. Ah, but look, the lock on the chain around the gatepost was open. For a second we wondered: Go in or not? Well, that was stupid. We had no choice. The cab had left.

As we took the lock off, three thoughts occurred to me: We're going to get shot, or chewed to bits by a slavering German shepherd, or (too late to save our lives) arrested.

We started tiptoeing through the prison camp. Every time a dog barked in the distance, we stopped breathing. The only reason I could imagine for the absence of the junkyard dog was that it was just too cold for the poor beast. At last we spotted our Renault. Fortunately, it was on the outside of a row, not blocked in. To get to it, we tiptoed past a little shed that had a faint light showing behind its curtains. We slipped quietly into the car and pulled on the doors until they latched softly; Larry eased the key into the ignition, turned it, and

WOMP BOMP A LOO MOP BA LAM BAM BOOM!!! . . .

The radio was still as we had left it, at top volume. Larry's terrified twist of the knob quieted Little Richard. We sat like stones, listening to the thud of our hearts. When we could talk, I whispered, "Larry. Turn it on and *floor* it."

The back wheels spun and threw rocks; then we were racing by the hut. Its door must have jerked open, for light spilled out onto the cars behind us.

"Hit it, Larry," I yelled. "Hurry!" The wind had swung the gate half shut, but neither of us gave a thought to getting out to open it. Larry bashed it open with the bumper and we skidded onto the street. After he got us around the corner and the lights of the yard were out of sight, we turned Little Richard back on and laughed, near hysteria, into the night.

8

Visiting the Visitors

Wherever we stopped this time, we wanted to hole up for a day or so to do calculations on the dash we'd just made from the southeast corner of Massachusetts across the breadth of Connecticut into New York State. It would be nice if we could do it in someplace lively. At seven in the evening, West Point looked pretty dark. We figured the cadets wouldn't have much time to chat. Larry said, "Let's push on to Princeton."

By half past ten we had checked in and hit the streets near the Princeton campus to look for a meal. At first the town looked as solemn as West Point. Quiet. "What do these people do on Thursdays?" I wondered. "Study?"

"Could be," Larry said. "This isn't California, you know."

A helpful passerby said to try a place called The Alchemist and the Barrister. Down an alley, securely secluded from the street, it was the place we'd been looking for—the picture-perfect Ivy League pub: well-dressed young men and women, some of them reading at their tables, all quiet conversation and lamplight, the atmosphere even warmer than the first impression of Malone's, and not a trace of a feeling that anyone had come in to get drunk and fight.

The one place to sit was a table in a booth already occupied by two young women drinking coffee. Both of them wore dark outfits that highlighted their faces, and both had strikingly healthy, natural looks, without much makeup (or much that showed). One had reddish hair slightly spiked up in a New Wave style. The other had long, dark brown hair parted on one side.

"Can we rent half your table?" I asked. They looked up, either puzzled or not amused. Okay, it was a dumb way to start. I tried

63

again: "Do you mind if we share your table? The restaurant is full."

Plain English worked better. "Sure, you are welcome," the dark-haired woman said in some sort of accent. They moved to give us room. When we got ready to order, I asked them, "Would you like anything? Since we've invaded your privacy . . ." The puzzled looks were briefer, and the dark-haired one said, "Thanks. Two coffees."

"You sound as if you're from Germany," I ventured. "Is that so?"

"Yes. From Darmstadt. That's near Frankfurt am Main, in West Germany."

"Oh," I blurted, "my grandfather is from Berlin. I'm half German. His claim to fame is that he had one of the first jazz bands in Berlin, in the 1920s. His name is Jack Stessel. Have you heard of him?" She saw no humor in that, either. Come to think of it, if she had cracked a joke in German, I wouldn't have gotten it. I plodded ahead anyway, talking slowly to be as understandable as possible. When Dark Hair got the gist of a sentence, she would translate it into German for Red Hair.

This was as tough for them as it was for me. Couldn't quit now, though. "What do you think of America so far?"

"The people are really nice. New York is huge. We only spend a day there, though. We live now in Princeton with a family—to earn money, we watch the baby, how do you say, baby-sit? My friend and I, we want very much to see California."

I caught myself talking slower and, as if it would help, louder. "Is America a place you would consider staying in? Have you thought of moving here?" How could I have said that? I'd always been ready to criticize the way we throw our weight around in the world and here, coming out of my own mouth, was the Ugly American assumption that any foreigner who sees this country immediately falls in love with it and wants to move here.

The way the women shook their heads conveyed two things: "No," and, "Are you kidding?" Dark Hair added, politely, "My home is Darmstadt. I was born there, I have lived there twenty-one years, my whole life. I would not leave my home. It is where I belong."

Grasping for a common interest, I remembered a song, "Ninety-nine Luft Balloons," by a big German rock star. "Are you fans of

Neena?" Red Hair heard a familiar name, smiled, and said, "Ah, Neena, yes."

"I really liked the song when it came out in German. Didn't understand the words, but that didn't matter. When it came out in English, I hope people listened to them. The antiwar message was very strong in the original, isn't that right? I hope it didn't get lost in translation." They nodded politely. The U.S. administration had been installing missiles in England and West Germany over protests from the public there, and we had been hearing of million-person demonstrations expressing fear and resentment of our behavior despite assurances from Ronald Reagan that our missiles were good for the people who lived in their shadow. "What do you think of our involvement in your country?"

Dark Hair shook her head again. "America is a very great country and we like the people very much. But your government is just using our country as a place to threaten the Russians. We have had bad experiences in the past with Russians, many of them, but I am made afraid by what you do now. A Pershing missile is now three kilometers from my family's house."

I thought of asking, "Does that make you feel safer?" but this did not seem a time for sarcasm; and she had already given her answer.

The hamburgers arrived. Larry attacked his. I was too caught up in the conversation to pay much attention to mine.

"Your government says it puts arms and soldiers in West Germany to protect Europe," Dark Hair continued. "Many others besides me believe that you really do not protect us, you protect yourselves and make us your . . . shield. You make us the target." The force of what she had to say pierced our language barrier, and she spoke more rapidly. "When we see American soldiers on the streets of Darmstadt, we think two things. We are furious to have them imposed on us, and we laugh because they are so useless, so ridiculous. I wish they would go home to this big country that has so much for them to do." She stopped. "I hope I do not offend you. Forgive me, please, if I do."

"You know," I said, "there are people in this country who agree with you."

At first glance, she had looked like a Princeton student. But she had been challenged as few of us, as students, ever had been. Many of us, it occurred to me, had hardly been challenged at all. Problems such as hers seemed far away, out of sight, and we kept pushing them onto someone else. Sitting in that booth, looking at that visitor from another country who was telling me something about my own, I wondered, How many twenty-one-year-old rock and rollers here speak that passionately about politics? Not enough, I answered myself. They don't feel their existence is being tested. It's somebody else's problem.

Red Hair said, *"Werden Sie nicht Ihren Hamburger essen?"* or something like it. At least that's what I wrote in my notebook.

"What did she say?" I asked Dark Hair.

"She said, 'Aren't you going to eat your hamburger?'"

9

The High and the Low of It

Luckily, Larry had an eye for comedy. We crammed so much energy into the little car that neither of us sat still for long. I switched radio stations nonstop, riffling through the buttons even when I liked a song, sure that something better was just a click away. Whichever of us was not at the wheel loved to reach over and beep the horn; drivers ahead would turn and glare at the innocent driver.

Some of the nonsense came from the relentless arithmetic of the kilometers, the cold that confined us behind rolled-up windows, the two weeks without a break from each other. Those trifling discomforts, which we amused ourselves by exaggerating, were no price at all to pay for the miracle of our mobility up and down a land so much bigger than anyone had ever told us it was. Still, we had to have our pranks.

In Princeton, Larry had shown me a new toy: the unexpected emergency brake. An icy parking lot, deserted in the middle of a weekday night, gave him room to demonstrate. You get up some speed. You yank on the hand brake—locking only the rear wheels, so you can still control the front—and then twist the steering wheel hard. The car whips into a skid that spirals it across the ice, leaving a donut-shaped track. A front-seat passenger could provide some thrills with the trick, too, even without the circles. As your driver approached a halt somewhere, say a rural stop sign, you could reach over and jerk the hand brake. It was stupid, childish, and a rush for both of us.

"Gimme a break!" Larry would yell. He'd turn on me, grinding his teeth and sometimes—not every time—laughing. "Make it your own fool neck! Not mine!"

67

He had only himself to blame for that one. By the time he showed me the donuts trick, he knew neither of us had much control over the high spirits we couldn't keep bottled up. Or over something else: The occasional tension that we didn't know how to release gracefully.

Tensions didn't always come from inside the car. The night we drove through Philadelphia, I made only two notes in my diary: "Rich Up—Poor Down," and "Rock at car."

What struck us both about our first quick look at that city was the huge gap between haves and have-nots. New York and Boston certainly had those gaps, but by the time we reached Philadelphia we were less awed and more aware of them. There was no escaping the cruel contrasts between the downtown City Hall area—the streets around its historic buildings filled with white, collegiate-looking armies of young professionals in suits of blue and gray—and the streets of South Philly.

There, the driving instructions on the schedule stopped making sense to us. We wandered deeper into a residential section where the faces were mostly black. We had our heads down, trying to decipher the map and making notes. When we looked up, some of the looks we got would probably have scared us if we had known what they meant. As we drove around looking for a missing street, the last of the daylight faded. On our third trip down one street, my head hit the roof of the car as I jumped at the sound of a stone bouncing off the door panel.

We did stick out: Two button-down white lads tooling around the neighborhood in a new car. But until someone threw the stone, we had been to preoccupied with our maps and schedule and lack of street smarts to appreciate just how far out we stuck.

As one week turned into the next, our restlessness carried all sorts of overtones: the high spirits, the occasional tension, and, I began to think, something else—something like the fitful waking spells of an uneasy night's sleep. I was starting to notice a worry that was hard to admit. Maybe this job was a mistake.

The torch run was getting us to places we wanted to see. We were getting good at our work and having fun. But . . . some of the time it left me feeling, so what? Kind of hollow inside, the way you do when you suspect you're wasting time.

We checked into the Washington Hilton around noon and walked to the LAOOC office on Avenue I. It was a compact place, decorated with the familiar official Olympic prints. The door was still closing behind us when we looked up and saw a delightful sight—Suzanne Lipps, running down a corridor toward us. She gave us both a hug, like a homecoming.

"You look great!" "*You* look great!" "Where you headed?" "Chicago. How about you?" And so forth, less a conversation than a babble of greetings. Before it went further, we heard loud voices from several rooms down the corridor.

"What's that?" Larry asked. "Ueberroth and the Russians?"

Suzanne just rolled her eyes. We walked into the room where the noise was, and saw Dan Triest and Mark Zangrando. The big argument was about how to get to Pittsburgh.

"Drive!" Dan said.

"Fly!" Mark insisted.

Dan, a former advance man for Jerry Brown's campaign for president in 1980, was about twenty-five and chunky, and had shown awesome ambition in the training seminar. He had preceded Larry and me to Boston, drawing up the schedule we'd been double-checking. Mark had left John Glenn's current presidential campaign to become a torch rat. His smooth Italian good looks and natty clothes gave him a frat-boy-turned-young-professional appearance.

Dan raised his voice another notch. "Listen, man, you're just too generous with LAOOC money, that's all I'm saying. We ought to drive and save the airfare."

"Ahh, come on, get serious," Mark countered, less noisy and more intense. "A day of our time is a lot more valuable at this point than a few bucks in plane fare. We've got priorities here. Let's try to keep them straight."

Larry looked over at me and we both grinned. So we weren't unique. It was some comfort to see that the pace could take its toll on others, too.

Later in the afternoon there was time for a run before dark. As I set out on a route that would give me a look at the White House, bureaucrats and businessmen and politicians and their support staffs were spilling out onto the streets. Some were headed home, some to dinner, some to bars like the one with a sign in its window ATTITUDE ADJUSTMENT HOUR. They made a sea of dark suits, identical haircuts, and sprinkles of tortoise-shell eyeglasses. Looking at one expressionless face after another, I couldn't help wondering, "What brings you here? Passion for issues? Hopes of changing the world? Power?"

I had wanted a Capitol Hill internship during college, but could never afford it, and always felt a little jealous of friends who did get one. To downplay my lack of opportunity, I had latched on to the opinion that people lose touch with the real America after they've been in Washington a while. I still figured they did. And still, I would have loved the chance to find out for myself.

At the corner of Pennsylvania Avenue, a right turn headed me toward my first close look at our most famous address. We had driven by it so fast earlier that I had failed to see the newly constructed barricade around the White House grounds. The thing looked very much like a freeway divider. It was a response to reports that "Libyan hit squads" were sneaking into the United States. Stopping across the street to take in the scene, I found it absurd and sad at the same time.

A man next to me lowered his camera, and we exchanged glances of agreement. Looking at the barricade that blotched one of our precious monuments, he looked troubled.

Beth Tucker, a good friend from UCSB, made time that evening to meet another friend and me at the Hilton. When she appeared, I jumped to my feet, as much from surprise as from manners. Beth had always been shy whenever a bunch of us got together to talk politics over a few pitchers at the pub; she was thoughtful and quiet, and used to slouch meekly into a room. Here, the person approaching the table seemed to have matured beyond me. The new impression came from more than just the flair of her navy blue suit. Beth was walking upright and assured, and her smile had a lively confidence that warmed us.

The presidential primary season would parallel the torch campaign, and she had just joined California Senator Alan Cranston's campaign. Dinner turned into a bull session about the virtues of various candidates, and of the much-maligned primaries. The season might be too long, its delegate rules might be confusing, but it was an X-ray of the politicians. It gave voters a crucial chance to see who was willing to dig into real issues, beyond the old flag-waving P.R.

"It's so easy to forget there are alternatives," Beth said. She wouldn't give an inch in her stand for her candidate, and you could tell that her loyalty had nothing at all to do with the glamor of power. "People can see intelligence and imagination," she said. "They see through gimmicks, when there's something better to see." In her heart, she put no trust in slippery tricks. She put her faith in the people she trusted to listen, the voters.

After our good-byes, I was left wondering. Beside Beth's idealism and commitment, my priorities looked kind of shabby. Face it. I missed politics. There was so much work to be done. Why didn't I put the rest of me where my mouth was, and if I thought some candidate was so worthwhile, join his campaign? What am I doing, spending all my time correcting computer printouts and driving all day counting kilometers for something that might be nothing more than patriotic hot air, when I should be doing something that mattered?

But Beth, now—Washington seemed to have changed her life. It might sound presumptuous to say I was proud of her, but I was, in the way you like to applaud a friend who has just done something great. She made me remember a side of myself that I missed. Maybe Washington wasn't completely filled with Mindless Bureaucrats.

10

Into the Heartland

Getting to Interstate 65 was a geography lesson. The night before, Chicago had looked big enough to reach the horizon, so it was interesting to see on a map that within minutes I would be out of the city, out of Illinois entirely, and into Indiana. Tonight's destination: Indianapolis and a first meeting with two new partners. Wally had assigned three of us to scout from the edge of Chicago to the edge of Atlanta.

Whiting, Indiana, was a new name to me; there it was, saying WELCOME when I thought I was still in Chicago, looking like one continuous oil refinery. Then, abruptly, the countryside. Traffic thinned out, and the newly rented blue Dodge glided past curious mounds with outcroppings of rock and gravel that turned out to be glacial moraines. The car carried me over streams with names like the clicking of rocks, the Kankakee, the Iroquois.

Across the Wabash River at Lafayette, some signs pointed to the Tippecanoe Battlefield, where General William Henry Harrison defeated a band of Shawnee Indians in 1811. Almost thirty years later he ran for president on the slogan "Tippecanoe and Tyler, too," Tyler being his running mate. What the Indians couldn't do in 1811, pneumonia did to Harrison in 1841. He caught it standing in the rain at his inauguration and died forty-one days later. The country got Tyler without Tippecanoe.

Every time I stopped and got out, people through here were less guarded, more friendly, than any I had met so far. Past the Wabash, a combination gas pump and convenience store looked good for a Pepsi, a bag of Cheeto Balls, and some advice about a tricky spot where two roads were supposed to join. According to the driving instructions from the torch committee, I should have passed it already.

This was no 7-Eleven chain store. It was a plain little ma and pa place. Ma, behind the counter, glanced at the Dodge out front, the only new automobile in sight, and asked mildly, "Are you from Chicago?"

"No, California," I said.

"Oh, *California*. Do you know Pomona? An old friend of ours lives—"

"Yes, but I don't know anyone there." I was downright curt about it. Evening was approaching, the weather looked like snow, I was not especially looking forward to what awaited me in Indianapolis, and I just wanted to get on with it.

That didn't bother Ma. She took my map and started studying it as if she really wanted to solve my problem. "Well," she said after a few moments of going, "Ah . . . hm . . . uh, huh . . . well, you'd get there easier by going out here"—running a finger up to a thick red line, glancing up to make sure I followed—"to the Interstate."

"Yes, but I really need to follow Route 52 here. I've got to see where Route 38 crosses it, so I need to stay on 52." I didn't want to get into any long explanations about the Olympics.

Ma looked at me with some curiosity. She said, "Let's see if Tommy knows how to get there," and called in a mechanic who was refilling the paper-towel container on the gas pump island. He had one of those blue gas-station shirts with "Tommy" embroidered over the pocket, a bulge of tobacco in his left cheek, and the same modest, friendly look that Ma had. Tommy started the same way she had: "You ought to get out to the Interstate . . ."

I cut in, my hurry starting to turn to impatience. "No, I gotta stay on this road. Have I missed the turn? Is it down that way? What can I look for?"

"He's from California, Tommy," Ma said.

"Oh," Tommy said. "I got a friend in Bakersfield. Don't suppose you know him—"

"Probably not," I said.

He gazed at the map, then looked at me. "Here's what you do. Route 38 here is Old Purdue Road, so if you see a sign that says that, you're all right. You still got about four miles straight down this road in front of us, so just stay on 52 here and you can't miss it."

A quick thank you and I was back in the Dodge shifting into Drive.

Less than a mile along, passing a farm, with the sharp, sweet smell of animals coming in the air vents and the sun nudging the horizon in the rear view mirror, I thought, "You schmuck. Those people stopped everything and came over to help, and all you could do was act like some general marching through."

The land flattened out, rising to an occasional ridge and dipping to the shallow valleys of streams like Sugar Creek and Raccoon Creek. Darkness and snow started falling together. By the time the car crossed I-465, the perimeter highway encircling Indianapolis, there was a thick cold blanket on the roadsides and the car hood. The Dodge and I were heading into a blizzard. David Halliburton had said on the phone to meet him and Jan Williams at a Howard Johnson's Motor Lodge near an exit from I-465, and something about his directions had made me ask, "How close is that to downtown?"

"Ten or twelve miles," he'd said.

"There's no hotels downtown?" We were going to be dealing with mayors, Indy 500 officials, and the kinds of people you find in the middle of a city. "How come we're staying so far out of it? Why not be in where we can get more work done?"

David had acted vague for a few seconds, then he had come out with it: He wanted to stay in Howard Johnson's Motor Lodges all the way because they gave bonus points you could cash in for prizes, and he was collecting points. Okay. But did I want to organize my next three or four thousand miles of American experience around bonus points? Well, we would deal with that later. Right now, here I was on a road bypassing the big city, peering through a torrent of snowflakes for an exit sign, any exit sign, looking for two people I wasn't thrilled about working with, still indulging in the cranky abruptness I'd shown the people at the gas station.

I had focused my life on getting this job. It was giving me a ticket to America. I loved it. Now it was sentencing me to two partners who were, from what I could tell, even more provincial than I was. "Guess who I got assigned to," I said when Mark Zangrando called from New York. "Donny and Marie."

Right, I had an attitude. I didn't know David or Jan well enough to justify likes, dislikes, or comparisons to the Osmonds. Little remarks here and there on the torch rats' telephone network, though, made both of them sound so clean-cut that I wondered who was going to translate for us when we had to talk.

David was a born-again Christian who had belonged to the scrubbed-up, upbeat Up with People group as a singer and promoter. He had grown up in Santa Barbara, on the right side of the tracks. Definitely not a street kid. The first time we met, I couldn't believe he was twenty-six years old; he looked like an untouched preppie with a good build and a careful haircut.

Jan was no street kid, either. She had grown up in Palo Alto, near the Stanford campus, in neighborhoods where people like judges live (her father was a Nixon judicial appointee). She had come to the torch run from a sports information job at Arizona State. Jan also seemed younger than she was. Her red hair, sprinkles of freckles, and diffidence suggested the nice kid in school who loves sports but doesn't play, so she works her way on to the team as manager.

I must have been nowhere near their first choice, either. They probably thought I spent my time stealing cars and bar-hopping through New England.

The three of us found each other in the motel by 10:00 P.M. and went next door for a snack. Jan had a beer, I had a beer, and David had a Tang or whatever he drank. Wally had said nothing to Jan or me, but David confided that the Southeast would be his region. Jan didn't seem to mind, and I certainly didn't. He would probably be good at it. David gave the impression that he always worked his butt off. He asked a lot of questions, even when he knew the answers, and he let it be known that he was giving a hundred percent.

We milled around in our seats, chatting and looking for a handle on how to arrange the next few days. By now we had all committed enough goofs and inefficiencies to rouse some ideas for improving the operation.

"You know," I said at one point, "Larry Silman and I just spent two weeks of fourteen-hour days together in a tiny car going over the first eight days of the run. If we had split up, it wouldn't have taken us that long."

David picked it up. "So we'd cover more ground if we drove separate cars and double-checked each other."

"Right. How about you guys taking the top part from Chicago down and me starting in Louisville?"

"That's fine with me," Jan said. David had no problem with it. He was entirely open, in fact, to the way our three personalities might complement each other. The deft work he did during the conversation to balance our strengths opened an entirely new possibility. We could end up being the best team in any region, without having to give up a single one of our differences.

11

Hero Worship, Lesson One

The telephone bell startled me out of a deep sleep. Grabbing for the receiver too fast, I wrenched my neck.

"It's only your old nine-to-five mother," said the voice, and I had to smile. Mom must have tracked down the number by calling the torch relay office in Los Angeles. "Where is the vagabond today?" she asked, and for a couple of seconds I didn't have an answer. Only five weeks on the road, and I'd started to think of locations by area code. Quick. The room-service menu. By some light leaking through the heavy hotel curtains I saw "Howard Johnson Motor Lodge." Indianapolis.

After a few minutes of banter I asked what time it was in California. "Ten," she said. Damn. That meant one in the afternoon here.

"Gotta run, Mom. I'll call you later this week."

David and Jan were sure to have left already for the drive north to start checking the route from Chicago. I'd better hit the road down to Louisville and the route south from there. Must have slept so long because it was so peaceful outside . . . Sunday morning. The blizzard had muffled us in a foot of fluff. Outside the curtains the snow was brilliant in the light of a clearing sky, and was already pretty much plowed off the streets around the hotel.

Packed and checked out, I wolfed down a pancake sandwich— three cakes, fried egg, crisp bacon, not bad—and scanned the Sunday *Star* for the Lakers score. Out in the parking lot, the Dodge looked jaunty under its cap of snow, so I brushed off the hood and rear window for safety and left the rest to the wind on the highway to Kentucky.

Interstate 65 runs generally parallel to Route 31, the southbound

77

two-lane road that the torch runners would take in May. We liked to stay on smaller roads whenever possible, so that spectators would see the runners up close. Driving a high-speed, eight-lane, divided superhighway today might prevent me from seeing much of the country along the exact torch route, but with a possibility of snow and ice patches on the smaller road, I would take the interstate. Even from it, though, the scenery rolling by the windows had an austere beauty: sharp ridges, the blue shadows of deep valleys, the rising roll of the foothills of the Cumberland Mountains.

From the middle of Indiana where Indianapolis sits as neatly as a navel, the Dodge had a gentle cruise for a hundred and thirteen miles to the Ohio River and the Kentucky border. The boundary between Indiana and Kentucky follows every wiggle of the river from east to west. So does the northern rim of Louisville, where the city and the two states share about eleven and a half miles of border. In my mind, that border divided the North from the South.

The South. I already had my mind made up about the South without ever setting foot in it. Most of what I knew of it came from television and movies. *Deliverance.* Stock car races. Sheriff Andy of Mayberry; Opie, Aunt Bea, and Goober. Gomer Pyle, the hick of the Marine Corps. I guess images like that are no less trite than the surfers, Valley Girl accents and hustling gurus that get used as shorthand for California. What also stuck in my mind, though, were harsher images from the sixties: Fire hoses blasting black teenagers. Cold eyes in smiling faces. Politics rooted in racism. "Outside agitators will be shot and buried." A regular gallery of preconceptions about a region I had not seen and people I had not met.

By half past five, the glow of a city skyline showed up ahead. The snow had thinned to just a frosting. Miles back, the slosh of tires on wet concrete had turned to a dry hum. The sun was gone. To my right the horizon still had some orange on it. To my left the sky shaded to purple, then black. Electric lights in the dusk looked warmer than the air outside. I had reached the only section of Indiana that glaciers never touched, the southern hills and lowlands. The fields and knobs that I could still see gave off a last little glow, blue-white from snow and limestone outcrops, tan and chocolate from patches of earth. At Jeffersonville I steered off I-65 onto Route 31, to pick up the torch route for the last mile into Louisville. And here came the border.

An openwork tunnel of steel girders ahead, capped by half a dozen peaked trusses, turned out to be the George Rogers Clark Memorial Bridge. The water below was dark, and smooth enough to reflect the city lights. A sign said OHIO RIVER. Another said WELCOME TO KENTUCKY. A third said LOUISVILLE. POPULATION 298,500.

Time to start thinking. An advance person looks ahead, sets up now as much as possible for tomorrow, extracts the most from the moment. What local color would make interesting media events? Where were the best backdrops for the runners? What I knew would fill a line and a half, at most, on the sports page: Louisville Slugger baseball bats. Kentucky Derby. Horses. Not much to hook the torch run to. . . .

Muhammad Ali! Wait a minute. The obvious is right under my nose. I'm driving over history here. This could be the spot where Muhammad Ali chucked his gold medal.

The story goes that when Ali was still Cassius Clay, he came home to Louisville after winning the light heavyweight boxing championship of the 1960 Olympics. Celebrities from television and radio lined up to make him a celebrity, too. The city gave him a parade. Then he took his family out for dinner in one of the ritzy restaurants overlooking this same Ohio River. The story goes on that the restaurant, in those pre–Freedom March days, found some excuse to turn the Clays away. After all the fuss over his heroic deeds, after all the politicians getting their picture taken next to him—this. A reminder from the white folks that he was still just a *Negro* hero (it would be a few years until we learned to say "black"). It must have seemed there would be no end to the insults and humiliations. He went to the river. He pulled his medal out of his pocket. He said something like, "If a man can't even take his family to dinner in his hometown in his own country, what is this thing worth?" and he dropped the medal in the drink.

The bridge fed the Dodge and me into a grid of one-way streets. I made some rights and lefts, checking the map, trying to get my bearings. Our little advance group was stretched so thin that we had no provision for logistics like calling ahead for hotel reservations, so I wasn't sure where to go. Every city has a Tenderloin, and from the glare of adult movie houses and raunchy shops on these streets I guessed I was in Louisville's. At night, Jefferson Street could have been Ninth Avenue near the Port Authority in

New York. I knew this city had better routes for the torch than this. Tomorrow I'd start finding them.

The first hotel I walked into had red carpeting that was frayed long before my time, and red flocked wallpaper in the lobby. Spittoons. A few chairs occupied by characters nodding off, either from fatigue or chemicals. I went up to the room (more red wallpaper) and washed my face, phoned in the nightly report to Wally in San Francisco, and called Mom back to apologize for rushing her off our conversation earlier.

Then it was time to go down and have a look around.

First stop was Happy Hour in the bar off the lobby. Not having to think about putting on a coat and tie until the next morning, I walked in wearing my cleanest University of California sweatshirt, jeans, Topsiders, and horn-rim glasses. A sharp smell greeted me, the one old bars get from lots of cigarette smoke and years of spilled drinks soaked into the floor. This was an honest drinking man's bar, and I looked like a kid who should be out on his paper route.

The other six people inside were paired up: The bartender and the cocktail waitress together at the far end, each with an elbow on the bar, chatting and surveying the place with that easy look of people who know they've made the team. He was younger than she, maybe forty to her fifty, and glossy, as if he spent his mornings outdoors in the fresh air. She was saying, "I can't believe she won't cover for me tomorrow, you know? You know how many shifts I've worked for her?" A couple at a table, probably my mom's age, whispered and smiled like two high school kids cutting classes. Whether they were having a fling or celebrating their anniversary I couldn't tell, but they looked happy. Two guys down the bar looked like buddies who had come in for a drink on the way home from some kind of work halfway between indoors and out— auto parts, maybe. Something about their long sideburns and flat cheeks fitted my formula for native Kentuckians. The work buddies kept their hats on. One wore a chewed-up cowboy straw, the other a cap with a National Rifle Association patch on the front. Each of them had a white belt holding up blue pants over a pretty fair case of Dunlap's Disease, the condition an old Teamster buddy back home defined as "where your belly done laps over your buckle." Everyone but me looked to be at least forty. The music was country, completely.

Maybe I'd never been in their state before, but those guys were familiar. Loading trucks for United Parcel Service before I went away to college, I'd got an early idea of what it meant to have power—or not have it. At last I was a Real Man to my stepfather, a Teamster, Local 234, who came home sweaty. And I was working my way up the pecking order. At the top was the pickoff man, who directed the flow of packages coming off the little brown local vans toward the big semi-trailers. At the bottom were the loaders in the Los Angeles Metro semi, working frantically for a six-hour shift inside the trailer to stuff thousands of packages in the right piles for hundreds of little towns.

In the middle of the shift, an alarm would go off and we'd have a fifteen-minute break. The last two or three minutes of it were GIT, General Information Time, for union announcements and safety information. In one of our GITs, the shop steward said, "All of you, write to your congressman and senator and Carter and tell them to lay off deregulation." President Carter's plan to deregulate the trucking industry enraged the Teamsters, who had their own ways of regulating it.

"Excuse me," I'd said. "I thought this was for union and safety stuff, not politics. Besides, maybe deregulation isn't such a bad idea." The next day, I was back inside the L.A. Metro semi.

But there was a pull to loading trucks. Even though I seemed to spend my life trying to get somewhere else, there were plenty of times when it looked like a pretty good life. When the shift ended, a bunch of us would turn our backs on the loading dock and leave it behind until tomorrow. We'd scout up some beers, and there would be talk about girlfriends, families, and the little victories at work that day.

From where I've worked, the country isn't all politicians and rich executives who can't explain exactly what they do. The heart of it, I bet, is tough-looking guys like the two buddies sitting to my right. They put in a day at some job that never gets written up in the paper, and they can tell you what they do. They leave at five and go home to their wives, who do a job that *nobody* gives them credit for, and they see their kids. And they've got each other for friends.

The work buddies were arguing over who wrote the song that had come up on the jukebox. It was Patsy Cline singing "Crazy." My stepfather listens to country music, so I've been exposed to it for years and some of it sticks. I knew the answer. Here was my opportunity to say hello. Except . . . part of me wished it would go away. No matter how confident I made myself look in high-powered meetings for the torch run, outside of those meetings the simple task of meeting people different from me was often a struggle. A job makes you a player in a game. It gives you structure, introductions, a vocabulary to start with. In a job, I could override my shyness. Here, though, in this supposedly relaxed setting where all I wanted was for somebody to talk to me, I wondered if I should add my two cents to the work buddies' argument. Part of me wanted to say hello by blurting out the answer; another part didn't want to invade their privacy. The part that wanted to say hello finally won. I leaned sideways for attention and, hoping to sound casually firm—an airline pilot drawl would have been perfect—said, "Willie Nelson wrote it." But the shyness choked me. My overture came out as a little croak. The work buddies glanced around to see who was croaking. What they saw must have fitted the voice they heard, a strange kid in horn-rim glasses looking tentative and embarrassed. They glanced at me and looked away as if I didn't exist.

There had already been a few nights when I never left my hotel room for fear of just this scene. Now that it was happening, it didn't seem so bad. There was still tomorrow. In the daylight I'd be scouting backdrops for runners, choosing a route, finding people who wanted to talk business. Most times I'd have given it a second effort, but tonight the shyness beat me, and I paid up and headed for the safety of my room.

Next morning I sketched a possible route and started driving to see if it worked. The city looked much more manageable, and a lot more handsome, in the sunlight. We would come over the bridge and loop through the redevelopment along Main Street near the river, including the gleaming Kentucky Center for the Arts at the Riverfront Plaza where the city holds Heritage Festivals; then head through several parks and up River Road toward the manicured gardens and imposing Old Kentucky homes in East Louisville. Nice. From there we would run southeast through bluegrass country to the state capital at Frankfort; Lexington; and turn south for Knoxville.

Between odometer checks I had plenty of time to wonder, "What are we going to do for a media event here?" Well . . . it's true, Muhammad Ali would be perfect. Past Olympian. Possibly the most famous man in the world. Long gone from Louisville, now living in Los Angeles—that was even better. The drama of the old story would attract journalists from everywhere: Muhammad Ali returns to run the Olympic flame through the town that wouldn't serve him dinner.

What about the difficulty he seemed to be having with his speech? People were noticing some slowness and slurring, and the rumors implied he'd been punched in the head once too often or might have something like Parkinson's disease. A week or so before, I'd stayed up to get my nightly dose of David Letterman's "Late Night" show, and there was Ali on the hotel television screen. He seemed tired, but his mind was quick and his grin was as playful as ever. Something else: Along with his humor, he projected a massive kind of calm dignity. Where he had once put together dazzling physical combinations with his feet and hands, now he was somehow putting together an emotional version of those combinations that was every bit as impressive. No, more impressive. What I saw was Ali showing real grace about his role at the moment. Unlike a lot of ex-athletes who can't deal with life after sports, Ali seemed to have no ego tied up in defensiveness about the old glories. He played along with Letterman's harmless needling, answering a question about what he did with his days: "Oh, I sleep until noon, eat lunch, take a nap, have a big dinner, go on a talk show. See, I don't do anything." He had fun with it, knowing, behind whatever he said, that people still follow him down the street like the Pied Piper, still write him so many letters that he can't get them all answered even though he works at it every day, and never stop asking him to lend his presence to their events.

Ali was one of my heroes when I was a boy. Boxing is not my favorite sport, but there is something about a person in any sport that you have to appreciate when the person towers among the best that have ever been. Ali's being a great fighter was not the only thing about him that I looked up to. There have been other great fighters. What made him special was the way he *thought*. He was intelligent. All that talk about being the greatest was great

83

show business; he knew how to please an audience then, and he still knows how. Then there was his outspokenness—his refusal to enter military service during the Vietnam War. Can you imagine some million-dollar athlete of the 1980s giving up three years of his prime to back up what he believes in? Ali had a conscience and was willing to pay for it. When he said, "Those Viet Congs never did nothin' to me" in 1967, he knew he would be stripped of the championship for which he had fought. A world champion twenty-five years old, whose livelihood was so perishable, so dependent on youth and strength and coordination, doing what he did—to me, that was valiant. Ali must have known the Army would not have sent him out where soldiers were getting killed. The champ would have been a showpiece on exhibition, an endorsement of the war. He would not lend himself to that. A lot of people did not admire him then and do not today, but to me he represented a peak of skill and intensity and integrity. There was nobody to compare to him.

One arm on the wheel, pushing sixty-five or seventy miles an hour, probably faster for a fast song, I was so caught up in my thoughts that I looked up and asked myself, "Who's been driving this car for the last half hour?" The Dodge and I were heading south from Lexington, out of bluegrass country into the Pennyroyal— "Pennyrile"—Region named for a variety of mint that grows there. The car rolled up and down hills, between fields with a few cows now and then, past silos and houses with real front porches, and no tractors or other cars—for the moment—ahead of us.

On two-lane roads like this I would often come up behind three or four other cars poking along. When I'd lean out to see what was holding us up, almost always there was a farmer ahead on a tractor, or sometimes in a pickup. It isn't that the roads don't have plenty of pullouts. You almost never see the tractors and pickups use them. You just have to wait, or risk roaring out into the left lane to pass everybody. After a while, you understand: You're on their turf. This is farm country. Those guys are not interested in what time you want to get to Knoxville. When you're on my turf, on the West Coast, you drive as fast as you can get away with, and that's how fast I was going at the moment I had the road to myself.

Another thing you don't see much on the West Coast is cemeteries. Maybe people there don't want to be reminded that they die. In any case, the dead are tucked away somewhere. Cemeteries in the East are a familiar part of the roadside scene, all green and white out there next to churches, showing off their headstones and fences and flowers. As I skimmed along at seventy miles an hour, I half saw one to the left. What happened then is probably impossible, but an instant after that casual glance, I realized I had picked one name off a headstone: Barr. Was that really what the headstone said, or was it fate saying, "Slow down"? Either way, I got the message. I hit the brakes and pulled over. The face in the mirror was white as the stripe on the road. Nobody would catch me driving faster than sixty for the rest of the torch run, anywhere.

12

For What?

Winter gave us a hint of spring with one of those Friday after-noons that pull you out to feel the air—sixty degrees or so, soft and full of clear light. I laced up my running shoes and jogged from the hotel toward the Tennessee River, hoping to bump into Ralph Boston in a way that would be less formal than calling ahead for an appointment.

Boston won the gold medal for the long jump in the 1960 Olym-pics, setting a new record at the time. I'd heard he now worked for AT&T in Knoxville, and that he coached a women's relay team that trained at the University of Tennessee track.

It wasn't just the weather that was warm. Knoxville turned out to be more of an easy and pleasant place to be with every day, a circumstance all the more surprising because I'd felt so recently that I was crossing into something like a foreign country. The differences from home were real enough to make you notice that they didn't cut down people's friendliness, or at least my attention to it.

"Ah kin tale yore not from rayon haya," the first waitress who brought me a hamburger said, looking me in the eye. "Yore ak-sayunt." We both smiled, delighted that she was using the old joke, probably for the five hundredth time, to give me an opening to say I really liked it rayon haya.

University of Tennessee sports are a dominant fact of life in Knoxville. Year in, year out, a hundred thousand fans pack Neyland Stadium for football games, and they give the same lively support to Volunteer basketball and track teams. The twenty-five or thirty people in warmup suits at the track this afternoon were there for serious practice. Relay runners timed their handoffs,

86

sprinters bounced up and down in the blocks. Nobody in sight looked like a coach, so I decided to do a few laps and see if one would show up.

The track was one of those springy modern surfaces that almost fools you into thinking you're some sort of runner. Even so, the scene had me a little intimidated. Back in a place like Malone's, people seemed to actually think I could be an athlete. Here, the athletes were real. Every step had purpose, every inch of muscle and bone was used fully. Those trim bodies made my own huffs and puffs sound awfully loud as I flopped around the track, and I kept carefully out of the way in the outside lane.

A tall man in a gray suit walked down from the stands. The stopwatch on a cord around his neck meant "coach." I pulled up about thirty feet short as he finished giving instructions to a couple of women runners, then went up and asked, "Excuse me, are you Ralph Boston?"

Pleasantly, he said, "Yes." He looked down at me through wire-rimmed glasses with photo-gray lenses.

As soon as I said "Olympic Committee," his face closed. Maybe this is just my imagination, I thought, and pushed on. "I was hoping we could work together on an event of some sort here at UT. . . ." More and more, the look in Ralph Boston's eyes forced my voice to trail off, as if I had said something wrong. He let a silence sit there for five seconds or so. It seemed like a month. Then he sucked in his breath.

"Look, Steve. Nothing against you personally, but I don't know if I'm interested." That was the last thing I expected to hear. Everybody said what a good guy Ralph Boston is, a gold medalist, works for AT&T, is coaching Olympic hopefuls. And he wasn't interested?

His voice cut harder. "You're not the first person from the L.A. Olympics who's got hold of me. Here's the problem. They want me to go out there and be a track and field commissioner at the games. Isn't that nice? Except they expect *me* to foot the whole bill. They won't pay my airfare. They won't put me up in a hotel. I won a gold medal, they want me there for their show, and they won't pay any expenses. It's not just the money, it's the chintzy attitude. They ought to take care of their own. They ought to treat us better than that." Behind the words was a passion and a bitterness that stirred me up. By God, he was right. How dare the people in power do this? At that moment I'd have turned around and fought for him.

But fight whom? With what? For what? "Mr. Boston, I wish I had some say in it. I see what you mean. It sounds rough. I don't agree with everything that goes on back in L.A., either. But I don't have a thing to do with that end of the games." His intensity had me so involved that it never occurred to me to ask, "What's the big problem? Other people get asked the same thing and don't object." All I wanted to do was get away, the way you want to when someone starts yelling in the office. A couple of track guys ran by and glanced over with looks that clearly wondered, "Boy, what did *that* guy do to Mr. Boston?"

The day had started with high hopes for working with a man who had accomplished a lot, and was ending with more doubts. Never mind my doubts; they didn't count. There must be something more, though, to Ralph Boston's indignation than just airfare and hotel bills; it had the taste of real bitterness. Maybe it had something to do with the pittance a black long-jumper got in 1960 compared to the endorsements and income a gold medalist commands nowadays. Maybe coming down from the heights to everyday life was a daily irritant. Or maybe he was saying something true about the outfit I'd gone to work for.

Ralph Boston was not the only athlete who had lost his reverence for the sacred Olympics. On the way back to the hotel, I remembered something a friend, Nancy White, had said. Nancy was on the 1980 field hockey team that couldn't go to the Moscow Olympics because of the U.S. boycott. She had a bad taste in her mouth about the Olympics, and not just from the politics of the boycott.

"I can't help wondering what the Olympics are really for," she had said. "A lot of the athletes feel as if we're just window dressing. . . . You know the toughest thing about living in an 'Olympic Village'? It's having to work every day, consciously, to remind ourselves that we really are there to compete with each other as athletes. In the Olympic atmosphere, that's so easy to forget. You hear so much talk about the endorsements a *win* will bring—if you're in the right sport. The whole time you're there, with that constant buzz about agents and contracts in the background, you're living in

dormitories, eating dorm food. When you look around at the lim-
ousines and the big suites in hotels, you know who you see in
them? The corporate big shots. I don't mean a hockey player ought
to live in a suite. I mean it's just so *obvious* that the games aren't
for the athletes. You get no recognition unless you can be used to
sell a product. Never mind the rhetoric the Olympic Committees
feed the public. Athletic competition isn't what the games are
about. They're about profits."

The next couple of weeks were a crosshatch of drives between
Lexington and Atlanta to research alternate routes in case Memorial Day weekend traffic jammed us up anywhere from Indianapolis
on down. It gave me a great chance to sing off-key and think I
sounded perfect, as long as the radio was loud enough to drown
me out.

Heading back to Knoxville one cloudy afternoon, I was taking a
first look at Kentucky Route 25E. Past Flat Lick, Four Mile, and
Pineville, I was expecting the Tennessee border when all of a sudden the road sign up ahead said VIRGINIA. I almost slammed on the
brakes. Had I zoned out and gone into some sort of space warp?
Virginia is up near Washington, D.C. Better have a look at the
map. There it was, a little sliver of Virginia poking down in here
like an extended toe, between two other states.

The geography of this old part of the United States still shows
some of the rich tangles that formed us. A mile later, another sign
put us in THE GREAT STATE OF TENNESSEE . . . WELCOME.

A few miles farther on, the music was still blaring and I was
looking forward to relaxing in Knoxville, when the traffic clogged
up and then stopped. Both lanes of the road appeared full of cars
and pickup trucks as far ahead as I could see. We moved a bit,
every four or five minutes. Stop, go, stop, go . . . mostly stop . . .
for no reason you could see. This was farm land, with no shopping
centers or factories that I'd heard of. If it was some horrible accident, I didn't want to look when we got to it.

Eventually we crept up to a place where there was a small one-
story stucco building on the left. It had no identifying sign that I
could see. There was no accident; a lot of drivers were trying to
find space in a little parking lot in front of the building, or stopping
on whatever shoulder they could find off the road. In the parking

lot, a big semi was backed up to the building. Three or four men were unloading boxes from it. That's what everybody seemed to want, what was in the boxes.

Then I noticed a handmade sign taped to the side of the building. In red letters on white cardboard, it said something like FEDERAL CHEESE SURPLUS PROGRAM. A line of people, thirty-five or forty at the time, was moving slowly past a table that was set up near the door of the building. There was something unusual about the people. Stopped by the traffic jam, I had time to sort out what it was. There was none of the chatting and joking you notice in lines at the checkout counter or the movies. Nobody looked ragged or poor. All the men and women in the line were white, all solid-looking people in denim or plaid work shirts and jeans or overalls, some wearing straw hats and some with gimme caps that read "Cat" or "Deere."

What seemed so familiar about them? Yes. A few evenings before, I'd seen a Bud Light commercial that featured two obviously substantial farmers in a huge expanse of rolling cropland. The commercial showed them pausing in their work, which was clearly important and clearly a source of pride, to applaud silently as a projected version of an Olympic torch runner (let's hope ours will look as good) went by. These people standing in line looked just like them, except that these people did not look proud. They were embarrassed. They were avoiding each other's eyes, slouching, not talking. Even from a passing car window you could see lines of pain cut into faces, teeth clamped shut. The people moved forward as if they were going to be executed, or castrated. Silence. The mood was as gray as the sky.

I sat there with the engine running, stunned. All I could figure was that they were men and women who had worked hard all their lives, done all right, held up their heads around their neighbors, and now had to come and accept charity—free cheese the government was giving to people who couldn't feed themselves—as if they were those big-city welfare recipients everyone around here shook their heads about.

My father had wandered away when my brother Mike and I were little, and he never sent our mother any child support. She took care of us the best she could. And she did it without asking for handouts. Just once, for two weeks when things were very tight, somebody persuaded Mom that food stamps were her due. I was nine. One day she sent me to the store with some stamps. I will never forget the pain of standing in the checkout line, keeping the stamps covered as long as I could, then handing them up quickly to the cashier. Her motion, as she held them up and put them in the drawer just as if they were cash, couldn't have taken more than a couple of seconds, but it made one of the longest moments I will ever live through. I was so ashamed.

Past the giveaway point, traffic thinned out again. For the moment, I couldn't stand the sound of the radio. Those people hadn't done anything extra bad. In fact, by the standards we all honor, they had probably been extra good. Yet I was the one free to drive by, headed for a comfortable hotel and an expense-account meal, while they had to stay back there. Why am I so lucky when the next guy isn't? That was a question I couldn't answer.

People see beer commercials and political promotions in which farmers are strong, homespun, upright, and proud, and think that's America. And in some places it is. Back up the road were farmers just as strong and homespun, but beaten down and ashamed. That's America, too.

13

Neither a Doctor's Son nor a Lawyer's

It must be amazing to look at the world as someone who knows more than one word for "green." The old Indians, I've heard, had dozens of words to describe plants that we just call green, according to what season the plant was in—putting out new growth, ripening its fruit, waiting for rain, bracing for winter. Across hundreds of thousands of acres from the roadside to the horizon, spruce trees, firs, and I don't know what else, dappled the land in more shades of green than anyone could count, much less name. The farther away they were, the more nearly blue the forest was in the haze that gives the Great Smoky Mountains their name.

The Newfound Gap Road climbed across the spine of the national park. To the left, Mount LeConte bulked up to 6,593 feet. To the right, behind a layer of cloud, Clingmans Dome rose (the map said) to the highest point in Tennessee at 6,643 feet. The rent-a-car was rolling through the most massive mountain uplift in the East and one of the oldest land areas on Earth, where for one stretch of thirty-six miles the main ridge never drops below 5,000 feet. Newfound Gap and the state line coincide at 5,048 feet. From there down to the foothills we were in North Carolina.

As vast and romantic as the Smokies are, south of them where the Nantahala National Forest begins is country with its own different beauty. The mountains are sharper, and in spots the edge of the road drops in a nearly vertical vista down a valley cut by a river—the Nantahala? the Little Tennessee? I didn't know—glinting far below. That stretch of Route 19 got my vote for underrated scenic wonder of the month.

In the midst of those wonders, I saw a sign that said QUALLA BOUNDARY CHEROKEE INDIAN RESERVATION. Toward the foothills,

92

both sides of the road showed an increasing clutter of cars that looked not just abandoned, but abandoned years ago. Farther on, in front of a little shack, a man who might have been seventy, wearing some paint on his face, tried to wave me down. He wanted me to come into the little shop behind him, under a sign that said AUTHENTIC INDIAN SOUVENIRS, and he pantomimed aiming a camera. The pantomime was well done and perfectly clear: I could buy permission to take his picture. From the look of the shop, and the look of him, I wondered if anyone had stopped there in years. The Cherokee Nation once inhabited much of the entire Southeast. Now a remnant of it was selling himself as a picture subject for tourists, standing out there with practically nothing to offer but self-mockery.

Coming out of the ancient Smoky Mountains through the rolling waves of trees all around them, driving through this area was a physical shock. It was an urban slum in the middle of the forest. A clump of young people stood by the road. One in particular was staring, just staring up the road, as if he were waiting for something to come along for him.

Murphy, North Carolina, fifteen miles from the Georgia border, came up around nightfall. Across the Hiwassee River, I pulled off at the BUSINESS 19 sign and slowed down to see what I could recognize of a town I was seeing for the first time.

Memories of Murphy, or what felt like memories, came from Peter Jenkins's book, *A Walk Across America*. On the left, as I looped through town, was what could have been the basketball court where Jenkins met the Oliver brothers, the three young black men who took him home to meet their mother and shared their mobile home on Texana Mountain with him for four months. No basketball players tonight.

With one foot in the motel office, I looked down and realized I looked more like a member of a stump-clearing crew than an Olympics salesman. Rumpled from the ankles up, unshaven since yesterday morning, baseball cap pulled low. Trashy. But it didn't matter. I didn't plan on any meetings until tomorrow. Nobody in Murphy knew me. I had the luxury of anonymity.

At the "ding" of the bell, a door behind the desk opened and the resident manager looked out, shushing a couple of children who were watching television in the room behind her. She smiled and pointed to a registration form. I wrote my name.

"Oh, Mr. Barr!" the manager exclaimed. "We've been expecting you."

I froze. Expecting me? This felt like an episode of *The Twilight Zone*. How could they expect me? I hadn't found my voice when she said, "You're going to announce the torch route." Turning back to a stack of newspapers, she rummaged until she found the one she wanted and held it up. A headline read OLYMPIC TORCH ROUTE TO BE ANNOUNCED. There it was: "Olympic spokesman Steve Barr will be in Murphy . . ."

An enterprising reporter must have tracked down Jan Williams on her initial trip through here, and from whatever Jan said must have manufactured a local hero. I drove in and they gave me the part.

In forty-five minutes I had dropped my things in my room, gone out to the local McDonald's, and brought a burger back to the motel. By then the manager had four messages for me from Howard Weston. The Los Angeles office had told me a Telephone Pioneer from Asheville wanted to get together in Murphy; that was probably Mr. Weston. The return number was the same as the one on my telephone. "Oh, yes," the manager said, "Mr. Weston has the room next to yours."

He looked like a true Pioneer. A little over five feet six, I'd say, stocky, gray hair, getting a little bald on top. A big smile as he opened his door, and not the slightest flinch when he saw what could have been a vagrant standing there.

"You must be Steve Barr," he said. "Come in, come in. How about a drink?" He motioned to the two bottles on the desk. My choice of vodka or Coke, or for all I knew, a combination. A few get-acquainted words moved us to a quick agreement that we would meet the next morning, and I thanked him for the glass of Coke I took next door to wash down the Big Mac.

"Seven-thirty," Howard said. "All the North Carolina Pioneers will be here."

That seemed odd. The torch was going to be in North Carolina for only forty miles, so why was the whole state coming to Howard's motel room?

Getting into my coat and tie the next morning—this was going to be a *meeting*—I could hear the sounds of about twenty people in the next room. The faces that greeted me when Howard opened his door were not smiling. Uh oh, I thought, I'm going to get it. Surrounded by men in windbreakers and caps, a few of them wearing ties, I took a seat on the table where the vodka and Coke had been. It felt like a prison revolt when they've taken the warden hostage. They started in:

"My region's being short-changed."

"The route doesn't go through enough of North Carolina."

"We get conflicting instructions—first AT&T tells us one thing, then your people in Los Angeles tell us another."

"Nobody ever calls us. You leave us in the dark."

"We make arrangements and somebody we never heard of changes them, and doesn't ask so much as a by-your-leave."

Mostly, they had a point. I listened for half an hour, then said I certainly understood their feelings:

"There's no villain in this. There's a lot of gray area, partly because this has never been done before, and we all have to work our way through it. There are just fifteen advance people, we're on the road all the time, and there probably ought to be forty to help you out. On top of that, AT&T has its hands full, what with the divestiture and all . . ."

At that they grumbled, "Yeah, damn AT&T went and abandoned us."

". . . and the fifteen advance people have the whole country to cover. You've got one state and I've got forty. I haven't been home since New Year's." I spread my arms. "I completely sympathize. What you say is right. All I can do is ask you to be patient."

Some of the men thawed a little, maybe because of my "overworked and underpaid" remarks. We decided to go out for breakfast. Over ham and eggs and biscuits and grits, Howard made friendly overtures, asking where I came from.

One of the men in a windbreaker, who hadn't said much to that point, looked across the table and ventured with an agreeable nod, "Your daddy's a doctor or lawyer, I guess?"

An innocent supposition. No big deal. Except that it absolutely stunned me. I had my assumptions about them, but until this instant it had never occurred to me that people would make such broad assumptions about me. How ironic. I worked at presenting an image—the Joe Cool manner, the David Letterman irony, the college sweatshirts, the natty blazer and tie—and it had not dawned on me until right now that I might be trying to turn my back on my real roots.

"No, as a matter of fact," I said to the man in the windbreaker, aware of a sudden heat in my face. "My dad left us when I was two. My mom raised us and she was a dental assistant. I loaded trucks for United Parcel to pay for college. Teamsters Local 234. My stepfather is a mechanic. My brother came out of the navy and spends most of his time on motorcycles. I never had a suit until this job, and nobody in the family even thought about going to college before me. We're blue collar, doing the best we can."

What a relief to finally say it. So many times in the past few years I had said my father was dead. Around Cupertino, having a dead parent was far better than having a divorced one. In school I had gone through all sorts of contortions to pretend we were better off than we were. No wonder being seen with food stamps had felt like such a disgrace.

It seemed to be a relief to the Pioneers, too. The men around the table sat back, relaxed, and started saying "we" instead of "you" when they looked in my direction.

We all got up, piled into our cars, and drove in a caravan to the Georgia border, imagining what it would feel like the day the torch came through. By the time we said good-bye at the Georgia line, there was no more "them" on one side and "me" on another. It was us together.

(Bill Mattman)

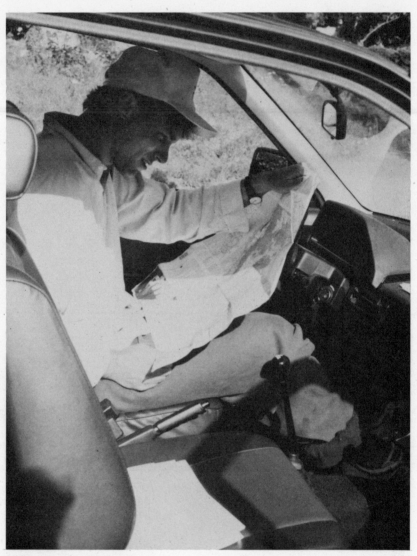

Here I am, lost in New Haven.
(Steve Barr)

Wally McGuire
(Bill Mattman)

David Halliburton, after
we'd realized we were
buddies, getting pictures of
Muhammad Ali in
Louisville
(Jim Long)

Chuckie Cunningham, assisted by his father, carrying the torch on the day of the real run through Morgantown, West Virginia, two months after he won our hearts on the practice run
(Bill Mattman)

Bronx welcome from the men and women of the New York Fire Department
(Bill Mattman)

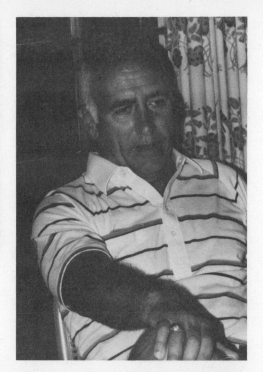

ABOVE: "God bless America,"
they sang on this corner and
hundreds of others
(Bill Mattman)

RIGHT: Dick Hamilton
(Dick Hamilton)

Afternoon in Oakland, New Jersey, May 12, 1984: The first of many homemade triumphal arches people put up to show how they felt
(Bill Mattman)

Kate Washburn and Lou Putnam, two of the three managers of the AT&T cadre runners who coached and cheered 3,436 sponsored runners—each representing a donation to charity in return for the privilege of carrying the torch—over 9,100 miles across America
(Bill Mattman)

Harold Littell of Akron, Ohio, Telephone Pioneer and guardian of the flame. "Daughter" flames of the original lived in the lamps Harold kept safe in Torch 10, the torch supply truck.
(Suzanne Lipps)

It didn't matter how early the runner came by. Someone was always there, and the applause just rippled along the line.
(Suzanne Lipps)

In Little Italy, Cleveland
(Bill Mattman)

Hoosiers
(Bill Mattman)

14

What Am I Doing Here?

ATLANTA, FEBRUARY 28

Red clay and green kudzu vines. The landscape of Georgia looked fertile even in winter. Come evening, the countryside gave way to a no-fooling big city: Atlanta. After checking in at the Sheraton, I dialed Dan Lee's number. Wally McGuire knew Lee from past campaigns; said he was now chief of staff in former President Jimmy Carter's Atlanta office; and suggested calling him. I didn't know why, exactly. What ex-presidents actually did with the offices they all had was a mystery I hadn't thought about much, but I did want to see Jimmy Carter's; he had been my first hero in politics.

To an earnest teenager, Carter's appeal was not just that he came out of a political nowhere, with no glamor and no old-school connections. It was, mostly, that he made an intelligent, serious run at the issues of the time. Just after he won the presidential election in 1976, *Rolling Stone* ran some excerpts from his Law Day speech of May 4, 1974, at the University of Georgia. That was a startling speech. It showed common sense; it went beyond the old emotional clichés of ordinary politics; it showed how Carter would run straight at the things he considered important. I remembered thinking with admiration, Jimmy Carter has guts.

What other politician would have the nerve to start a speech to the most powerful lawyers in his home state by pairing up references to his reading of Reinhold Niebuhr and his friendship with Bob Dylan? He said Dylan songs such as "The Lonesome Death of Hattie Carroll" and "Like a Rolling Stone" and "The Times They Are A-Changin'" taught him to appreciate the dynamism of change in a modern society. He recalled reading in Niebuhr that "the sad duty of the political system is to establish justice in a

sinful world." Then he told the lawyers why he was so deeply concerned about "the inadequacies of a system of which it is obvious
that you're so patently proud." He said scientists "probe, probe
every day . . . for constant change for the better." So do farmers.
But not lawyers.

"The powerful and influential have carved out for themselves or
have inherited a privileged position in our society," Carter said.
They are therefore, perhaps unalterably, reluctant to change. Every
one of the lawyers listening to him, he concluded, "ought to remember the oath that Thomas Jefferson and others took when they
practically signed their own death warrant, writing the Declaration
of Independence. To preserve justice and equality and freedom and
fairness, they pledged their lives, their fortunes, and their sacred
honor."

The *Rolling Stone* photo showed Carter in a work shirt and
jeans, hands on his hips, with his head cocked rather pugnaciously.
I liked his stance.

When I started paying attention to politicians, it seemed to me
that they always invoked the Great Depression or The War, the
two big events they had lived through. I had not lived through either, and didn't feel a connection with them. From Carter I heard
very few of those emotional clichés. In Carter there was an hon-
esty that touched me. A lot of people laughed when *Playboy*
quoted his saying he had felt lust in his heart, but his insistence
that he was not superhuman impressed me. "I'll never lie to you,"
he said, and a lot of people would say later that that was his down-
fall. If he had lied, been more of a flag-waver and less of an analyst
of the national malaise, maybe he'd have done better. He had a
good message, even though as it turned out, he was not a good
messenger.

So I was curious, and pleased when Dan Lee came to the telephone. "Ah, yeah, my old friend Wally. What's he up to? Sure,
Steve, come on by in the morning. If you want, we'll set you up
with a place to work here." The voice conveyed a calm, confident,
pleasant, sweet Georgia style.

Now it was time to take out my contact lenses and have a quick
shower. My room on the twenty-fifth floor had a good view of Atlanta. It also looked at some rooms in another wing of the building,
but they all looked blank. I was alone. That meant I could open the

curtains wide and keep the sliding door to the balcony ajar. I wandered out of the bathroom, toweling my hair, wearing nothing but socks and boxer shorts and a pair of horn-rim glasses, and flicked on the television set to see what programs would be keeping me company. Well, it could have been worse. That night we had the Grammy Awards. I laid out a batch of receipts and trip notes on the bed and paid little attention to the award show in the background, until Herbie Hancock started blaring out "Rocket" and the dancers started doing the Michael Jackson moon walk that makes you look as if you're gliding backwards on wheels. What on earth did he do with his feet to move backward while he seemed to be walking forward?

Up off the bed, I studied the screen, then tried to do the step. Heel, toe, confusion. Socks don't slide well on carpet, so I got some loafers out of the suitcase. They completed a pretty funny-looking costume. I practiced for four or five minutes, left heel up, right toe up, step, step, getting completely absorbed. Then I thought I heard laughter that wasn't coming from the television set. Looking up from my feet, out the window, to the hotel wing at the left, I saw half a dozen people with drinks in their hands, leaning on the rail of their balcony, nudging each other and laughing as if they were at the zoo. When I looked out at them, two or three applauded.

It would have been uncool to dash over and jerk the curtains shut. Ignoring them was impossible. So I waved at them like a performer going offstage and did my moon walk back into the bathroom. When I looked in the mirror, I saw a fuzzy-haired geek with a silly smile, and said aloud, "Remember, boy, they don't know your name."

The spectators were gone when I came out. Still, I closed the curtains in case I had any more outbursts.

At the close of the Grammies, a teaser for the late news said, "Dramatic upset in the New Hampshire primaries. More at eleven." My head jerked up. Receipts fluttered to the floor as I jumped up to twirl the dial to a ten o'clock news show. My heart started pounding. Maybe I really was in the wrong place. Maybe something I had assured myself couldn't happen was happening. My early disillusionment with politics, plus the signs that the organizations on both sides had everything boringly under control, had let me convince myself that there was no point in working on the 1984 campaigns, or even caring about them. Now, Gary Hart had just whipped the Democratic organization's candidate, Walter Mondale, thirty-nine percent to twenty-nine. He had pulled one of the most exciting upsets since Jimmy Carter worked his way out of Georgia. The question hit me harder than ever: What am I doing on a torch run when I could be working for something I *believe* in?

Wally was still awake out there in San Francisco. On the telephone, he talked faster than usual, as if he, too, were excited that Democratic politics had come out of the seventies into the eighties. Before I could stop myself, I said, "You know, Wally, I really wish I were part of that Hart campaign." As it came out, another thought flashed through my mind: What am I saying? I can't tell my boss I'd rather be in another job.

Wally said, "Yeah. I miss it, too."

Tuning from one news show to the next, hungry for information on what was happening, I put off going to bed until six the next morning. A couple hours' sleep set me up for the walk over to the Federal Building, where I expected to see an officeful of sharp, bright operators working for the former president of the United States. The elevator doors opened to a foyer made immediately impressive by white columns outside the inner sanctum. Inside, the offices looked as if they could be in the White House: paneling, carpeting everywhere, official portraits of Carter with this dignitary and that. It felt like a little shrine. The secretaries out front were pleasant. They were talking about—the fresh wind blowing through politics? No, about the Grammies and Michael Jackson's white glove.

Dan Lee's office looked busier, with telephone consoles and blinking lights, and Lee himself on the phone. He waved me to a seat. While he finished up, I wondered again, What do they do here?

"The president" was out of town, unfortunately. Everyone in this office always referred to "the president." Rosalyn Carter's office was empty for the day, Lee said, and I could operate from there. His easy way of trusting me seemed a clear sign of friendship and respect for Wally.

The most prominent feature of Mrs. Carter's office was a life-size portrait of their daughter, Amy, on the wall across from the desk. There's something incongruous about writing out directions for a motor caravan and calculating kilometers for a bunch of runners with a huge portrait of a child staring down at you. But it was no more odd than the idea of me conducting business from the office of a woman whose accomplishments I'd be lucky to come anywhere near.

The place had a neat, clean, unused feeling. It was hard to imagine Mrs. Carter hanging out there, making calls and drafting speeches. Many's the time I've sat at someone else's desk and wondered what was in the drawers. It isn't right to look. Here it was as unright as it could be—and here I gave in to temptation. What got the better of me was not Mrs. Carter's eminence. That, and respect for the Carters' principles, actually delayed my peeking. What nudged me over the line was curiosity. Did anyone actually use this immaculate desk?

I inched open the top drawer. Sure enough, it looked unused—a neat array of pencils, pens, and things someone might have arranged in case Mrs. Carter ever wanted to do something in there. A legal pad with no indentations from ever being written on. The bottom drawer held blank white presidential-looking stationery imprinted with Rosalyn Carter's name. That covered the secrets in this office. Hastily, I pushed all the drawers shut and sat staring at the door. What would I have said if someone had walked in while I was invading Mrs. Carter's privacy? Would a guilty look betray me now?

Lunch time. Dan Lee appeared in the doorway. "Want to go to the Mondale rally with us?"

The rally site was a shopping mall. The crowd-builders had been working. They had a band playing, and they had rounded up the usual supporters: a group of black women, many of them old, wearing Carter-Mondale hats they must have saved from four years before; a group of union men in windbreakers and work jackets; and a batch of curious shoppers. A worker came around to put Mondale buttons on all of us. The five other people in our group each took one, and I declined. They gave me a look. "I'm sorry, I'm not for your man," I said.

A little stir at the back of the crowd started the band playing "Happy Days Are Here Again," and some of the supporters sang the words. Maybe I was just feeling my own mood, but the enthusiasm seemed artificial. By and by an entourage arrived with Mondale in the middle. The clutches—the aides who always buzz around a candidate even though nobody knows quite what they're doing—escorted him up to the platform. By standing on a chair at the back of the crowd, I got an unobstructed look at him. Even from a distance, Mondale's smile seemed forced. His face was waxen. The bags under his eyes were darker than ever. His eyes looked worried. My impression was that he was concealing a lot of pain, and was working very hard to get that smile out. You had to feel sorry for him. His well-oiled machine had just started making awful noises.

During that night's call to Wally, I said, "Remember all that whining last night about missing politics? Well, I think it might be a lot more fun right now as an observer."

Wally laughed. "This'll cheer you up," he said. "I have to go to Ueberroth in a couple of days with a filled-in national schedule, and New Mexico isn't going to be ready if we don't do something fast. You're going to go help Joyce Tate in Albuquerque. Leave tonight."

15

Wally Isn't Going to Like It When They Find My Body

I was happy to go, to tell the truth, because I'd heard for years about the Albuquerque Dukes, the Dodgers' number one farm team. They didn't play in the winter, of course, but I figured that once I had a toehold in the city I'd be back to see them in the spring. Also, this was a place dear to the heart of a Bugs Bunny fan. Whenever Bugs popped out of his tunnel and found himself staring into the twin muzzles of Elmer Fudd's shotgun, he was likely to reflect in his best Brooklyn accent: "Ehhh . . . I musta took a wrong toyn at Albakoykee."

Joyce Tate described what she needed: Somebody to drive over the chunk she hadn't done yet, from Santa Fe north to the Colorado border. A snap. Just a quiet day of making notes on benchmarks and distances. Out of Santa Fe, the route was straightforward: A few small towns and ninety miles of nice four-lane road past the San Juan Mountains. I could continue to Denver, borrow a corner of the Burson Marsteller office to catch up on some paperwork, look up a friend, and fly out from there.

The car this time was a big new Thunderbird, a good solid American machine to navigate the open stretches of the American West. Santa Fe was a leisurely hour and fifteen minute cruise up Interstate 25 from Albuquerque, and a world away.

If Albuquerque looked like a long blank road being devoured by shopping centers, Santa Fe looked like a town that has kept its soul. Its tan adobes are gentle reminders of the different strands of cultures that meet there: Indian, Spanish, Mexican, Anglo; church, state; commerce, art; old, new. Evidence of the past, and the emphasis among the present people of Santa Fe on arts and crafts, are so pervasive that the place would feel downright quaint if it didn't also have the vigor of a state capital and a steady flow of young tourists coming through to ski, or hike, or just look around.

The Inn of the Governors, my destination for the night, was a couple of blocks from the famous Plaza at the center of town. Strolling over there to look at the *palacio* that the first Spanish governor, don Pedro de Peralta, started building in 1609, I couldn't help thinking that present-day architects are still learning from the efficient designs that Pueblo Indians developed in this area more than a thousand years ago. Since then, four flags have flown over the *palacio* as governmental center under Spain, Mexico, the Confederate States of America, and the United States. The history of our buildings may not reach back very far in comparison to the Old World of other continents; still, reading that this city is the oldest continuous seat of government in the United States gave me some minutes of quiet reflection.

The quiet lasted only as far as my next stop. Looking for a bite to eat on the way back to the hotel, I stepped into a place running at high decibels and realized that practically everyone in it was young. The nearby ski resorts at Taos were in full swing. All around me, people had glowing skiers' tans with reverse-raccoon white goggle marks around the eyes. The only exceptions were several rougher-looking cowboy types at the bar. The sunburns on them went right up to the eyeballs, but stopped halfway up the forehead. Some of the cowboys were watching a basketball game on the TV over the bar. The Lakers, no less. A scuffle under the basket, a rebound knocked away by a big guy in glasses, a fast break and a stuff for the Lakers, and a yell from the cowboys for one of my Laker heroes: "Yeah! Rambis!"

Now the question about tomorrow was, should I turn around at the Colorado border, drive back to Albuquerque and fly to Denver from there, or drive all the way up? The waitress looked like someone who knew the lay of the land, considering her tan and her white goggle marks. "Oh, it's only a few hours' drive," she said. "Nothing to it. Go for it."

The next morning I skipped breakfast and got a quick start. The sky was overcast, but not threatening. I did notice Route 285 climbing steadily as we moved north, but the T-Bird wouldn't have too hard a pull; Santa Fe started at 7,000 feet and the highest pass ahead was North La Veta, well into Colorado, at 9,416.

A few snowflakes showed up in Tres Piedras at the foot of the San Juans when I stopped for a snack. They didn't stick, though. The border was about twenty-two miles away, so I'd soon be in Colorado and scooting toward Denver. At the border, the snow started to stick. The flakes were not so much falling as shooting across from right to left in a steady wind. Still, no worry. Satisfied that I had closed the last gap for Joyce, looking ahead to a reunion in Denver, I never considered that I was in the Rocky Mountains thirty miles east of the Continental Divide.

By San Antonio, two miles into Colorado, the snowflakes had turned into a genuine blizzard. A glance at the map kept my hopes alive. If I could make it over to Interstate 25, the big road through Pueblo and Colorado Springs to Denver, I'd be all right. And the road I was on was no slouch—four lanes, other cars to keep me company. We'd be okay. But we wouldn't be fast. The driving snow cut visibility to a couple of dozen yards and the roadway was mostly white, so those of us who would normally be moving at forty-five or fifty miles an hour were going twenty and slowing down every few yards. Without chains, my best strategy was to stay in the tracks of the car ahead and hope the T-Bird's tires would keep a grip on the road.

The three miles to Antonito took fifteen minutes that seemed like an hour. The edges of the pavement had disappeared. From Antonito to Romeo, scarcely more than five miles, there was nothing to see outside the car but milky, moving masses of white. I tucked in behind a big truck and held the T-Bird's left wheels in the ruts of his tires, but soon got uncomfortable trying to keep up with his speed and lost him.

In the mountains you lose the FM radio signals first. I switched to AM for music, talk, weather reports, anything to keep me company. When AM radio faded to just a hiss and an occasional meaningless word, I was cut off.

There were no lights in the roadside business section of Romeo. A gas pump, closed; a little market, closed. Who could blame them when it was getting dark on a Sunday and a blizzard had driven everyone indoors? I would have loved to see a motel or a ROOM FOR RENT sign. Nothing. At a stop sign where Route 142 branched off to the right I touched the brakes and the car kept sliding, turning lazily sideways until it hit something and stopped. What it hit was a post holding a board saying that Route 285 ahead was closed.

Well, okay. Route 142 was just a two-lane road but it headed east toward the interstate, or at least a town where there might be shelter for the night. Right or wrong, I was committed now. It was dark and the road behind had probably drifted over. Maybe this assault of snow was local and I'd come out of it in another few miles. Maybe there will be something in Manassa. On the map it looked like two or three miles. Crawling along for five miles, I saw nothing. Must have missed it. Now the snow was piled up the height of the stakes holding the roadside mileage signs, almost to the signs themselves.

Not that I could see the signs until I was right next to one. It had been a while since I'd seen the lights of any other cars. In fact, I couldn't see the hood ornament of the Thunderbird. All there was out there was white. The wipers pushed aside a layer of snow with each sweep, and new snow immediately coated the windshield. It was as if someone cruel had a huge brush and kept re-painting everything white. By then I was so tense that my back felt ready to snap. Never mind Denver—all I wanted was to get to San Luis. But that was thirty miles away. Nursing the gas pedal but still losing traction more and more frequently, I crept past a couple of cars snowbanked off the edge of the road and apparently abandoned. Finally, I gave up the fight to avoid being another one of them.

The car was barely moving. I couldn't see. I pulled over and turned off the engine. The silence shut me in. No radio. No light. The only sound was an occasional moan of wind probing for an opening on the surface of the car.

At least my suitcase wasn't in the trunk. My things were on the back seat where I could reach them. I wasn't scared so much as seriously concerned. How long would this last? Through the night, certainly. After half an hour, I pushed on the door to look out and see whatever I could. It wouldn't open. Snow must be jamming it shut.

Once in a while I started the engine to make sure it still ran and to get some warmth. The odd thing was, it must have been well below freezing outside but I didn't feel any danger of frostbite. I had pulled on all the clothes that would fit, layer after layer, and the car wasn't all that cold inside. It must have been like an igloo, insulated by all the snow packed around it. The seat reclined, and I tried to sleep. Through the night I would wake with my knees drawn up and my arms clutched around me in a ball, run the engine for a shot of heat, and doze off again.

It was great time for reflection. One early thought was, "I'd love to bury that waitress in the snow. Sure, there's nothing to this route. In the summer." But nobody said I had to take her advice. Next: I don't have any food and haven't eaten anything but a Twinky since last night. At least I can bring in some snow and melt it for water. If I can't see out, can anyone see in? What happens if I'm here for two or three days? If I had just done my job, driven up to the border and back to Santa Fe, I wouldn't be in this position. I'm going to die here, and I'm not even supposed to be here. When they find my body, Wally's going to be pissed.

The night was not very restful. Dreams about the Donner Party woke me a couple of time. This was getting frightening. Maybe I'd wake up and hear somebody knocking on the door.

That is pretty much what happened. At first light, I awoke to the first civilized sound I'd heard in twelve hours, a diesel motor. I ran down the power window, and a bank of snow fell into the driver's seat. A few feet away was a big yellow plow with a flashing light on top and a driver waving to me from his cab. That man can have my vote for president any day he wants it.

He plowed as close to the car as he dared. I braced against the passenger door and used my feet to push open the driver's door. "You okay?" the snowplow driver yelled. "Yeah, thanks," I yelled back. He turned as close in front of the T-Bird as he could, then together we cleared away most of the snow piled ahead of it. He bounced the front of the car a few times to loosen the snowpack, and little by little I eased it onto the roadway.

The snowfall was just an occasional flurry. Now that I could see, there was another car fifty feet ahead. The man inside and I could have spent three days there without suspecting one another's presence. There were others at intervals farther on. At each one the plow stopped, the driver cleared and bounced, pulled some out with a chain, and we all joined in a caravan behind the plow. After a few miles we came to a stretch of road that had been cleared earlier, and the plow pulled over. One by one, we passed, on our own again, and waved good-bye to our rescuer. Up there in a little cab was a man who, thank God, had not called in sick that morning. He gave each of us a cheery wave as we pulled around and left him behind.

I hadn't eaten for thirty-six hours. I looked like a tramp. I had to go to the bathroom. This was still not luxury freeway driving, our top speed was still about thirty, but I had been in the car so long that I was determined to get to Route 25 and some sort of city before anything else could happen. Near Pueblo, I pulled over at a gas station to call Wally. We hadn't talked since Atlanta, and we had a meeting coming up in Washington.

Standing in a phone booth, freezing, starving, frazzled, dazed by fatigue, I dialed his home number. Pat, his wife, answered with her always pleasant greeting, "How's it going, Steve? How are you doing?"

"Oh, fine," I said. "Is Wally at home?"

He was. But before I could start filling him in, I glanced out at the attendant pumping gas. A pickup truck with a little driver whose head barely showed above the dashboard was backing toward the side of the Thunderbird, the vehicle that had started every time I asked it to, that had grabbed the road when there was nothing to grab, that had protected me from a Rocky Mountain blizzard and my own stupidity, and had come out of it unmarred. Oh, no . . . Bang! The pickup hit the T-Bird behind the driver's door. The car that had pulled me through without a scratch now had something to show for its ordeal.

16

Countdown

It was time for a trial run. Two months from now, when the real torch relay started, would be too late to find out that something didn't work. So the whole organization was about to have a dress rehearsal.

The simulation run was to be real in most respects, except for two: The flames in the torches would come from ordinary matches, not the sacred site in Greece; and we would not solicit the big crowds and celebrations we'd want later.

We would run the test on an eight-hundred-mile section of the torch route across parts of eight states, starting in New Jersey and ending in Michigan. It had inner cities, mountain roads, political and police jurisdictions going by so fast that there was bound to be a foul-up, and probably every weather problem except summer heat.

"The point," Wally said, "is to push the system so hard that if something's going to break, it'll break now—while we still have time to fix it before the real thing." He intended to test everything that could conceivably go wrong. "Are the motors in the caravan dependable? Do the radios work? Are the volunteers clued in? Can we keep storms from snuffing the flame? Do we know how to adjust when a runner doesn't keep up the pace? Are the torch rats' plans accurate? Am I asking the right questions?"

He expected many of the answers to be "No." He wouldn't bother with a trial run that he thought was going to go perfectly. "So don't waste time worrying about the mistakes that show up," he said. "Just correct them." Still, our work was about to get its first public judgment. As the fifteen torch rats converged on the Mayflower Hotel in Washington, at least a few of us felt some big-game jitters.

Wally called a countdown meeting before every major event. He had brought in people from all over the country for this one. And he'd brought in the torch rats for something else, too: A party, to give us a few hours with each other before we scattered again. One by one that afternoon and evening, in the lobby and in hallways, we came back together—some of us friends who had been on the road together just days before, others who hadn't seen each other since the training seminar in Los Angeles. We waved, headed for each other with smiles, sometimes even embraced. For dinner, Wally laid on food and drink in a private dining room. We were in a hotel, surrounded by tablecloths and silverware and bright lights; yet very soon we felt like a clan that had gathered around a campfire to tell our tales far into the night.

The next morning was all business. A meeting room: note pads, dark suits, white shirts, and red ties. We were ready to check and double-check arrangements with managers from AT&T, P.R. people from Burson Marsteller, the security team loaded with former Secret Service agents, and various Los Angeles Olympic Committee honchos.

Wally had wanted the schedule completely blocked in by the middle of March, and it was: A total of 14,645 kilometers. From a New York sidewalk to the rim of the L.A. Coliseum, the flame had 9,100 miles to travel, every inch of the way in somebody's hand, propelled by somebody's feet—3,436 Youth Legacy Kilometer torch bearers, each representing a donation to charity, plus two hundred AT&T cadre runners who would fill in the stretches where there were no sponsored runners. We had settled where the runners would go. Now we had eight weeks to settle every other detail of what was going to happen. The trial run that was about to begin should help turn our illusions into realities.

Early in the meeting, Wally showed the Bud Light commercial. There were the two farmers; there, way down the road, they saw some kind of light; there drawing closer, was the flame they had been waiting to see, in the hand of a lone runner; there, solemn and proud, they stood straight and clapped slowly as he passed by. It was a superbly emotional piece of moviemaking. A number of people in the room were seeing it for the first time, and had the same reaction I did. Many of us were blinking away tears when Wally turned the lights back on. And, once again, I couldn't help imagining those same two farmers standing in line for a block of cheese.

One of the last presentations of the day came from Bonnie Warner, a powerfully built woman with short blond hair who had taken part in a shorter torch relay that led up to the 1980 Winter Olympics at Lake Placid. The perspective she brought to our little enterprise was interesting: A reminder that there had been other torch runs before, and a warning that they did not always go as they had been planned. Some of her stories about breaches of security, about spectators running *at* the torch, were sobering—for instance, the woman who brought out a bag of local upstate New York apples to be hospitable, thrust it at a torch runner, and knocked the runner down.

We had all wrapped ourselves in the logistics of the job, and I for one had not even begun to think about the problems Bonnie Warner described. It was sobering. Telling a group of Telephone Pioneers in Murphy, North Carolina, that a cross-continental torch relay had never been done before was good showy speechifying (and, incidentally, true) and I had loved the way it pulled us all together that morning. But the reality behind that sort of speech was now starting to show its teeth.

We had no idea what would happen when the trial run started. I had thought, back in Los Angeles, that we could stage a torch relay and control it like a campaign appearance. But now I was not sure at all. The thing had so many elements, and no room for mistakes. We started imagining mishaps that would make the Olympics, AT&T, and America look like buffoons.

We could send the caravan on a wrong turn. Can't you see the headlines? GUESS WHAT, FOLKS. THEY GOT LOST AGAIN.

Somebody could misplace a two-line entry on the immense printout of the schedule, and a person in shorts, holding a torch, would be left standing somewhere—probably a city full of TV cameras—with nobody to give it to.

A terrorist could blow up the runner and several vehicles with one mine in a manhole.

This operation was one of those things you get yourself into and then just go ahead and do, and keep on doing, and don't let yourself stop to think about how it's going to look if everything goes wrong.

No one could give any guarantees that it was going to work.

17

A Touch of the Power

"You're going to screw up *everything I've been working for!*" the guy snarled.

Now here was somebody who revived my old notions about Telephone Pioneers. Maris Segal and I had stopped by his office in Pittsburgh to confirm arrangements for our leg of the trial run. We were responsible for tomorrow, Wednesday, in the hilly corner where West Virginia meets Pennsylvania. The runners and support vehicles on this leg of the practice run would come down from the Allegheny Mountains in West Virginia tomorrow morning, pass through Morgantown at midday, and reach the outskirts of Pittsburgh that night. And tomorrow, this Pioneer knew, was not in good hands.

His telephone had been ringing with reports of problems they'd had in Philadelphia: Traffic jams (nobody expected a lot of onlookers—the advance teams were putting out no publicity, this being a test of machinery and the fit between planning and reality, not of crowd-building); timing goofs (quite possibly from an advance team's miscalculation); weather delays (maybe we'll meet Whoever is responsible for the weather, but not today, I hope). And so on and so forth, all of it our fault even though we hadn't been in Philadelphia.

"You dipshits didn't even get 'em a torch that would *light!*"

That's why you have a trial run, we assured him. To straighten out mistakes.

The truth was, though, we didn't feel so assured ourselves. All our preparations so far had been on paper. We had no idea of how an actual torch run would go. The level of tension was about to hit the top peg, and not just for that Pittsburgh Pioneer. Maris seemed a different person from the confident woman she had been in Oregon. Even at the training seminar in Los Angeles, radiating the in-charge competence that made me vote for her and Suzanne Lipps as most likely to succeed, she had been slender as a dancer. She had lost even more weight. All day she had been darting between one checklist and another, snapping at the heels of everyone on the team. We were all showing some strain.

A gloomy rain over Morgantown added weight to our apprehensiveness about what could go wrong when the torch arrived on Wednesday. Yet it also added a gleaming wash to the tree-shaded, settled charm of the community. Of course I had anticipated that in West Virginia, we'd see coal miners all over the place. We were in the Scott's Run bituminous coalfield, true; but this was no raw open-pit town. With its big trees and decently kept up buildings downtown, Morgantown carried its age comfortably. West Virginia University, divided between a downtown campus and a nearby Evansdale campus, provided the atmosphere of a picturesque little college town. On top of that it offered a striking high-tech apparition: Overhead trams carried people between downtown and the Evansdale campus. "That's the PRT," a pharmacist said while he rang up my toothpaste, "Personal Rapid Transit system. Computer controlled. A guinea pig, you might say, for engineering students and urban planners."

I was downtown with a couple of local Pioneers, driving the next day's route over the city streets. The way Maris and I had divided it up, she would guide the torch entourage to Morgantown and I would take over once it was in the city. Maris was at the Holiday Inn a mile and a half north of Morgantown where we had set up our command post, calling tomorrow's runners to triple-check that they would show up in the right place at the right time. We were both making notes for the evening's countdown meeting, the first one either of us had ever organized. In our uncertain state, we were grateful for Wally's experience and his decree that we should have those meetings the night before the torch caravan's arrival. They promised to be a reassuring ritual, allowing local officials, torch rats and security people, Pioneers, and other important volunteers to verify that we were all working from the same agenda.

At the motel, we had set up our headquarters exactly as Wally instructed us in the training seminar: Get three adjoining rooms—

one for each torch rat and the third for an office. Have the beds removed from that one if possible, to make space for typewriters, extra telephones if you can get them, tables for the local volunteers you recruit to hold the fort while you're out, and a message center. Our message center was a batch of envelopes with names Magik Markered on them and taped to the mirror, where volunteers could drop incoming notes.

The volunteers Maris had rounded up were half a dozen young women from the university who chose this way of doing the hours of community-service work their sorority required. They brought their homework over and kept each other company when we didn't have them actually jumping around. They had all been in the motel for most of the day.

When I called from downtown, Maris asked for a couple of pizzas and some drinks for the crew. The instant I got there with the food, she yanked me aside.

"Where have you *been*?" she whispered. "The countdown meeting starts in an *hour* and look, the Pioneers told the blind boy's *father* he could run alongside and the rules say it has to be a cadre runner, not the father."

Until recently we hadn't even known who the five runners on our downtown leg were going to be. In our vocabulary, there were two types of runners, "sponsored" and "cadre." Sponsored runners were people who paid for Youth Legacy Kilometers. Cadre runners were AT&T running buffs who carried the torch on kilometers that didn't have sponsored runners. Tomorrow, some of the people were going to be sponsored runners who would carry the torch in the real relay in the summer, and some were friends of the local Pioneers, filling in for this rehearsal. Cadre runners were scheduled to run alongside all the way, and help out people like eleven-year-old Chuckie Cunningham, who we had heard was not only blind but partly paralyzed on his left side.

Maris's whisper bounced off the walls. The volunteers looked at each other, at Maris, and at me standing there with two pizza cartons in my hands.

"How 'bout those Knicks?" I said, uncovering the pizzas with a mock flourish, in a weak attempt to defuse a tense situation. Maris gave me a chilling "I've been pushed far enough" look. The sorority girl closest to me laid down her paperback copy of *Catcher in the Rye* and tilted her head with a sympathetic smile, like a fond sister who knows you're going to get it good.

Before Maris could tell me how immature she thought I was, we heard a knock at the door. On the other side stood Jan Williams and Larry Silman. Jan and Larry were responsible for this day's run, and weren't due here until the torch caravan bedded down for the night in the mountains to the east. We didn't expect them until eleven thirty or so, and here it was only half past six.

"What are you doing here?" Maris asked.

"We've got snow in the mountains, a blizzard," Larry said. "They called it off early. The caravan's holed up in some place called Redhouse." That was strange, his saying "they" called it off, not "we."

I asked, "How did the day go, anyway?"

Jan and Larry glanced at each other. They looked dejected in a way I hadn't seen either of them look before. "You know," Jan said, "it was weird. We kinda got pushed aside."

"Huh? Pushed aside? Who did that?"

"It turns out, when the torch is actually running, we don't get in on the decisions very much," Larry said.

Now we had a new mystery. But there was no time for more questions. We had to get to the meeting. In my room getting into a suit and tie, I thought, Wow, this is supposed to be our payoff. Gratification. Months of practice and now we're in the game. But Larry looks as if somebody just cut him from the team. What's up?

After the meeting we all went back to the room with the volunteers. The remains of a pizza lay on one end of a table that took up a corner. I stretched out in a straight-backed chair and rubbed my face. The *Catcher in the Rye* woman came across the room to pull off a slice, and we smiled again. She sat down.

"It's cold," she said, looking at the wedge of dough and cheese in her hand.

"That's when it gets good," I said. Such a man of the world.

The woman was tall and slender, with dark brown hair and lively, intelligent eyes. A lot of people are good-looking, but she was interesting-looking besides. She also had a graceful way of letting a dumb remark slide by, neither taking it too seriously nor making fun of me.

"Are you reading *Catcher in the Rye* for a class?" I asked.

"Nope. Just for fun."

"What do you think?"

"It's amazing how well it holds up," she said. "I mean, Holden Caulfield doesn't seem at all like somebody left over from the forties. He's still alive."

"Yeah. You know, it scares me when I meet somebody our age who already knows what their whole life is going to be," I said, grateful for her company. "Don't you think there's some of Holden in everybody?"

"Remember when Holden talks about the field and the cliff?" she answered. "And there are children running through the rye, and it's over their heads so they can't see, and he wants to be there to catch them before they go over the edge?"

"Sure. Sometimes I feel like one of the kids, not Holden."

"Me, too." She had an elbow on the table and looked at me with a kind of clean composure that made talking easier than it had been for quite a while. "Close to the edge, you mean?"

"Scared . . . oh . . . of the future, wishing there were some way to be sure of what things mean. I woke up this morning in this motel wondering, 'What the hell am I doing here?' I get so homesick when I'm on the road, but when I'm home I get restless. Sometimes I don't know where I belong. Well . . . well . . . who knows?" I felt so sorry for myself that my eyes teared a bit, and so did hers. "Sorry. I'm babbling."

She shook her head. "Your babbling hits awfully close to home."

Our conversation in the corner had one unintended effect; it was outlasting the other volunteers. They peeled off one by one to go home to the sorority house, until the only people left in the room were Larry, Maris, one sleeping volunteer, and the two of us. I couldn't help wondering what it would be like if the talk were to move on to more intimate matters . . . but no, that was unthinkable. Not with a local college girl, and me the equivalent of a traveling salesman.

"Is there something wrong with your neck?" she asked.

"It's a little sore," I admitted.

She moved behind my chair and started kneading my shoulders and the back of my neck. Instead of relaxing me, her kindness brought back my tension, because of the looks Larry started lobbing at us—those nudging he-man grins that guys give other guys in the locker room.

Eventually she trailed her fingers in a last stroke down my back.
"That really did help," I admitted. "Thank you, very much."

The other volunteer woke up and said good night. Maris left. I
know what they're thinking, I thought. They probably think I
think they're in the way. Maybe they're right. On the other hand,
maybe I'm making all of this up. She'll probably be the next to
leave. By then, Johnny Carson was on television, talking to Jerry
Lewis and exclaiming over snapshots of Jerry's little dog. Larry
gave me the last of those macho-buddy looks. He too said good
night, and we were alone.

All the little moves and countermoves, the laughs at each
other's jokes, had brought us to a point at which I didn't know
quite what you were supposed to say next.

"Um . . ." I said, "would you like to go next door and watch
David Letterman?"

She glanced at her watch, then looked up, smiling only in her
eyes. "Sure," she said.

We turned on the television set and sat on the edge of the bed.
What now? College hadn't taught me much about this sort of moment.

She solved the problem. "Why don't you lie down on your stomach? I didn't quite finish rubbing your back."

She hadn't, and I was glad she wanted to. Her hands were
soothing this time, and kind. The room was quiet, and for the first
time that day we both relaxed fully, just enjoying each other's
company. "I'm glad you're here," I said sometime in the next couple of hours.

I realized something scary. I didn't want to leave in the morning.
I wished there were a way to stay in this motel room forever, not
having to leave and not having to worry about whatever I was
looking for with this silly trip. But I did have to leave. When I did,
maybe I could help Holden Caulfield in his dream of catching the
little children in the rye field before they fell. If that included being
yelled at by middle-aged telephone men, so be it. It was okay. This
was the first time in months that I'd felt any warmth. I felt comfortable, secure. Just before my eyes closed, my wise sorority
friend, perhaps sensing some of my uncertainty, looked along the
pillow with a knowing smile and whispered, "How 'bout those
Knicks?"

MARCH 22

Four hours later, I drove and Maris navigated as night gave way
to cold gray skies over the Alleghenies. I wanted to be excited. We
were headed for our first look at the Olympic Torch Relay—not
just numbers and paper, the real thing. But I was tired after three
hours' sleep, and sad. I couldn't stop thinking about how warm last
night had been. It was sad that I'd never see my generous dark-
haired friend again. We had given each other addresses and phone
numbers, but we both knew that was more courtesy than anything
else.

Maris, meanwhile, bubbled in the passenger seat, as rested and
bright as I was weary. She had her notes out, prepared to a fare-
thee-well, and we were barely under way before she started on one
of her checklists.

"Wally said we should include the state police in countdown
meetings and we just had the city cops last night.

"Wally said we should have access to a Xerox machine, and we
don't.

"Wally said . . ."

My melancholy evaporated an hour later as we pulled up to an
awakening portable city. We shut off the engine. Maris and I sat in
the car and stared, amazed. We felt as if we had come to graduation
day and they had delivered our presents. People probably gaped like
this when the circus came to town in the twenties. Here it was—
twenty vehicles and more than a hundred people, all to make sure
that one runner could light a torch for the next runner, who could
light a torch for the next, who could light a torch . . . in an unbroken line from New York to California. This was our first look
at the fleet.

At first it looked like a whole parking lot of big rigs lined up like
a brigade of sleek elephants. Even under the sunless overcast, their
white paint glistened, with rainbow stripes and Olympic Torch Relay emblems on the sides and AT&T and GMC emblems proudly
displayed on the front. Custom-built GMC motor homes. Custom-
engineered Buicks. Customized four-wheel-drive utility vans. Trac-
tor-trailers. Here we had about half of the forty-one vehicles that
would accompany the runners starting in May.

We had arrived early, so there was time to look into some of the vehicles. The motor homes had more conveniences than any house I've ever lived in. Some were sleepers for the AT&T cadre runners and for drivers and food-crew members. Not only did they have beds, sinks, refrigerators, generators to make their own power, closets and big picture windows, they had air conditioning, color television and video games, stereo tape decks, swivel chairs and telephones. One of the big GMCs was "Torch 1," the command vehicle—an office on wheels full of photocopying machines, telefax equipment, and computers. Another truck, Torch 10, carried a couple of the miner's lamps that would keep alive the original fire from Olympia, Greece. These "mother" lanterns of gleaming glass and gold stood about ten inches high, and threw a soft glow on racks holding hundreds of the spun-aluminum, bronze-coated torches that would be lighted for each runner. The Pioneers had other mother lanterns distributed around the caravan, and in the actual torch run they would guard them with a care that bordered on reverence, ensuring that no matter what happened, at least one original flame would survive. It was very important for people to know they were seeing the true Olympic flame, the eternal fire.

The biggest truck was a forty-three-foot tractor-trailer with a stainless steel kitchen inside. The most spectacular was the Emergency Medical Service (EMS) vehicle, a hospital on wheels. It carried all the homey amenities plus a doctor, nurse, physical therapist, Jacuzzi, massage table, complete hospital bed, and assorted other important doctor stuff. Most of the motor homes traveled as a supply train that looped ahead of the runners each day, accommodating visiting celebrities and setting up overnight stops for the "core caravan."

The core caravan was a cluster of vehicles that traveled with the runners, surrounding them at every step. The first vehicle in the core caravan belonged to the local police. Then came the Olympic Committee lead car, one of the Buicks that had been engineered to grind along at eight miles an hour (in some stretches, as little as five) for up to twenty hours a day, for three months: Heavy-duty coolers on engine and transmission, hand throttles, separate power supply for the radios and phones. The lead car, a convertible, would always have its top down except on days like this one, when the rain would have turned it into a bathtub. In motion, it held a driver, a trip director, an advance person (Maris, me, etc.), and a

Pioneer who supposedly knew every inch of the route. A platform on its rear held two mother lanterns for a quick re-light if wind blew out a runner's torch, rain doused it, or it just plain fizzled. Then came the runner. Behind the runner came the security van, a GMC Suburban with former Secret Service agents riding the running boards. Behind the security van was the EMS, which, in addition to its other attractions, was the only vehicle in the core caravan that had a bathroom. Bringing up the rear of the core caravan was another police car. When we anticipated especially good photo opportunities, we could insert a flatbed truck for photographers in front of the runner. The whole core caravan moved at the pace of a running human being. That meant driving across the United States in first gear.

Except for the core caravan, I didn't see the point of the technological overkill. Why couldn't this little army stay in motels and eat in restaurants, like everyone else? Who needs to have a semi driving along with a crew of cooks fixing dinners of chicken gumbo, spinach salad with hot bacon dressing, chicken breasts in bordelaise sauce, lobster tails with drawn butter, wild rice, vegetable lasagna, asparagus spears, Harvard beets, amaretto cheesecake, and chocolate truffles? But then, why not let the corporate sponsors show off?

Each time we ducked out of the rain into a motor home, we got a suspicious stare from the Pioneer in charge of it. That was natural enough. They had survived an ordeal of mountain driving in a blizzard just the day before while we were, to their minds, relaxing in our motel. But that wasn't all. The curt replies to our "good mornings" said, clear and simple, that they considered this operation theirs and theirs alone. Until now, we torch rats had thought we could walk in anywhere without question—didn't they know we were the people who made all this possible? Nope. This was Telephone Pioneer turf.

Milling around like a convention of clutches were ten or fifteen other AT&T men in badges and blue suits. Where were those guys when Evelyn Barham was getting out aspirin and heating pads for me in the middle of the night?

Start-up time. People headed for their vehicles and engines kicked over. I found Jim Suennen, the trip director for the day. As in a political campaign, trip director is a strange position. The trip director is the final authority on movements in the field. Yet he seldom knows where the parade is going. He needs a guide, someone who has been over the route before. Us. Maris was going to ride in the lead Buick as far as Morgantown, and I would take it in from there. So I asked, "Jim, where do you want me to be?"

Suennen looked around in a cool sort of way and said, "Well, I don't have a walkie-talkie for you. I guess you can hang out in the EMS."

This was starting to feel really odd. We had been promised walkie-talkies so we could maintain the contact with each other— and with people ahead and behind on the route—that we had kept unbroken since the third of January. We were supposed to be the experts on the route, and this trip director wasn't even going to keep himself in touch with half the advance team in case something unexpected came up. Larry hadn't been imagining things. We really were being pushed aside.

The EMS was crowded with cadre runners, AT&T men in suits, Pioneers, doctors and nurses, and a writer from *Time*. I couldn't get near the windows in front. The engine rumbled. We moved. After two and a half months of work, I didn't rate high enough to see the torch runner. I was in the back of the EMS next to the donuts, the farthest person in the caravan from the flame. So this is what it all amounted to. I should have known.

Half of me was exhausted. A good chunk of me was pouting. My ego grumbled, "This is what I haven't had a day off in ten weeks for? Here we go again, the old power trip. Big fish eat little fish in the good old U.S.A., the way they do in every other pond in the world." Haven't the grunts always done the work and watched the officers grab the glory? Sure.

The rain came down the way I felt. Heavy. Gloomy. Everything in the universe was obviously focused on harassing me. Obviously it was even raining because of me.

Eleven o'clock. We were an hour from Morgantown. Maris was out there somewhere, and if I didn't find a way to talk with her soon, we'd have a fine mess at our changeover point.

There was one walkie-talkie in the EMS, and George Broder (son of David Broder, the columnist) from the LAOOC News Department had it. Which is to say, he had power. If you had a walkie-talkie, you were part of the caravan; if you didn't, you were just hanging around. My mind chattered away to me: "All Broder has to do is service the *Time* correspondent. Why does he have a walkie-talkie when you don't? Especially now, when you have a legitimate use for one." I pushed my way up to the front to get near Broder.

"George," I said, "it's not in the printed schedule, but Maris and I are going to switch at the Morgantown city line. Could you let Jim know that, so he can hold the lead car during the torch exchange, just long enough for me to run up there and Maris can come back here?"

"Yeah, yeah," Broder sighed. "I'll call 'em. I've got to go up to the flatbed then anyway, so they'll stop." He resumed looking out the window and talking with the *Time* guy.

Almost noon. Out a side window, I saw the benchmark for the exchange. The EMS stopped. We would have the fifteen seconds it normally took for a runner to light the next runner's torch, plus whatever extra seconds the trip director allotted for swaps like this one between Maris and me.

"George, let's go!" I shouted, and flung open the door on the side of the EMS. He jumped out ahead of me. The rain was monsooning. In two steps, our suits were soaked. We had run a couple of car lengths, less than a third of the way to the head of the caravan, when the engines rumbled and the whole thing started rolling. I yelled, "George, what the hell is going on?"

"I don't know," he shouted. "Just keep going."

I felt like the Defiant Ones running to catch that train at the end of the movie. The torch bearer who had just taken the flame was one of the cadre runners, an experienced racer who went a lot faster than I could, even if I weren't wearing a suit and loafers in a drenching rain. We were going to have to haul ass for a kilometer, or get left behind. Broder had his walky-talky up to his mouth, trying to yell into it as he ran and managing to hit himself in the lips a few times, but he got no response.

Great! Great! I fumed. The last thing I need is a six-minute run at this pace, in the rain, stepping in holes full of mud, just as we come into my section of the day. We were falling behind. The EMS passed us. This is going to be impressive: The first day of the torch run, I get left behind. I'll have to call a cab to catch up to the thing. After what seemed like an hour of effort, we had fallen fifteen car lengths behind the EMS. Then it stopped for the next exchange.

We ran and ran, past the EMS, past the security van, past the runners, and got to within a few strides of the back steps of the flatbed just as it started again. I had passed Broder in a final desperate sprint, and I didn't have more than a few more strides in me. There was no hope of reaching the lead car. If I missed the truck, I was through. I lunged for it, stretching my right foot toward a step. The foot hit the second step up without breaking stride. As I reached for the rail, a bolt of pain shot all the way up my back as if someone had hit me with an axe. At the next step up, I realized I had done something really serious to myself.

Three photographers in slickers stared at the apparition in a clinging wet suit, hair matted by rain, face contorted by a combination of oxygen debt, rage, and desperate pain. One recovered his wits enough to stretch out a hand and pull me the rest of the way up, and I staggered past them to the front of the flatbed. Standing there doubled over, watching my gusts of breath steam in the forty-degree air, I felt Broder heave up beside me. We clung to the side rails, unable to talk. He glared at me as if he wanted to say, "This is all your fault."

I croaked, "You never called, did you?"

He said, "You should have let me know earlier."

The next thing I'd have said was, "One more word and I'm going to bust you in the mouth, you son of a bitch."

But it never came out. I was distracted by a curious awareness that the sounds around us had changed. Where there had been silence, there seemed to be applause and yells. At the end of the truck, the three photographers had their backs to us, oblivious to our combat. They were focusing on something going on back in the area of the runner.

My first glimpse of the torch included not one runner, but two: A big man with a mustache, wearing an Olympic Torch T-shirt over a blue sweatshirt, was looking down with a proud smile at a dark-haired, skinny little boy, and holding the boy's right hand as they ran together. The boy had the torch in the same hand. He ran with a pigeon-toed wobble, a gait so unsteady that it seemed he must ordinarily be almost unable to walk, much less run. His eyes did not see us. He was blind. But not deaf, not at all; he turned his head from side to side, picking up voices.

His most prominent feature was a huge, huge, shining smile on a

131

face that radiated as much happiness as a human being can show. His twisted knees, his unaimed eyes, disappeared behind the immense, luminous smile.

Then I started hearing the words of the yells. The photographers were calling, "Go, Chuckie! You can do it! Attaboy, Chuckie!" And there were—I couldn't believe it, we hadn't arranged this— there were people streaming out of buildings to the sides of the street, calling out:

"Yay, Chuckie!"

"God bless you, boy!"

"You're doing great, Chuckie, you're looking *good!*"

At the left, a swarm of people came running down from the university campus to see what was going on. What had been a person here and a person there hurrying to get out of the rain was swelling into a throng of hundreds, and hundreds more were drawn out to get in on whatever the others saw. Morgantown had no idea what was happening to it. Spontaneously, people from every corner of the town were running toward Chuckie Cunningham.

Many of the people were feeling the same sensations I felt. We were seeing an Olympic torch for the first time. They came up, curious, and saw a child with an incredibly joyful smile, and heard people calling encouragement to him. They joined the chant and pulled in more people behind them. The next thing, after the chants, were the tears.

About a third of the way along, Chuckie began slowing down. His one good arm trembled with strain. If he was collapsing, his smile didn't show it. His smile reached out even more strongly to the crowd than it had before. People from behind were now running to get back up where they could stay in touch with him. He slowed some more, almost down to a walk. He was going to need some help to keep the torch from falling. His father adjusted to guiding him with a firm touch on the shoulder, and hefted some of the weight of the torch for a few dozen steps every now and then until Chuckie's strength came back up to holding it alone. Chuckie's initial rush of adrenalin was gone and the reality of his handicaps was getting to him. His father's look of exaltation took on some concern. You could see him think as he looked down at his son, "Is this too much for him?" The crowd saw. Chuckie's steps faltered.

Chuckie's smile, though, never faltered. No matter what pain he was going through, he was not smiling at us or for us. He was just all smiles.

"Go, Chuckie!"

"We're proud of you!"

"God, Chuckie, we love you."

"We're with you, Chuckie, hang in there!"

Ten minutes before, people had been in calculus class, or buying a pair of pliers, worrying about their grades, or whether a haircut looked right, or stewing about some jerk at work. It might have been ten years since some of us had said, "I love you." Here were people calling out in front of several hundred neighbors and strangers, "I love you, Chuckie," and letting tears stream down their cheeks.

The rain had slowed to a sprinkle when Chuckie got the flame. Now it had stopped. Chuckie's halting run became a walk, a painful and slow walk. I turned to check where we were. Over the cab of the truck, the exchange point was three blocks ahead. Turning back to Chuckie, my eyes met George Broder's; his were red and brimming with tears. For the first time, I noticed my own tears.

I finally found my voice. "Only three more blocks, Chuckie," I yelled. The crowd all around picked up the cry:

"Just three more blocks."

"You can do it, Chuckie!"

"Hang in there, boy, you're almost there."

People were still running in from both sides, stumbling and craning their necks, some in back hopping as high as they could while they ran to catch a glimpse. A little boy with a smile as big as West Virginia had a whole town in the palm of his hand. I couldn't imagine this happening many times, here or anywhere.

I hadn't spent much time here, so I didn't know, but I wondered what all those people had thought was important fifteen minutes before. We were everybody: business people, auto mechanics, people on welfare, college students, housewives, journalists, Republicans, Democrats, non-voters. George and I had been at each other's throats over a walky-talky. All of a sudden it all seemed so unimportant compared to Chuckie Cunningham's next three blocks. Everyone rooting for him pushed aside everything else for that moment and gave all they had to him. It was the first time I had ever seen a whole group of people showing their best qualities all at once.

I didn't know if he could ever do it again, but this time Chuckie made it. At the exchange, his father guided his hand and Chuckie lighted the next runner's torch. Everybody burst into cheers of gladness. The boy had led the town and the visitors into an accomplishment that took us totally by surprise. Who among us would have predicted an hour before that we would be standing out on the street on a Wednesday afternoon crying like this?

People began to compose themselves, and I headed for the ladder to get down from the truck. The crowd of students was still enthralled. One face came into focus: my friend from last night. She was smiling again; only now she was letting tears spill, like the rest of us.

I had cried before. Now, for the first time in my life, I was crying for happiness.

18

Hero Worship, Lesson Two

We walked into one of those restaurants where half the people eating their eggs and bacon and grits seemed to know each other. This was David Halliburton's setup. We had a little over a month to finish and patch each day's route and re-check it; as time went on, our focus would shift more and more to shaping media events. David couldn't have made a better contact to start our second swing through Louisville than Jim Long of the Kentucky Derby.

Jim was still in his thirties even though he'd already had a career as a banker and, apparently, was a first-name friend of everyone in the place. He guided us to a table through a ripple of greetings: "Hey, Jim, how you doing?" "Gimme a holler, Jim. . . ." From every side, hands touching, pats on the shoulder, waves, smiles.

Within half an hour he had erased my caricature of what a southern accent means. It sure doesn't mean you're Gomer Pyle. Behind the extra vowels and easy pace, Jim's mind was scooping up every ball we hit in his direction and some we didn't even know we'd hit. He was sharp. And warm. And man, was he effective.

An advance person's dream is to come into town and find one person connected to everybody in the community, an ambassador who can push the right buttons and show you every shortcut. That was Jim Long. From that morning on, every time one of us said we needed something, we had it.

"Jim, we need a wire sent." Done.

"Jim, I need a check cashed." Done.

"Jim, we need printing donated." Done. Really well done.

Before the eggs arrived, he asked, "Where are you fellows staying?" We told him. "No, no, let me call my friend over at the Galt House and we'll work something out. People here want the Olympic torch to go first class."

Who else were we planning to see? Jeffrey Hutter, director of communications in Mayor Harvey Sloan's office. You generally check with the mayor before you come in and start poking through his town. "Good, Jeffrey's the man you want. We're old friends, so let me call him first."

David mentioned another name. "Don't spend any more time with that horse's ass than you have to."

When I mentioned Muhammad Ali, Jim smiled. "Not bad. As long as he's in good enough shape." He approved our notion that the Kentucky Center for the Arts would be a handsome backdrop for Ali to take the torch; a fifteen-minute run from the Second Street Bridge, the center's black glass exterior would make dramatic reflections for pictures, and the acoustics in front are among the best in America. Jim said he would set up a high-school band to play for the crowd. He offered to put us in touch with Michael Berry, administrative assistant to the governor.

The Good Old Boy network was giving us a front-row look at how it excels. By my reckoning, Jim Long should have had very little time to spare for us. Derby Day, the first Saturday in May, was six weeks away, and preparations for it were coming to a boil. But you'd never know it to look at him. I had a question: Where did he get all that confidence that things were going to work the way he said they would? Is there some secret to getting things done in Kentucky?

His answer was brief. "In Kentucky, nobody is a stranger. Everybody's a friend."

The mood was lightening up, too, because of something even Jim Long could not have arranged. The sun had come out. We finally thought we might be done with snow.

In this part of the country it did seem that when the flowers bloom, the people bloom. The businessmen in this town gave the women real competition in dressing for work. Their spring colors included plaid pants, pink shirts, yellow shirts, madras jackets, ice-cream suits, all neatly cut and coordinated. By contrast, Jim's navy blue blazer and gray slacks looked like a Wall Street lawyer's.

We said good-bye to Jim and walked over to the mayor's office. This was the real test of my Ali brainstorm. None of us had mentioned it yet to Muhammad Ali himself, since we didn't know if the city officials would give their cooperation. With it, we could get rolling. Without it, we weren't sure what we would do. Polite and slightly formal in that way we began to recognize as the way they did it here, Jeffrey Hutter motioned us into his office.

I started selling: Back when Cassius Clay was known as the Louisville Lip, he helped put the name of the city on everyone's lips. Now, the Kentucky Derby even has its office on Muhammad Ali Boulevard. Hutter listened patiently while I built my case. Finally he grinned and said, easy as you please, "Absolutely. No problem." He had stayed quiet to let me get the sales pitch out of my system. "The mayor's a good friend of Ali, you know. I'm sure they can get together on this. In fact," he said, "we ought to have the city sponsor Ali's kilometer. We could show some appreciation for a favorite son and a great Olympian. Whatever we can do to fit into Ali's schedule, we'll do."

Jim Long wasn't just woofing about people being friends. This morning he, and now Jeffrey Hutter, had made sure we no longer felt like strangers.

Word of the torch run had been getting around, and people started turning up with ideas about doing something unusual with it. Two U.S. Marine Corps captains who ran recruiting offices, Daniel Miller and David Breen, got the idea that sponsoring a kilometer would, as Captain Miller put it, "re-seed patriotic values." A platoon of officer candidates from the University of Louisville campus had raised the money. They held a raffle and netted $2,611. They chopped down trees and sold the wood for $65 a cord to raise the rest. Then they donated their kilometer to a member of a city Boys' Club. It was an advance man's dream, a perfect human interest story. It had a catch, though: The Marine platoon wanted to run along with their beneficiary. And I was pretty sure I wasn't going to be able to let them do it.

One person at a time was the Olympic Committee's rule. No team runs. If word got around that the LAOOC had said yes to one group, every torch bearer would have an entourage. Crowds would get messy, security would be impossible.

Sergeant Jack Olinick called a couple of times and then came by the Galt House. He was a career Marine, my age, about five inches shorter—five foot nine, maybe—a pleasant-looking guy with close-cropped blond hair and a firm way about him. He was very correct, very polite. And he had a valid point.

"We've done a lot, Mr. Barr," he said. "We would really like to run."

It's strange how a suit and tie and a little authority get people calling you "Mister" even when you're both the same age—more strange to me, probably, than to someone who grew up on the East Coast. First names are one of California's principal exports. Back home, everybody uses your first name whether you like it or not; I don't know how many times I've called big offices for the first time and asked to talk with some executive who's never heard of me and the receptionist has said, "Yes, Steve, I'll see if he's in." I asked Jack Olinick to call me Steve, and we both managed to relax.

"You know," the sergeant said, "Captain Miller's right when he says Marines are always doing something like this. We believe in traditional stuff, Corps and country, God, Mom and apple pie. And we want to carry the flag for our torch runner."

The situation didn't look hopeless, I said, just delicate. "You sure ought to have a chance to run. You see our problem, though. If it gets out that I said yes, some entire town in New Mexico or someplace is going to say, 'I heard those Marines in Louisville got to do it, so why can't we?' But let's keep it flexible. We're still a long way from locking everything in. No commitments, and I really hope we can figure out something that'll work."

The torch rats had come a long way, and not just in miles. It had seemed impossible, when we first met, that David Halliburton and I would work well together. He came across so earnest and neat; I acted so flippant and casual. He came from the wealthy side of the tracks, listened to religious rock in the car, and if you asked would talk politely about his born-again Christianity. I came from the other side and thought of myself as more cynical, not to say realistic. He was positive and enthusiastic; I did what I could to cover up feelings that might look too gentle or sentimental.

Through days together in hotel rooms and automobiles, David and I discovered that we played well off one another in negotiations with local power brokers. Not only that; we became friends. We put up with each other's quirks: He tolerated my schedule being arranged around Laker games; I tolerated his quest for

Howard Johnson bonus points. Each of us could make the other laugh. At the countdown party in Washington, everyone had been surprised to see us being good buds, getting along like the Odd Couple. We took to greeting each other in thick fake Ivy League accents, mimicking the last few lines from the movie *Trading Places:* "Looking good, David." "Feeling good, Steven." We had asked Wally to let us work together again.

For the rest of that first week in April we buried ourselves in logistics: Re-checked the route, fitted sponsored runners into the schedule at what we thought were the most beautiful parts of Louisville, huddled over our calculators, transmitted data by telephone to Los Angeles.

On our second Monday in town, we quit at nine in the evening and agreed it would be good for both of us to break the rhythm with a quiet evening alone. David headed for his room, and I went to mine. The sports page had fascinating news—a Dodgers-Cubs game was going to be cabled from Los Angeles by WGN, the Chicago superstation. I was flooded by a longing to see that game.

It wasn't just that I'm a Dodger fan. It wasn't even that sports are such a relief from the rest of the world. (When Earl Warren was Chief Justice, somebody asked him why he read the sports page first and he said, "The front page shows man's failures. The sports page shows his accomplishments.") It was also that I was just plain homesick. There had been summers when friends and I went to so many games at Dodger Stadium that going there, with the green grass and the little white ball and the people who all had something in common to talk about, felt like going home. This night, I would do almost anything for a chance to see the familiar sights.

The Galt House didn't get WGN. I had to find someplace with cable television that would play the Cubs game. And the place had to stay open long enough for me to watch the game, which started late by eastern standard time. I didn't know what the chances were on a Monday night in the South. There was only one thing to do. Get out the Yellow Pages, look up "Cocktail Lounges" and "Taverns," and start calling bartenders.

"We don't have cable." "We won't be open that late." Call by call, the answers grew more discouraging. But I just couldn't give up. Miraculously, at the last number in the book, the woman who answered said, "Yeah, we get WGN. Yes, we're open till two."

The bartender's directions were a list of lefts and rights scribbled on a page of my journal. Where they led, I had no idea. That didn't matter to a Dodger fanatic on a mission. I went downstairs, put our rented car in gear, and started driving. The directions took me from the center of town into a residential area. The houses got smaller and smaller. The lawns got scrawnier. The cars got older. The poorer the area got, the more people you could see standing around outside. This was going to be a neighborhood tavern, not a slick cocktail lounge.

Finally, there it was, the words CIRCLE BAR painted on one of those glass signs that lights up from inside. The sign was dark, but the bar was plenty visible. It occupied a corner of the street, with a front door that cut slantwise across the corner. The front windows were decorated with a couple of those neon signs that beer distributors give out: BUDWEISER. MICHELOB ON TAP. I saw a parking space several cars short of the door and edged into it. As I rolled up the window and started getting out, I noted that the dozen or so people in front of the bar were black, and they were all looking at me. The car I was about to leave behind was a silver Thunderbird with red upholstery, newer by at least eight years than the worn Chevrolets and Pintos surrounding it. I realized I was dressed in my casual uniform, an Oxford button-down shirt, khaki pants, and Topsiders.

Suddenly my heart was pounding fast. Everything about me seemed exaggerated to the point of awkwardness. I noticed my own fast breathing, the pounding heart, the way I put my foot out the door onto the sidewalk, my attempt to stand straight—but not stiff, not too straight. Just walking felt like climbing a huge wall. The fact is, I was terrified.

So many impressions flashed through my head so fast that I can't say they came in words; the language came later. I don't belong here. This neighborhood belongs to the guys who are staring at me, not to me and my friends. Why do I wear khaki pants and button-down shirts? Because where I usually hang out, they blend in. They sure don't blend in here.

"Here" was a sort of block party where people familiar with each other could be comfortable and hang out together, and all of a sudden it was disrupted by a conspicuous misfit. The clothes were the least of the problem. What a huge distinction we make of skin color.

You can *want* color to make no difference, you can try pretending it makes no difference, and still it jerks your leash. You could probably walk into a crowd of white people naked without feeling any more exposed than I did on the sidewalk in front of the Circle Bar. Maybe Billy Reed, a friend who was one of the few blacks at UCSB, felt like this twenty-four hours a day. He didn't talk about what it does to you to be black in a white world; the rest of us didn't know enough to ask him. Now, since about sixty seconds ago, we could share a few impressions about fear, and alertness clicking on like a gun being cocked, and the looming importance of every shape and motion in the corner of your eye. I had stepped into a zone of deep and powerful colors, and I felt very pale.

There were just two ways to go. In, or out. Well, there was no choice. I couldn't let myself act like the reactionary I don't want to be—too scared to get near people whose language I don't speak, or too arrogant to meet them on their terms instead of mine. The person I want to be believes in heroes. He would open the door and see what's on the other side.

The people, most of them men, moved barely enough to get out of the way as I started walking toward the door on the corner. They kept looking. The music from inside was so loud you could hear it on the street. Marvin Gaye. The day before, Marvin Gaye had been shot dead by his father. Marvin's been shot and that's what we're going to listen to all night, "Let's Get It On" and "Heard It Through the Grapevine" and all his hits. As I opened the door it was "Sexual Healing."

If you remember the *Animal House* scene when the college kids blunder into the roadhouse and everything stops, you know what this looked like. The place must have had a hundred people in it, crammed around a bar that really was circular, sitting at tables along the walls, and dancing in whatever space they could stand on. The music didn't stop, but heads turned and everything else did. The light was low in there, but from what I could see of clothing and faces the crowd was a mixture of men and women of just about every age and a lot of occupations. There were leather jackets and jeans, cotton dresses and shirts over skirts, work pants and slacks, plaid shirts, flannel shirts, some white shirts, but no silks and big jewelry that I could see.

I didn't want to make myself conspicuous by looking around. It is true, though, that you can feel eyes on you. There were a lot on me. The only other person in the place who was not black was the bartender. She might have been part Indian and part black. Her look at me was different from the rest—amused, as if she were thinking, "What's this white bread think he's doing in here?"

Diagonally to the left from the door, I pressed in at the bar next to a quiet old man, about seventy-five with a stubble of gray beard, and his slightly younger companion. The bartender leaned over so I could shout in her ear that I was the one who'd called about cable television. She said, "Oh, yeah, the Dodger game." Just like that, she walked out from behind the bar to the wall behind us where the TV was bolted to a shelf and turned it on. The set was too old to have a remote control, but it had a color picture. As soon as the screen lighted up I got even more stares, probably from people wondering if the jukebox was going to go off.

It wasn't. It completely drowned out the sound from the television set, but that didn't matter. The two acquaintances who had moved over to make space for me didn't seem to feel a need to talk a lot, even to each other; they had long since reached that point of familiarity with the place and each other that was beyond the desire to chatter. Without a word, though, they gave me some camaraderie. In the midst of the Marvin Gaye extravaganza the three of us were the only people who turned around to watch the ball game. I felt so grateful, I almost thought they did it for me. But I knew better than to be that conceited; baseball is a big sport here, what with the hometown Redbirds, a St. Louis Cardinals farm team, being the most successful minor-league club in the nation, and this being the home of the great Pee Wee Reese and the Louisville Slugger bat factory just across the river in Jeffersonville, Indiana.

The man with the stubble, who also had no teeth, was wearing a blue knit watch hat perched over a pair of old horn-rim glasses, and a work uniform that had been made a long time ago: green shirt of the sort gas-station attendants used to wear, brown corduroy flight jacket with imitation fur on the collar, baggy blue pants, and worn work shoes. His companion had a faded red baseball cap with an "L" on it, a gray sweatshirt over a long-john undershirt that showed through a couple of holes at the elbows, tan bell-bottom pants, and worn-down black Chuck Taylor hightops. He kept a stub of a stogie lit with steady, gentle puffs. Each of them had a long-neck Bud that he took occasional pulls on. They seemed accustomed to making a beer last a whole evening.

About the second inning I realized I needed to go to the bathroom. A lot. Even though I was acting a little crazy this evening, I wasn't *that* far out of my mind. If I go in there, I thought, I may not come out. I'll scrinch up and sit here a while and see what happens.

The music blared on, and people kept partying—a little sadly, because of Marvin Gaye dying. On the screen a left-handed batter came up, and I saw two of my buddies in the seats for which we split season tickets. Southern California had put on one of those balmy nights that makes the TV people want to show the palm trees, and the homesickness really hit me. There's a place I would love to be, I thought, at a Dodger game with my friends, drinking Dodger Beers and eating Dodger Dogs. And I'm watching it in a bar where I don't know a soul, with two hundred eyes hating me.

The three of us watched the game so intently that when Tommy Lasorda changed pitchers I was startled to hear a voice next to me say, "What happened? Why pull him out?" It was the guy in the knit hat, saying it not so much to his friend or to me as to himself. Without thinking, without taking my eyes off the screen, I said, "I think he's got an arm problem." This time intruding into somebody's conversation at a bar got me a response: "Uh *huh*."

Now I felt I had a connection with somebody else in this bar. Just getting that "Uh huh" back as a reply was all the acceptance I could ever want. For people watching baseball, that much conversation is practically hugging and kissing. I had a couple of compatriots now. If one of the dancers had come up to turn off the TV, I felt I'd have some company wanting to keep it on.

The station broke away to a commercial while the relief pitcher warmed up. Knit Hat said to Baseball Cap, "You know, I like the way that Landreaux swings a bat."

Baseball Cap said, "Shoot, Landreaux couldn't hold Lou Brock's jock. Brock was hungry, man. That's a bunch of millionaires up there now. Nobody as hungry as Brock."

The ice was already broken, so I chimed in. "I used to go to Lou Brock baseball camps when I was a kid. I sure miss seeing him on the basepaths."

143

Baseball Cap looked me in the eye and nodded. His smile said, "You and I know something, all right." Just then Tom Niedenfuer finished his warm-ups and we all went back to watching the game. Niedenfuer struck out Ryne Sandberg to end the Cub rally, and the three of us turned to the bar. The Buds in front of my two friends were empty, so I said, "Can I buy us all a drink so we can toast Lou Brock?" They both nodded, and they each gave me a little grin. The brooding, semi-bored men of an hour ago were different now; smiles do bring a face to life.

"Sure," Baseball Cap said. "Lou Brock's a *good* reason for a beer."

After our toast, I got up and headed around the bar, past the pool table in the back, to the rest room. It was a slow journey, squeezing through the tightly packed groups with an "Excuse me" now and then when one dancer would bounce me into another, but much less tense than my entrance. The wall-climbing I had created on my way in was eased, if not gone. Standing at the urinal, I looked sideways into a mirror that was cracked so that half my face showed to the right of the crack. To the face, or about it, I murmured, "What a jerk! Whose idea was all that drama?"

Coming back out, I still took a few stares. Mostly, though, the people whose tavern I had invaded were ready to let me be there and have a good time. I actually was having a good time. The Dodgers were winning, a couple of regulars had let me buy them a round of beers—we weren't exactly palling around, but we had a bit of baseball in common and they would talk to me.

The Dodgers won the game. My neighbors at the bar said good night and reached out to shake hands as they left. The crowd thinned out. A thought started, "Now I've got to walk out to the car." I didn't want the thought, but there it was. And there outside at the curb sat my new silver T-Bird, flanked by dented old cars, untouched.

19

Real and Ideal

David felt as shaky as I did, but he gamely took the wheel for a drive east to the capital in Frankfort to talk—courtesy of Jim Long—with Governor Martha Layne Collins's aide Michael Berry. A violent stomach flu had hit both of us, and we hadn't left our rooms for two days. The sunshine and fresh air were a relief; they made us feel like trying for a comeback.

The beauty on both sides of U.S. 60 amazed us. We had heard about the horse farms around Lexington, and here they were. White plank fences bordered long green fields where gleaming animals ran for sheer pleasure. The smells of springtime soft in the air . . . Suddenly I realized what a gift spring is when you're coming out of a cold winter. All of this slipped inside my guard while I was still wide-eyed in surprise at the warmth of the people who were helping us. The nature of the landscape—the openness, the expanse and the details of buildings and tended earth, the age and calm permanence of it all—pressed around me almost physically, as the air grabs you when you step from a chilled office to a warm afternoon.

"Hey," I said to David. "Do you think they're using Southern hospitality on us?"

The Kentucky State Capitol is a real beauty—shining limestone walls ornamented with Ionic columns outside, a lot of marble, murals, and paintings inside. We felt as if we were walking into some kind of French palace.

"Funny you should mention that," Mike Berry said outside his office. "The original of the dome is on the Hotel des Invalides over Napoleon's tomb, and that big flight of stairs is modeled on the

Paris Opera." His clothes were straight Kentucky, though, like Jeffrey Hutter's: crisp pastels and saddle shoes like David's, except white where David's were (to my mild but probably irritating amazement) blue. David gave me a glance that said, "See, it's okay."

The governor's ideas about the torch were perfect for us. She wanted to host a nice reception at her mansion—"If that's all right with you," Berry would say at every new point, as if we were doing Martha Layne Collins the favor instead of the other way around. She would like the torch to run past the front of the building so the guests could see it—"Is that okay?" What a change from people elsewhere who wanted us to beg. Berry walked us through a garden on the approach to the mansion. "See those little *shrubs*?" he said, his voice taking on an edge of irritation. "They were beautiful high hedges until that . . . the former first lady had them chopped down."

Pleasant as Michael was, I felt queasy and weak enough that I asked if we could shorten the tour and finish up. "Sure," he said. "Let's go see if we can find the governor. I know she wants to say hello." Back in the building, we stopped at what must have been the big office. The guardian outside saw Berry and barely looked up when he pushed the door open and went in for a minute, then came out and said, "She'll be here in a minute." So, I figured, she's in there. We stood around and nodded to various assistants. I picked a piece of hard candy out of a bowl and gnawed on it to change the taste of the flu. A woman came up behind us and shook hands—mighty firmly for an aide, I thought—and joined the conversation.

After a moment or two of chat, she asked, "Are you going to run the torch yourself?"

I wasn't rude, exactly, but I did want the governor to show up so we could trade greetings and I could go off and be sick. "Hell, no, I can't afford three thousand dollars," I said and slapped her on the back. "How about you? Got three thousand bucks lying around?"

She laughed loudly, the way a politician laughs at something that isn't all that funny. Then she said, "Well, so long," and walked into the big office.

Michael looked at us and said, "So, what did you think?"

David nodded pleasantly. Then it dawned on me. "Oh, yeah." I

146

couldn't let on that I hadn't known all along that we were meeting the governor of Kentucky. "Nice lady."

We hustled on through the Bluegrass to the night's stop just outside Lexington. In the morning we'd scout Keeneland Race Course as a possible campsite for the caravan. First, though, was an evening I'd been looking forward to—a visit with a favorite professor from my alma mater.

Art Stevens had been one of the top people at the Library of Congress before he moved to UCSB to teach political science. Some of us political science majors had been excited that we were getting a professor from the real world of Washington politics. With my usual tact, I managed to have a disagreement with him right off the bat because I thought better of the Carter presidency than Art did. Even though Art came originally from Kentucky, he was not much charmed by Carter's Southernness. Rather, as part of the Washington, D.C., establishment, he regarded Carter with some suspicion.

Art and Judy Stevens had since moved back to his home town, Danville, about thirty miles south of Lexington on the road to Tennessee, and he taught at Centre College. I was still at the stage of my travels where I craved familiar faces. At the same time, it was strange to sit in a warm living room chatting with this person I'd been used to seeing at the head of a classroom.

"Well," he said once he had me settled in a chair, "what do you think of Kentucky?"

"It's nice, really nice. I haven't met a single person who isn't completely helpful and . . . nice. I even roughed up the governor today and she took it as if she thought I was funny."

After a long, late dinner, Art and Judy sat up with me to ruminate about politics and people who had grown up through the sixties. We picked up our running discussion of Jimmy Carter, with me suggesting that people, including old Washington hands who had been around the South long enough to know better, were prejudiced against Carter because of his accent. Look at me: Talking as if I hadn't had all sorts of notions about what "Southern" meant before I came here a couple of months ago. Art wasn't buying the proposition. Then Judy, who had been sitting quietly by the fireplace, said, "Art, what he's trying to say is that if Carter had a Harvard accent you wouldn't dislike him so."

A few cognacs later, toward half past one, Art said something so poignant that at first I was unwilling to believe it: "Of all the students I've had in all the years I've taught, you know who I saw as the most idealistic? You. You took some basic notions of decency and actually went out and worked with them. You got into politics, you got involved, you wanted to do something with them. I've had four or five others I'd call idealistic at all, and I don't know how willing they were to get their hands dirty."

A lifetime of teaching, and only five? And the most idealistic sitting there swirling a last sip of cognac, looking stunned? What a thing to live up to.

20

Road Games

Who would think a place so far away would be so natural to settle into? We never did settle anywhere; but I would leave Knoxville and come back to it so often as we covered the South that the sight of the Sunsphere from the 1982 World's Fair, rising toward the sky like a twenty-five-story Tootsie Pop, would get me thinking, "I'm almost home."

A one-day membership at the YMCA near the motel cost five bucks—the least of what it was going to cost me to work off the pancake sandwiches that had collected around my middle. I checked out a rather worn, lopsided leather basketball and headed past the lobby through a swinging door into the gym.

A basketball player's delight: an empty gym. At three in the afternoon, the only other people in the place were a couple of joggers on the track overhead. The yellow light, the scuffed boards, the worn fittings: This basketball court had character. Each bounce of the ball on the crickety old floor made a deep, full, echoing sound as I dribbled toward the basket to my left. I lobbed my first shot from near the free-throw line and it hit the front of the rim, then the back, and settled through the long, thick net. Older gyms are a paradise for shooters, because the years of balls bouncing off a rim loosen it and let more shots fall in.

I warmed up, by habit, the way I always had. Five minutes of shooting. Then dribble-down sprints full court toward the far goal, simulating bringing up the ball on a fast break and pulling up suddenly with the jump shot. Winded after a few minutes of sprints, I settled back to the western basket.

The gym door swung open, and in walked a lanky teenage girl followed by a bald, stocky man. They started working the eastern basket. The man barked instructions as the girl went through numerous shooting and dribbling drills. She wasn't bad—probably had a high-school girls' team built around her. But boy, that guy is tough, I thought. She must be some player to get the coach over here for special sessions like this.

I kept shooting and sneaking looks at the two of them. After a few minutes the door swung open again and a fourth player, a short, muscular young guy, walked in. He hadn't finished lacing his shoes when the coach called to the new guy and me, "You two wanna play two-on-two?" The words were technically a question, but the booming, authoritative voice seemed to say, Get over here *now*. The old jock reflexes never would let me disobey a coach's command.

The man threw me the ball and said, curtly, "You two against us—go ahead and shoot for outs." I put up a do-or-die shot from the top of the key and hit nothing but net. The girl looked at the man and he ordered, "Well, get on him," as if to say, Guard him close, he can shoot from outside. She jumped up within arm's length to guard me as my partner inbounded the ball. We were a good thirty-five feet from the net and she was right on me, way too close. Fake right, then past her easily to the left for an easy lay-up. The coach shot her a stern look and she dropped too far off me. We were playing winner's outs; when I got the ball twenty feet to the right of the basket, she was five feet off me, so I lobbed an uncontested set shot off the backboard and in. The man said, "Time out," and walked the girl over underneath the basket. His loud whispers and frantic hand gestures gave her a merciless scolding. The fourth guy gave me a puzzled look and mouthed, "What an asshole."

They broke from their huddle and the girl once again got on me way too close. She looked embarrassed and confused. Her face was already beaded with sweat, and more poured out from under her hair. The worst of it was that she wasn't having any fun. She couldn't have been more than fourteen, maybe fifteen years old. This coach was riding her, demanding too much, and she was scared. For the next minute or so I didn't shoot, trying everything I could to set up my partner, but he clearly hadn't played much and didn't seem to enjoy having his lack of skill showcased. Finally the coach pulled me aside.

"Look," he said. "The best thing for her is for you to just play your game and let her learn from that."

Yeah, well, I thought of saying, the best thing would be for you to cut her a little slack. But I went along with it. We beat them three games in a row, lopsidedly, and it was no fun to watch the act any longer. I finally said I had an appointment and had to go.

"Sure you can't play a little longer?" the coach asked. As I said, "Sorry," I could tell he knew I was lying. Coaches and mothers always know when you're lying.

I had almost reached the door when I hear the girl's voice slide up to a high pitch: "I'm sorry, Daddy!" I turned around, furiously. The bald man looked quickly toward me. The girl had her head on his shoulder, crying. He folded his arms around her and patted her gently. The only sound in the gym was his daughter's sobbing. I turned away, and as I pushed through the old swinging door it was a relief to hear the sudden boom of the leather ball hitting the floor.

LOS ANGELES, APRIL 30

A schoolyard on opening day, that's what it felt like. People drifted into the big conference room, looked around at the clusters that had already formed, and joined the one with the most familiar faces. From the safety of their own faction, they could appraise the others.

The torch rats were the smallest faction. The Pioneers were far and away the biggest. Counting thirty-three state coordinators and their lieutenants, there must have been eighty in the room. I looked for Evelyn from Oregon, or any other Pioneer companion from the road. There—Harold from North Carolina. Time for a re-union and a little banter.

"Hey, Harold, good to see you. Can I get you a vodka and Coke?"

Harold gave it one cool chuckle and a brief, "Hey, Steve, how ya doing?" before he turned back to his group. Walking back to the torch rats' side of the room, I thought, Wow, I thought Harold and I got to be buds in Murphy, but there's no room for me in that bunch. This really feels as if we've gone back to Us and Them.

A torch rat in my cluster nodded across the room at a bunch of

Pioneers and said, "Have you ever worked with somebody really rude? Try that Hamilton guy over there someday." I'd heard the name several times before. Dick Hamilton was the Pioneer coordinator for New York State.

"Which one is he?" I asked.

"The one with the short hair and green pants." The rest of her remarks about him faded into the background as I watched the group that had formed around Hamilton. Short hair and green pants; you could measure the distance between the factions forming up in this room with any number of yardsticks, and appearance was the easiest.

Overall, the Pioneers in the room looked like a union meeting. Most were between forty and sixty, few were as lean as they had probably once been, and their outfits ranged from leisure suits to work shirts. They struck me as the sort of guys who devoted themselves to their jobs and spent little time worrying about what to wear to the club. By contrast, the AT&T brass could have been at a board meeting, in their hundred percent cotton button-down shirts and neat dark suits. The P.R. guys from Burson Marsteller looked even more like investment bankers. Executives from the Olympic Committee news department and torch run, and the fifteen torch rats, came as casual young professionals in blazers, slacks, and polished loafers. The crew around Bill Mattman, the ex–Secret Service agent in charge of security, bridged all the factions by looking simultaneously corporate and tough.

But clothes were not what set Hamilton apart. When he talked, everyone in his group paid attention. He stood about five feet ten, stocky but with no body fat, a man of about fifty who looked as if he worked out every day. His tan, and his yellow polo shirt, suggested that he might have just stepped off a golf course, except for one Pioneer touch: the outline of an undershirt. He kept a pair of horn-rim glasses propped at his hair line and an unlit cigar in the corner of his mouth. Muscles in his arms bunched when he jabbed a finger to emphasize a point, but the finger was unnecessary. He compelled attention with a voice that carried, not so much loud as intense, not obnoxious but commanding. The guy must have been a Marine at some point. He looked like Bull Meechum in *The Great Santini*. It was easy to imagine him leading a Marine platoon over a hill on a twenty-mile hike, and loving it. All those elements together should have made me want to stay a mile away from Hamilton. Instead, I kept glancing over to check out what he was doing.

Wally leaned into a microphone at the head table. "Time to get started," he said. In a week, the torch would start its journey in front of the UN building in New York. Wally had pulled together all the different—and sometimes conflicting—sections of the operation to boil out any lingering problems.

He started presenting the "block schedule," the overview route of the runners and core caravan from New York to California. The presentation ended up taking all day. Questions, arguments, and grievances from one faction or another made the meeting sound at times like a bigger version of the motel room in Murphy. Being a torch rat often felt like working alone against everyone else, and here it was again. We were the ones who said, "No, it has to go here, not over there." More than we'd like to admit, we brought some of that isolation on ourselves. We saw our attitude as practical. You couldn't blame a Pioneer for seeing it as snobbish, when it was essentially this: "We finally figured out the route for you. Now take your toys and go play on it. You've got the shiny trucks, the uniforms, the torches, and that's all you have to worry about." It was not, however, all they worried about.

Some Pioneers complained: "But where's the lunch stop on my section?" Not Hamilton. He was there to examine the core caravan schedule, and saw—as we did—everything else as a separate issue. And he was blunt about it. Mark Zangrando was describing some detail of the route when Hamilton boomed, "You gotta be kidding. There's no *way* to do that." But he didn't discriminate against torch rats.

"For the love of Pete!" he exclaimed as one Pioneer went on about when and where the motor homes were supposed to pump out their holding tanks. "Poop stops have nothing to do with the schedule we're talking about here. Get on with it, for Chrissake."

I got up at one point to report on arrangements for Louisville. Muhammad Ali had given the mayor there his promise to run. That led to questions and comments, some of them so skeptical that I began wondering if what we were doing was right.

"Is he coherent?" people asked. "Slurring? In shape? Can he make it?"

Of course, I assured them, of course. This man has never let anybody down and I know he won't let the Olympic torch and the people of Louisville down.

Did I really know that? No. I had never met Ali. This was more a defense of my boyhood hero than a reasoned argument. Whatever reasoned argument we did have, though, was persuasive enough. My interest at that stage was still mainly in what the pictures were going to show. Anybody can walk a torch for three-fifths of a mile; he wouldn't even have to run if he didn't want to. He would have a flame in his hand and it would be Muhammad Ali in Louisville. It was a natural.

We plowed through to the end. Finally, Charles Mitchell, the top AT&T man there, stood up for a rousing half-time pep talk: "We've come a long way . . . a lot of people have put hundreds of hours of their own time into this . . . let's all pull together. . . . And don't forget the banquet AT&T is giving for the torch relay tonight at the Sheraton Miramar. Everyone come and have a good time."

It was a good party. There was dancing after dinner, and the atmosphere was a little—just a little—looser than it had been in the meeting. Dick Hamilton didn't miss a dance; the man never seemed to sit down. When the band swung into a polka, Maris Segal took my hand and said, "Come on, I'll give you a lesson."

Only half a dozen other couples stayed up for this much exercise. Maris had a lot of room to work in, and soon had me dropstepping and whirling across the floor. The more confident I got, the less I looked where I was going, until I slammed into something that felt like the wall. It nearly knocked me out of my loafers. It did bounce me on the seat of my pants. When I looked up, there was Dick Hamilton grinning around his cigar, reaching down to give me a hand.

21

Okay, We'll Show 'Em . . . Won't We?

Everything around the U.S. Military Academy was lush and green. The cadets in their uniform gray with black trim looked like a whole camp of student body presidents. No fat guys, no nerds. As Capt. Tim Pfister, the public relations officer, walked us around, the cadets were all alert to Pfister's rank; we walked through wave after wave of salutes. Our first day of the torch relay, as it happened, would be Armed Forces Day. The spot where Captain Pfister stood us on the high west bank of the Hudson, looking over the water to Constitution Island, would be perfect for the first exchange of the flame.

Wally had assigned Mark Zangrando and me to work together for opening week. We were to handle the torch run on May 12, starting up the Hudson River at West Point and ending after dark at Rider College, just outside Princeton.

Mark took off on an errand while I went back to the Hotel Thayer to check us in. Carrying bags into the huge, high-ceilinged lobby of the old gray stone building on its hill above the Hudson felt like checking into a mansion. The desk clerk handed me a message. Dick Hamilton was in town. He would be back in an hour to set up a meeting. Oh, God. Here we go. I felt like a Marine recruit summoned by the drill sergeant. I had already seen him in action. He had knocked me down.

Precisely an hour later, he rapped on my door and strode into the room, cigar in place. He was wearing a red windbreaker and a brand-new cap—a really handsome cap, white, with the torch relay runner in motion trailing rainbow colors across the front. The Pioneers must have gotten them for volunteering, I thought; none of the rest of us had one.

"Nice to meet you," I said. "If there's anything Mark and I can do to help you, just ask."

"You can start by telling me what the schedule's going to look like," he said. We looked at it. He seemed astonished that I even showed it to him. So far, so good. He didn't seem terrifying, yet. He looked at his watch. "Six o'clock. You guys up for some dinner? I'm going down to the lobby for a drink. You and Mark meet me there when you're ready." Off he went.

Noises next door meant Mark was in. I knocked. "You hungry? Dick Hamilton's taking us to dinner."

"Yeah, right." Mark wasn't going to let me make a fool of him. "Who you kidding?"

Hamilton had it all planned. We were going to an Italian restaurant in Highland Falls. There, the hostess didn't break off her chat with a waiter the instant we crossed the threshold. Hamilton boomed, "Young lady!" and she jumped to his side. The waiter was slow in arriving. Hamilton raised his hand and snapped his fingers with a crack like a whip, and his voice cut across the room: "Waiter!" His drink was Scotch and water. Mark ordered bourbon and soda. Ordinarily I'd have had a beer, if that, but this seemed one of those nights when I'd better be one of the guys. Gin and tonic.

Hamilton settled back and started quizzing us about our impressions of the torch organization. What was McGuire really like? How well did we know some of the other brass at LAOOC headquarters? In turn, he answered our questions. He was an engineer in middle management from Albany, husband to a wife he plainly loved and called "a beautiful girl," father of a college-age daughter.

For all the friendly tone of the talk, it was easy to see where some of the tension between the Pioneers and the advance team came from. To a twenty-year man in management in a company run on semi-military lines, we probably looked like smart-ass college kids with an irreverent way of getting the Olympic flame across the country. Some of the abruptness might just be a test of mettle. Hamilton asked about us. Where did we come from? What had we done? He came on gruff, all right; yet he listened.

"My pop's the hardest working man I know," Mark told Hamilton. "He spent a lot of years on the road selling, but a day never went by that I didn't know he did all that stuff for us. So I do my job right—

sort of letting him know I'm paying back his investment, you know?"
The intensity of Mark's feeling for his family caught Hamilton's eye.
He seemed to like my rough and tumble, too—growing up with
my mom, living on Army reservations a couple of times while she
worked there, taking the blue collar to college.

Mark's glass was almost empty. Crack! The finger snap brought
a waiter almost at a run. Without a word, Dick jabbed his index
finger down at the glass. While the drink was on its way, he said,
"I like you guys. I walked into Stevie's room here and it was the
first time I didn't hear one of you advance people start in with, 'I
need this, I need that.'"

Another finger snap. "Some matches, please."

The waiter who brought them looked at the seat next to Dick
and said, "Great hat. Think I could buy it?"

Dick didn't look up, but he did put his hand protectively over
the hat. "Not a chance."

He held a flame under the end of his cigar. I said, "I've been
waiting ever since L.A. for you to light that sucker up." He pulled
out two more from an inside pocket and handed one to each of us.
Mark smokes a cigarette once in a while, so he bit off the end of
his and plopped it into his mouth. Dick lit it, then put a match in
front of me. I hesitated; I had never smoked anything.

"Ah, come on, Stevie, cut the crap," he said. "Put the thing in
your mouth." I followed orders immediately.

Dick put a generous tip on the check, and we were almost out
the door when he excused himself and headed back to the table. He
put down an extra five, nodded to the waiter, and turned back to
leave with us.

In midafternoon the next day, Mark called. "I'm done with the
posters already. You know what Dick did? He pulled half a dozen
guys off their jobs and sent them over to help. Did you ask him for
that?" No. Dick was making it clearer and clearer that in terms of
factions, it wasn't the torch rats and the Pioneers against each
other. It was the rats and the Pioneers together. We were the people on the front lines who had to produce the results.

MANHATTAN, MAY 8

On a Tuesday morning in a steady rain at the United Nations
Plaza in New York, Gina Hemphill and Bill Thorpe, grandchildren

of Jesse Owens and Jim Thorpe, started the torch on the first of its 14,500 kilometers across America. They put their hands on one torch and ran together up First Avenue.

With that gesture they linked the memories of two great Olympians whose triumphs hadn't paid off for them with the recognition that America routinely gives other heroes: The black man whose four gold medals foiled Hitler's rhetoric about a master race, and the Indian who lost his medals to petty officials because he played one summer of semipro baseball. As chairman of the Los Angeles Olympic Organizing Committee, Peter Ueberroth acknowledged a debt on behalf of all of us.

The evening before, Mark and I had sneaked into Manhattan to see it happen. We wanted to reward ourselves with the sight of the great beginning we had been playing and replaying in our imaginations since December.

In our hotel room, we flipped channels on the TV, trying to find some coverage of the torch. Dan Rather talked mostly about a threat from the Greeks not to let us use the flame. I muttered, "cynics," and then Rather talked about the great diversity of runners who would be carrying the flame. The screen showed pictures of Jane Fonda and Muhammad Ali. "All right, Muhammad!"

On our way to some food, we asked a cab driver what he thought of the big event tomorrow. He scratched his head and said, "Oh, yeah, it'll probably fuck up traffic all day. Glad I have the night shift."

I woke up at six-thirty and ran downstairs to the hotel lobby to buy a *New York Times*, eager to see what the nation's greatest newspaper would say about our big day. Ah! There! A headline at the bottom of page 1: OLYMPIC FLAME TO START ODYSSEY ACROSS U.S. A map, a schedule, a nice picture of Abel Kiviat, America's oldest living medalist, and a story by Frank Litsky beginning, "The pageantry of the 1984 Olympic Summer Games will begin at the United Nations today. . . ." Bingo! What a thrill to see the article, even the details. Kiviat, a cheerful-looking five-foot, one-inch great-grandfather, had shared a cabin with Jim Thorpe on the boat to Stockholm and won a silver medal in the 1,500-meter run. He would take the flame from the grandchildren, Gina and Jim.

We dodged up First Avenue toward a large beige canopy covering the ceremonial stand at the UN, and stopped across the street. The crowd was thin. The rain started coming down hard, and a little forest of umbrellas sprouted in front of the platform.

Turning away for a second, we spotted a short, pudgy man in an official Levi's Olympic warm-up suit selling what looked like bathroom night-lights in the shape of Sam the Eagle holding a torch. I drifted over to check out the lights. "Um," I asked him, "who are you associated with?"

He said, "I'm an AT&T Pioneer, wanna buy one?"

Something about him looked less genuine than the other Pioneers, but maybe he was just a type we hadn't met before. "Hi, I'm Steve," I said. "What's your name?"

"Fred."

"Glad to meet you, Fred."

"Yeah. Wanna buy one?"

The speakers—Mayors Ed Koch of New York and Tom Bradley of Los Angeles, Ueberroth, and AT&T Chairman Charles Brown—showed a fine sensitivity to the wetness of the crowd. They kept their remarks brief. Then Rafer Johnson, the 1960 decathlon gold medalist, touched off a big saucer of flame. Hemphill and Thorpe lighted their torch from it. And off they went.

Is this all there is? Mark and I looked at each other. Sure, it was raining, but where was the crowd? Besides the crowd, something else was missing. Why, on this island where seven million people are crammed, home of the most powerful communications organizations in America, did it look as if only the parents of the band musicians and a few phone company employees had come out for the great send-off?

The torch run had become personal for us. It had worked its way into our hearts as such a pure and positive undertaking that we gave ourselves to it completely. But if no one else cared . . . maybe that meant our devotion to the project was misplaced.

After breakfast, Mark took the Ford to Trenton to pick up more posters and I rented a different car to get back to West Point for a meeting with Captain Pfister about Saturday's event. Just out of Manhattan, Route 9 disappeared into a fog bank so thick that cars kept pulling off the road. I made my fourth or fifth pullout at a diner to call the captain to tell him I was going to be late. Leaving, I overheard an old man with a hunting cap say to no one in particular, "Who needs the stinkin' Russkies anyhow?" and thought

159

he must have been arguing about politics. Inching the car northward, I was peering into the fog and twisting the radio knob to get a clear station when I heard, faintly, the words, "Olympic boycott." Then a staticky top-of-the-hour newscast from New York: "The big story today—The Soviet Union shocked Olympic officials by announcing today in Moscow that they will not participate in this summer's games in Los Angeles. . . ." It felt like a punch in the stomach.

Early editions of the next day's *Times* conveyed the mood of May 8. Frank Litsky's lead at the top of page 1 read:

> The absence of a Soviet team would drastically diminish the quality of competition at the 1984 Olympic Games in Los Angeles. . . .

Back on page 16, coverage of the relay began:

> The Olympic Torch Relay began here yesterday, surviving a steady rain, to mostly blank stares from the relatively few spectators and the Soviet Union's announcement of its boycott. . . . Spectators were especially sparse in Central Park, and at times most were motorists who found intersections blocked by police cars. Inside and outside the park, a few people applauded as the relay passed. Many stared blankly. A Trump Tower doorman in a long red coat watched, hands on hips, obviously bored.

Sports columnist Dave Anderson's comments were headlined, THE OLYMPICS AREN'T WORTH IT.

What a flop this whole thing had become. What a fool I was, what a fool. Sure, I'd started off wanting just to see the country, but I had actually let myself care about this thing. We all had. We all worked so hard, only to be taunted by doormen and journalists. Frustration breeds disenchantment, and I felt myself slipping back.

22

Day of the Patriots

One of our torch bearers called to say she couldn't make it. (I'll name her Joyce, with apologies; two years of searching haven't turned up my lost notes of that day's conversations.) Joyce regretted giving up the honor of the run for which she had paid three thousand dollars, and she hoped we could pass it along to someone who would get a kick out of it. When she mentioned that her mother lived near Princeton, I asked, "How about letting her run in your place?"

Joyce said, "She's sixty-six years old and not athletic, and if you can talk her into it, good luck." Forty-five minutes later we had our fifty-third torch bearer, and Joyce's mother had a promise that I would personally run or walk alongside her.

MAY 12

Right on time the next morning, Canadian runner Pierre Caplette passed the flame to Joseph Schuh, from Ithaca, New York. The Canadian and the American were an ordinary mailman and plumber on any other day, but on this Saturday morning, hundreds of West Point cadets cheered them as heroes and honored celebrities.

The corps of cadets was studying for finals, but hundreds of them emerged from the library and other old stone buildings to see the torch. Some cheered: "Go for it! Run it!" Some even saluted. As Joseph Schuh passed with the flame held as high as his arm would reach, he ran through wave after wave of salutes.

West Point was affecting me in a totally unexpected way. The whole army officer scene, backed by the beauty of the place and its impressive traditions, the uniforms and parades, the atmosphere of duty and honor, started looking glamorous and attractive. I was attracted and at the same time uncomfortable about being attracted. If *I* can be drawn to it, I thought, what about people who start off less inclined against militarism?

Mark stayed with the runners as they left West Point under skies that glowered with rain one minute and beamed with sunshine the next. Dick Hamilton picked me up at the south gate of the Military Academy in a Pioneer advance car—another white Buick with the runner-in-motion rainbow on the sides, not a convertible but a four-door hardtop with a yellow flasher on the roof. We headed for Mahwah, at the New Jersey state line. There I would take over from Mark, at sponsored runner number twenty-three.

For several hours we drove, stopping at every kilometer so Dick could check out the Pioneer marshals at the points where each runner would pass the flame to the next one. Hours ahead of the torch, pockets of people were forming along Routes 9W and 202, the crowds thicker and thicker at the exchange points.

To one side of the crowd in Mahwah, a platoon of New Jersey state troopers stood ready to take the handoff from the New York police. Along with them, a dozen New Jersey Pioneers in their jackets and treasured caps like Dick's waited to take over from New York Pioneers. A little boy about six looked up at one and I heard him say, "Mister? That's a great hat. Can I get one?" The Pioneer looked down and told him, kindly but with the iron pride I'd seen so often in Dick, "Sorry, son. The only people who get these are Telephone Pioneers. We have to earn them."

A strange sight came up the street behind us: a sky blue Buick towing a trailer painted red, white, and blue. On the trailer was painted a sign, WE ♥ U.S.A.'s TORCH RUN. At the wheel of the car, in the official warm-up suit, was the nightlight huckster from First Avenue in New York. I nudged Dick. "Do you know that guy?" I asked. "Is he a Pioneer?"

Dick turned to look. "Hell, no," he said.

We all had walky-talkies. At a quarter to noon, Mark's voice came through: "Ten minutes."

We were on schedule. The caravan rounded a corner with its lights flashing, and the cheering rolled toward us. It was time. Dick turned, we each stuck out a hand, and his big, hard grip gave me a firm shake. He said, "Great job. Let's stay in touch," and turned away.

The core caravan reached us. Mark jumped out of the lead car and loped back to the EMS. I got into the seat he had vacated. A Security voice on the walky-talky said, "Proceed."

Just then, I heard a familiar voice bark, "Hey, Stevie!" There was Dick, five feet away with his hat off, exposing his scalp to the sun. He swept his arm forward and his Pioneer cap sailed into the car. The runner and caravan headed into New Jersey, and I settled Dick Hamilton's hat on my head.

MAHWAH TO LAWRENCEVILLE, NEW JERSEY, MAY 12

As we left the New York state line, I was finally in the relay.

People stood two and three deep along Route 202 almost every yard of the way. Rarely in the hundred and eighty miles we would travel that day was it quiet enough to reflect or chat with the other people in the lead car. As the torch approached, people started clapping and yelling.

"God bless you!"

"We love you!"

"Hold it high!"

"Go for it!"

"Good luck!"

Everybody waved or gave us thumbs-up. It was just amazing: Again and again clusters of people started singing "The Star Spangled Banner" or "America the Beautiful." They hadn't rehearsed, obviously. Singing their feelings was just what occurred to them to do as the flame passed.

Were we making all this happen? No. We set things up the best we could, we spread the word about times and places. We let it be known that people had invested their time, their passion, and their money in a chance to hold the flame high and run with it for a kilometer. But we could not possibly have arranged the crescendo of emotion and energy these crowds were producing. They saw the Olympic flame, a supposedly neutral symbol for faster, higher, stronger human achievement in general, and they were appropriating it. They were making it their own.

The patriotism wasn't all upbeat. Here and there a young guy, or a little gang of them, would yell, "Fuck the Russians!" A couple of hand-lettered signs said RUSSIA SUCKS and USA YES, USSR NYET. Nationalism has a way of reducing people to good guys and bad guys. But there was little time and little reason to be bothered by a sour note on one of the most exciting days in our lives.

Just outside Oakland, New Jersey, Mark came on the radio: "Five or six feet . . . eep . . . fire trucks agrahrusee. . . ."

"Say again?" I yelled. "Can't hear you!" There was so much noise behind him, crowd roar and what sounded like fog horns or truck klaxons, that the transmission made no sense. A couple more tries and we pieced together the message.

"Crowd here is five or six deep. Fire trucks as far as you can see. Everything's where it ought to be; we're not going to be stuck behind the Fireman's Parade."

That parade, a hundred fire trucks strong, could have been a major bottleneck if the torch got stuck behind it, but the mayor was keeping his word to hold it back until the runner had passed. I stood up in the convertible. Ahead, people crowded along the road as far as I could see. Fifty fire trucks on one side of the street entering Oakland, and fifty on the other side, were clanging their bells and blowing their horns. The fire engines on one side had joined their ladders with ladders from the other side, forming arches over us. The bells and horns and the cheering made talking impossible. Mark's eyes met mine in the middle of the glorious bedlam, and we both had smiles from ear to ear.

Around three o'clock, munching a sandwich, I spotted the next runner waiting up ahead. She was an older woman who looked unusually nervous. I put away my lunch, jumped out of the car and ran up to her.

"Hi," I said. "Are you Joyce's mother?"

"Yes," she said. "You must be the rascal who got me into this." Her tone gave no clue to whether she was kidding or not.

We ran and walked together. The moment we took off, her anxiety melted. Here was a grandmother of twelve, holding the torch over a neatly arranged gray hairdo, hearing people cheer even louder than ever when they saw her coming. After she touched her flame to the torch of the next runner, I asked, "That wasn't so bad, was it?" She just turned and hugged me.

As we approached Morris Plains, the crowds let up a bit, and with a chance to take a breath and look around, I got my first strong hit of how beautiful this strip of New Jersey was. I thought back on driving this part of the route in January at night in the snow, on the tedious hours of work, on forgetting for days at a time to appreciate that the work was allowing me to see the expanse of this unique country. This was an America I hadn't known about.

More well-wishers broke into the thought. I looked at the families on the edge of the pavement: proud parents hoisting up babies, people taking pictures and then running along or ahead to get one more shot. Old and young with broad smiles, some waving three-by-five-foot American flags like banners, many holding up little palm-size flags. Schoolchildren stood by signs they had made: MORRIS PLAINS ELEMENTARY SCHOOL LOVES THE TORCH in big crayon printing, and all the students' signatures.

A lot of folks would run alongside for a mile or two. Runners and bike riders kept peeling in from the sides to make themselves an unofficial part of our caravan. A young man with a Yale T-shirt and a big American flag finally pooped out in Morris Plains after running fifteen miles. Two men around thirty, wearing shirts printed "Here comes the torch," preceded us by a couple of hundred yards through Morristown.

The weather kept changing from sun to rain showers, to clouds, back to sunshine. On the approach to Far Hills, the sky ahead was black, but the manicured green estates on either side of us glowed in sunshine. This was AT&T country. Just ahead was Bedminster, home of the corporation's national headquarters. Friends, family and co-workers cheered some of the local AT&T runners along. Bedminster welcomed the runner with fireworks. A fifty-foot banner strung across Route 202 said, simply, GODSPEED.

Someone tossed a bouquet of flowers to Kate Washburn, an AT&T worker from nearby Peapack on temporary assignment as one of the managers of the cadre runners. I had mixed feelings about AT&T, but not about people like Kate; she was gracious, reliable, courageous, a fine runner, and almost always radiant. Especially now. This was a well-deserved tribute from the people of Far Hills and Bedminster to their own.

Just outside Bedminster, we hit a quiet couple of miles, the first time all day with just a person here and there along the road. Little

clusters of two and three in rolled-up sleeves and pastel cotton
dresses stood together, some holding the hands of their youngsters.
Some were alone. The groups liked to clap when the runner came
into sight. Single people clapped, too, though some stood in silence, drawing themselves a bit more erect as the flame passed by.
A few called softly, "Hi." One said, "I'm proud of you. Keep it up."
Even when all we heard in the lead car was the purr of the engine,
the slap of the runner's shoes, and an occasional voice, we were
still soaring on adrenalin. What a day.

A pile of purple clouds ahead rumbled as if they might have
lightning in them—the only weather that ever stopped the torch
run. We would run through cloudbursts, heat, wind, anything, but
we wouldn't leave that natural lightning rod in anybody's hand if
there was a chance of its being struck.

Rounding a bend, we saw a guy about seventeen or eighteen
standing on the hood of an old Buick parked to our right. He wore a
black T-shirt with a Van Halen album cover printed on it, and
wrinkled, frayed old jeans. He had one of those beards you sometimes see on kids in their teens who want to look rough but can't
quite get the hairs to work, all tufty and scraggly, and his hair was
long and dark and parted in the middle. A real heavy-metal type.
He also had one hand behind his back. The Security men's heads
all snapped to the right. In the first week, Security was not as sure
of itself as it soon got to be. Then he pulled something out from
behind his back, and it was a trumpet. In the first silence we'd
heard in hours, the kid raised the trumpet to his lips and started
his song: "Oh, say can you see . . ." We looked at each other with
our eyes full of tears as he wailed out our anthem.

We caught up to the clouds, and the sky spat a lightning bolt.
Immediately we pulled off as a cloud burst on our parade. Three-
quarters of an hour later the spring squall passed, the runner
emerged from the EMS, and we were on our way again.

Night fell. The people came out, and came out, and came out,
waving and cheering. Mark joined us in the lead car, so pumped up
by the emotions of the day—as I was—that they got to be too
much for him. Without a word, he hopped out of the back seat of
the Buick and started running along beside it, still in his blue
blazer, tie and buttondown, gray slacks, and penny loafers. He

looked like a Secret Service man, running with one hand on the car for half a mile, a mile, two miles. . . . "Mark," I finally yelled, "What the hell are you doing?"

"I don't know," he yelled back. "I can't . . . There's no way . . . I can't *not* do this!" A couple of runners later, he climbed back into the car, drenched with sweat, and beamed, "Ahh, I needed that."

Toward midnight, we found Princeton quiet, with a couple of people here and there applauding as the runner passed by. The caravan came upon a fraternity house on the right with lights blazing from every window. The members lounging on the front lawn, and their memberettes in gowns and bare-shouldered dresses, saluted the torch with monogrammed tumblers. In unison, as if they had rehearsed for the moment, they called out, "Drop trou!"

It sounded so silly that we all laughed, Mark the loudest of all. What did that mean? I asked him. The eternal frat boy said, "You mean you don't know? I mean, old man, everyone who's anyone knows. It means drop trousers."

The adrenalin must have burned away hours before, and we were punchy. Mark and I lapsed into giggles, like a couple of little boys making faces in church. We drew some stone stares from the exhausted Pioneer at the wheel.

What with the lightning and a few other delays, we were about an hour and a half behind schedule. Close to one in the morning, the countryside between Princeton and Lawrenceville should have been asleep. We were awake but barely conscious after sixteen hours of raw emotion, propped against each other in the back seat of the convertible. The torch bearer had a lot of quiet company now. The team of AT&T cadre runners had been on duty for a full week, so they would be replaced in the morning by a fresh team. All of them were running the last mile, tired but glowing with pride.

Near Lawrenceville we did notice a group of young people, then another larger gathering, and another. College students, judging by the plastic beer cups they held. Ahead, the sky took on a glow. A couple of blocks from the Rider College campus we started hearing noises, the rise and fall of voices, laughs and shouts, loud music, like a huge party. A right turn into the campus, and there was the support caravan, drawn up in its overnight array. All around it was a churning sea of people.

Hundreds and hundreds, maybe two thousand students, attracted hours before by our circus wagons coming to town and jazzed by the approach of the torch, were milling and swaying and leaping around in front of several bonfires they had built in the field behind the caravan, streaming to and from kegs of beer, and now heading, all of them, toward us.

The crowd was so thick, and the noise so deafening, that the core caravan stopped short. We realized there was a chant emerging from the general uproar, something with a four-beat rhythm that we hadn't heard before:

"Los Angeles! Los Angeles! Los Angeles!" A few dozen repetitions, then a general din while a new chant gathered force, then the new three-beat rhythm took over: "U-S-A! U-S-A! U . . . S . . . A!"

The pandemonium brought us wide awake. The crowd surged over the cadre runners and surrounded the car, chanting almost frantically and rocking the Buick playfully. Hands kept darting out of the mass to offer us cups of beer. Other hands came from all sides, clawing for Dick Hamilton's sacred hat, a piece of sweatshirt, anything they could reach. Friendly as they were, the intensity of the faces and the huge surge of the crowd, one immense creature, were overpowering and a little frightening.

Dick Boehner, one of the cadre team managers, had the torch. The cadre's last act of each day was to douse the flame—not the mother Olympic flame, which lived on in the miner's lamps inside Torch 10 and the back of the lead car, but the last torch carried that day. Boehner took the little snuffer (it could have been a little orange-juice can for all anyone knew) and started lowering it over the flame.

"No!" somebody yelled, and the crowd made it into a chant. "No! No! No!"

They didn't want to see the flame die. Playfully, as if heeding their plea, Boehner pulled the snuffer away.

"Yay! Yeah!" the crowd cheered.

He egged them on, threatening the flame again.

"No! No! . . . Yes! Yay! . . . No! . . ." The pitch rose with each swing back and forth, and Boehner looked as if he realized he was creating a monster he'd better quiet, no matter how cheerful it was, before it ate us all. To a long, good-natured groan—"Ooohh nooooo"—that had Mark's voice in it and mine, he extinguished the torch.

23

Fly on the Wall

Mark's heart went out to the industrial Midwestern cities where people must wish they had never heard the words, Rust Belt. "You see a factory roof covered with snow," he'd said in the winter during one of the phone calls that kept us in touch, "and for a minute, you don't realize what that means: The furnaces are cold. Where are the people who used to work there?"

He was so passionate about Cleveland that we nicknamed him "the little mayor." His reasons for asking Wally to assign him there were pure Zangrando: He loved the great Little Italy section, but even more, he loved the city for being an underdog—butt of jokes about the Cuyahoga River catching fire—and a fighter. When Cleveland almost went bankrupt in the 1970s, its people didn't get discouraged. They did a twelve-week study, came up with six hundred and fifty ways to save money and improve services, acted on more than ninety percent of them, and pulled the city out of default. The first two places that sold all their torch kilometers were, predictably, Los Angeles and New York. The third was Cleveland.

"You ought to see it, Steve, you gotta see it," he said. "Six, seven different cities in one! This is a melting pot that hasn't melted. These people are still themselves!" He wanted every one of the neighborhoods to have a piece of the torch celebration. "Irish on the West Side. Slavs and Poles on Fleet Street. Hungarians on Euclid. Jews in University Heights. Serbians on Solon. Italians in Mayfield Heights. People live their lives in their section, some of them never leave it. And it's still America. I hope we never smooth out all those differences. They're what make us rich, you know?"

So here we were at dinner in a warm restaurant fragrant with marinara sauce and herbs in the bosom of Little Italy. Our guest,

Dale Baich, was a major contact in that part of town, though an unlikely-looking one. Dale was as un-Italian as you could get—a fair-skinned Anglo-type lawyer in a three-piece suit, cool and precise and composed. He represented Mayor George Voinovich in Little Italy restoration projects, without showing a trace of Italian blood. At the moment, he looked as much out of his element as I did, with his knees under a red checkered tablecloth in a restaurant full of Italians forking up linguini and raising glasses of Chianti to each other all around. Mark had met us there from one of his fifty ethnic meetings, and Dale sat quietly, a bit cautious about us.

"Mark!" the exuberant little woman waiting on us cried when she spotted him. "Come, eat something! Mark is a good boy!"

Dale looked bemused. They knew him here, too, but all of a sudden they were giving this outsider all the affection. "See, Mark, your sign," the waitress said, "in my window." She pointed to one of the COME SEE THE OLYMPIC TORCH notices Mark had distributed. Beaming, in his thickest accent, he replied, "Grazie, Mama, mille grazie."

ALONG LAKE ERIE, MAY 20

Rain again. If some higher power were arranging these days as a test of people's spirit, the people were winning. This Sunday, from Bay Village westward along the Lake Erie shore, they stood out in the wet, refusing to let a mere monsoon make them leave their places along the road. There they were, water streaming down them, waving hello to the torch. We weren't so brave. We put up the top of the lead car.

At Vermilion, where it looked as if every one of the eleven thousand residents was out by the road, a sweet-faced, gray-haired woman ran up to the car with a rounded bundle. She offered it in the window, and when I pulled off the paper we had a chocolate cake.

"For the runners," the grandma called, "for the runners and you." For once, we disobeyed Bill Mattman's orders not to eat anything handed to us from a crowd; there just couldn't have been any razor blades or rat poison in that woman's cake.

Jeff jumped into the lead car just before noon, outside Sandusky.

I drove ahead in our rented Volvo. The land along Lake Erie had once been under the lake, as its flatness and occasional swampiness indicate. Angling northwest along the shore toward Toledo and Michigan, it showed less and less habitation. A few farms interrupted the emptiness through Ottawa County. The only other thing out there in the open was a nuclear power plant, just the sort of place Mattman had urged us to avoid in plotting the route: "You never know what those nuclear crazies, those Fonda-Hayden types, will do."

My meal for the day so far had been a hunk of chocolate cake. The Lakers were in a playoff game with Denver. So when the diner showed up near the Toledo city-limit sign, *and* had a TV antenna on top, I pulled in. Crunching across the gravel parking lot, I counted five other cars there—Chevies, Dodges, a Buick. A bumper sticker on one read BUY AMERICAN. Here I was, fifty miles from Detroit, in a foreign car. Good planning.

Inside, the counter ran off to the right, several tables to the left, and catty-cornered on a shelf at the end of the counter a color television set showed a Detroit Tigers game that nobody seemed to be watching. Seven or eight heads turned as if I had walked into their living room, not resenting my arrival, just curious to see someone they didn't already know. One man leaning against the counter was asking the room, "What time's that torch thing supposed to come by, anyhow?" Five-thirty, I knew. A few voices answered, "Five, it says here." They were right. That is what it said. We usually announced a time half an hour early so that latecomers wouldn't miss the event.

A stranger can't just ask a crowd of old friends to change channels for him. First I asked the counterman—a giant about six feet eight, one of the few people I've had to look up at—for a cheeseburger and root beer. Once I was a paying customer with some rights, I asked if anyone would mind if we watched the Lakers-Nuggets playoff game.

"After the Tigers game, sure," he said in a deep voice. He handed over the root beer and threw a burger on the grill. I took the drink to a table near the door. The guy at the next table might have been in his middle forties, or maybe his world-weary look added a few years. He was fiddling with a long-neck Bud, turning the bottle in its own puddle and looking up idly every now and then. The woman with him smiled and said, "Hi." Her windbreaker said

"Mud Hens" across the back, and so did the man's, which probably made him her husband. She was getting ready to use an El Marko pen to write something on a piece of sign board on the table.

"Come on, guys," she called to the room, "give me a hand here. Should I write 'Bill's Diner Loves The Torch'? Or 'Toledo Loves The Torch'?"

Nobody answered immediately, but they were thinking about it. I began to deduce that their being here together was no accident; they were actually having a pre–torch run party. The cook flipped the burger and rumbled over his shoulder, "Yeah, Jeannie, 'Bill's Diner Loves The Torch' sounds great." She smiled and started lettering. Her question had primed a flow of conversation around the room:

"How do you think they keep that thing from going out on days like this?"

"Who gets to run it?"

"It's right there in the paper."

"I wonder if it's going through South Dakota so my brother can see it."

I could have answered them all. But then I'd have had to give up being a fly on the wall.

Jeannie finished her sign and held it up to her table mate. "What do you think, honey?" He grumbled something that sounded like, "Whatever you want, who cares?"

She dropped the board on edge and looked down at him. "Paul," she said in a new voice tightened by who knows how many years of put-offs, "don't you give a shit about *anything*?" A wave of uneasiness flashed through the room, or at least through me.

Just then a new couple pushed open the door. They eased out of raincoats so as not to drip on the counter, and the woman said to the room at large, "Hey, guys, wait till you see it! It just surprised the hell out of us. Looked like everyone in Sandusky came out, and it was raining just like here, and you've never seen so many flags in your life. We got ahead and watched it a couple extra times—no, three—it's so exciting. You see those runners holding that thing up and something happens to you."

That picked up the spirits, except for Paul's, who was damned if he was going to change his mind at this point. He kept his eyes on the ball game.

"How far off is it?"

"When do you think it'll get here?"

"Jeannie, show 'em your sign." Jeannie held it up, shy and proud.

"Really nice, Jeannie, way to go."

Paul broke his silence. "Come on. It's the same old bullshit. They wave the flag and hope we'll forget half of us are on unemployment. It's politics. Who you kidding?"

Jeannie said, "Well, you couldn't do this in Russia. Why don't you just go over there and give it a try?"

24

Teammates

The sky cleared over Toledo, and probably Bill's Diner, in time for a sunset spectacular. It seems that every city in the United States has a redevelopment program, and I wouldn't be surprised to hear that the best of them are modeled on Toledo's. This city—and I do mean the whole city of 354,000—was celebrating a beautiful renovation of a former slum along Lake Erie, and embraced the torch along with it.

Under a glow from the western sky, tens of thousands of people on both sides of the street crammed the sidewalks, waving their flags and pumping their signs up and down, holding babies overhead, breaking out of the crush to run up and get a second look at the torch.

In one sense, these scenes were already familiar. In another sense, each one set a kind of hook deeper into us. The way people stood out there for hours on city sidewalks and country roads, the emotions they let out when the runner flashed by—that was more than just excitement. What was it? I didn't know. One thing I did know already, though. When we had thought we could stage a response to the torch, we just didn't know any better. The response had a life of its own.

Of course, you'd never have known it from the national press. The people were there by the roadsides, but where were the reporters? The people got it. How come the networks didn't? And the *Times*? And *Newsweek*?

Toward dark we headed into quiet countryside. Like last Saturday in New Jersey, we felt the adrenalin drain out. A new Pioneer jumped into the lead car at the Michigan line, all fresh and thrilled that his moment had finally come, full of anecdotes and local history:

"George Armstrong Custer lived near here before his army days. This is just like *Blue Highways*, you've read *Blue Highways?*"

One or another of us kept up what conversation we could. Eventually, the dark swallowed everything beyond the headlights and the quiet got to the Pioneer, too. For long stretches, all we heard over the chirp of crickets in the fields was the runner's footfalls and an occasional slap as someone tried for a mosquito.

The Security man at the wheel still had plenty of pep. Rich Green, a chunky guy with a full head of gray hair, had retired from the Secret Service to sell real estate in Memphis. "Detroit tomorrow," he said to break one silence. "Last time I was there with the Secret Service, we were on a detail with Muskie, and we took him to Tiger Stadium. Nineteen sixty-eight—what a great Tiger team."

That woke me up. That was the year my mom took us to live at Fort Leonard Wood, Missouri, for as long as her opportunity lasted; I had watched the life on the army base with a crew cut and a G.I. Joe doll in one hand, and a vague sense that the soldiers pouring through there had a bad feeling about going to Vietnam. It was also the year I started following baseball. "Ah, yeah," I said, "when I was eight, I wanted to be Mickey Stanley."

"They had Al Kaline in right," Rich said.

"And Norm Cash at first."

"And Gates Brown in left," he picked up.

"He always wore that batting helmet in the outfield," I added. We were in a game of Dueling Tigers now, reconstructing the lineup that beat the Cardinals in the World Series, four games to three. A moment of silence—crickets, runner's feet slapping pavement, soft purr of engines at eight miles an hour.

"Awk." Rich's walky-talky crackled. He had it on, as the Security men always did. "Bill Freehan at catcher."

"Awk"—a different voice on the radio, from somewhere behind us in the caravan—"don't forget Lolich and McLain."

"Awk"—a third voice from somewhere else—"yeah, thirty-one games worth of McLain."

We got the whole lineup set, except for third base. Rich couldn't remember. Neither could I. Neither could any of our invisible teammates in the walky-talky network.

Shoulder to shoulder in the car, ear to ear over the radio, we laid our heads back in the warm night and savored the trivial things we all shared. It was hard to imagine ourselves clustering in hostile factions at the countdown meeting in Los Angeles. Without anyone coming out and saying so, the sights and rhythms of the run were melting some of the divisions between us.

25

Hero Worship, Lesson Three

Whether we invent the best parts of ourselves, or borrow them from the lives of others, we often hope to resemble our heroes. I do, anyway. But look closely, and you notice something surprising about heroism (the real thing, not the myth)—its fragility. The people who use it to do the most good are the ones who treat it with the most care.

It was a shock, and a gift, to come face to face with one of my heroes and discover there is more to him—and his heroism—than I ever imagined.

Monday. Suzanne Lipps was at the Galt House, where she had set up our three-room command center for a torch approach. Jim Long came over for a drink and a review of the logistics for the coming week and our long-awaited day with Muhammad Ali. Seeing Jim was like rejoining an old friend, with the extra pleasure of noticing that he was really pumped up about the torch. Jim was going to help all week in every way he could.

Jeffrey Hutter had delivered on his promise to work out the Ali arrangements with Mayor Harvey Sloan. The mayor had asked the city council to sponsor Ali's kilometer, and within an hour they had appropriated the three thousand dollars. Hutter and Sloan were the ones who had contacted Ali, got his approval, and arranged his flight from Los Angeles.

Here's our part of the plan, we reminded Jim: The torch leaves the Indy 500 parade next Saturday. On Sunday, May 27, it reaches the Second Street Bridge at twelve-thirty in the afternoon. As the runner crosses to the Louisville end, the paddlewheel steamer *Belle of Louisville* on the river below will play "My Old Kentucky

Home" on its giant calliope, and a huge cloud of balloons—red ones, white ones, blue ones—will go up. Suzanne will be in the lead car for this leg. I will be at the Kentucky Center for the Arts. We can pick each other up by walkie-talkie when Suzanne is on or near the bridge. Landmark checks by radio allow us to cue the band and time announcements to the minute. It is much like political campaigning. If anything goes wrong with the radios, the calliope is my fail-safe signal that the torch is six minutes away. At the arts center, Muhammad Ali is at the top of the steps with the reflecting glass behind him. We've roped off a section in the shape of an inverted V so the spectators push up outside the legs of the V. As the runner handing off to Ali climbs the steps to meet him, the cameras pick up the crowd in layers converging on both runners and the sky reflected in the glass behind them. The band from the Performing Arts School is playing, and we release another batch of balloons. At exactly one o'clock, Ali gets the torch and runs a triumphant kilometer through Louisville.

That was the picture we wanted to paint. Now we had two major concerns: The crowd and the Marines.

Everyone in Louisville kept assuring me that since Ali was coming, we would have all the crowd we could possibly want. But crowds really do not just happen. To get people to leave their houses and show up where you want them, you have to give them a reason to be interested. No matter how big a hero is, you can't just say "Muhammad Ali" and go to lunch. You don't wait for crowds. You build them.

The technique of building a crowd includes getting your event hyped in the press and using paper—leaflets. First people read an article about it; but they read a lot of articles. Then they might see it on television. That second hit starts to raise a bit of interest. Then they go to the shopping center on Wednesday night and somebody hands them a leaflet:

1984 OLYMPICS—TORCH RELAY HERE

Sunday May 27th
Kentucky Center for the Arts, Fifth and Main Street
Noon
Come be a part of an official Olympic event. And play a part in his-

tory. Cheer the runners on their way across America from New York
to Los Angeles for opening ceremonies of the XXIIIrd Olympiad.
Special torch bearer Muhammad Ali

We'd give latecomers an hour of slack this time instead of half an
hour, considering the size of the event.

Now they're getting interested. Maybe they go to the movies on
Friday night, and there's another leaflet. You're starting to build
not only a crowd, but some enthusiasm. They talk to Uncle
George, and he says, "Did you get that leaflet for . . ." and they
say, "Yeah, they're all over the place. We ought to check it out."

It works almost every time. For every one hundred sheets of paper you pass out, you're guaranteed between five and ten people in
the crowd. I had paced off the grounds at the arts center and figured
it would take two thousand people, yelling and waving and clapping, to make the event look good on television. So:

"Jim, can you find somebody to print up thirty thousand leaflets
by Wednesday?"

"Sure, no problem."

"And get it donated?"

"Done." Jim didn't even blink. (As it turned out, this time
AT&T paid the bill, but Jim was ready.)

MAY 22

Tuesday. My second meeting of the morning was with Sgt. Jack
Olinick of the Marines. I had called Wally to review the situation:
People magazine had published a big picture of the Marines and a
story saying they were going to be "a fleet-footed honor guard. . . ."
They were constantly in the papers in Kentucky. Saying no to their
running plans would cause a big stink; on the other hand, we
didn't want to say yes and cause problems for some other advance
person down the road.

Jack took time off from work to come by the Galt House. Again
it was like a meeting of old friends, and since we both knew what
we wanted we could get to the point fast.

"We all want you guys to run with Chris Buehner," I said. Chris
was the sixteen-year-old member of a local Boys' and Girls' Club
whom the Marines were sponsoring. He was scheduled to run in

Cherokee Park, four hundred and nine acres of golf links, play-grounds, and handsome greenery in East Louisville. *"And* I can't give you formal authorization. But . . . if you're in the park, and if you happen to run in his vicinity, and if you don't get in the way of the Security people, nobody is likely to do anything about it."

We were practically winking at each other. Jack Olinick had be-gun to think his platoon was going to get some sort of order not to run, even though they had thrown themselves gung-ho into the project for the boys' club. Now, as he said, "I understand," he was beaming.

"Remember, if anybody asks, 'Did you get authorization to run?' the answer is 'No, we just happened to be here.'"

"Fine." Both of us really did wink. We laughed like school pranksters.

Why not? These guys had done something noble. Why shouldn't they get some pleasure from it? Besides, spontaneity is great. By definition you can't plan it, but in a way we just had, and what a sight it would be, the Marines chugging up a hill with their torch bearer.

Wednesday. By early afternoon I was looking forward to getting out on the street and handing out some paper. Jim Long had put us in touch with the Key Club at Western High School. Around three, as promised, half a dozen nice-looking athlete types came to the door in open-neck, button-down shirts and chino trousers, quite a bit more preppie-looking than we were in my Key Club days at Cupertino High. Beyond saying hello, they offered a minimum of conversation. But they started loosening up and even had a few laughs as we got into my talk about the joys of leafleting and the mechanics of doing it right:

"Don't worry about feeling nervous, standing out there on the sidewalk offering pieces of paper to strangers. We all feel like that at first, until we see that nobody cares. You'll each have your own box of these things. Spring on someone going by, smile, say, 'Hi, how are *you*? Come see Muhammad Ali on Sunday,' and shove it in their hand. Always say something or they'll think you've handed them a pizza menu or something and might not even look at the leaflet. Have fun with it. And you might. You have the per-mission of the Los Angeles Olympic Organizing Committee to use these leaflets to pick up girls. If you see a good-looking prospect walk by, you can effect a meeting. . . ."

Something was wrong. They weren't laughing. A couple of them looked as if a flying saucer had landed behind me. I looked around and saw the problem: Suzanne. Rather, Suzanne's outfit. She had strolled in from her room wearing what she would have worn on a warm day at the beach—tight shorts, a small T-shirt, and a cheery smile. In L.A., standard attire. In Louisville, in a hotel room with six ripening male high-school juniors, a major distraction.

"Glad you could come. How's it going?" Suzanne said, and they turned to her as if she had brought them each a free Walkman. Figuring I'd never get their attention again anyway, I herded the whole crew out the door and we hit the street.

Were we really going to get the crowd we wanted on Sunday? Everyone except me kept saying "No problem," but I was nervous about it. Ali's run was going to happen on a Sunday afternoon, in the middle of the Memorial Day weekend, and what if people had already made plans to be gone then?

We also had a little conflict. The local organizers wanted to publicize the route, and I didn't. In advance work, you don't want to compete with your own event. If the *Courier Journal* and the *Times* publish a map of the route and Mr. and Mrs. Louisville notice that Muhammad Ali will run right by their house, why would they drive downtown to see him? Fifty thousand people could see the torch in Louisville that day, yet if the cameras show a spotty crowd of one thousand at the arts center, then as far as the rest of the country is concerned, Muhammad Ali drew a spotty crowd of one thousand. You can put on a great event, but if the cameras don't see it, it's put down as a non-event.

I kept explaining my holdout on the route with the worst excuse an advance person can give. The Security people hated it, the newspapers hated it, AT&T hated it, and I kept saying it: "Security reasons." Not true. But I was playing poker. I wanted to hold the cards as long as possible, to make people think the only way they could be sure of seeing Muhammad Ali would be to go down to the arts center.

MAY 24

Thursday morning. AT&T had a press conference in front of the arts center for Louisville's sponsored runners, except Ali. He would arrive from L.A. on Sunday morning. Afterwards the principals gathered inside to go over the final countdown—Jeffrey Hutter from the mayor's office, the police chief and the chairman of the Louisville Crime Commission (security contacts), Jim Hurt from the regional AT&T office, president Khristy van Howe of the arts center, Jim Long and other several other powers behind the scenes, and me.

A visiting organizer's agenda doesn't always make sense to the people he's visiting. I wanted an event to look good on television. They wanted the spectators to be comfortable. They might ask Muhammad Ali to come, but they didn't want to rope off their neighbors and squeeze them into a weird-looking triangle. They had misgivings about Sunday's arrangements.

Jim Hurt, the AT&T man, wanted to change the setup. The crowd was going to be too big for my layered arrangement up the stairs; people would not be able to see; would surge forward into my open space; would jump the ropes.

I kept trying to explain that there won't be that many people; if we have enough security and the place is well roped off, they will not jump over. No sale. The thunderclouds of an argument were building up. That was a dismaying prospect. These people had all worked so hard on the event, they were no longer just contacts. They were friends. I didn't want to fight anybody, and I didn't want to be the cause of any fights among people who would go on living next to each other long after I left. As voices started rising and fingers started pointing every which way, I thought, "There must be an easier way to see America than this. Why didn't I just buy a used car and drive it across the country?"

"Of course," Hurt was saying, genially and softly, as I came back to the conversation, "it might be hard to understand if you aren't from here, but Muhammad Ali is a very big attraction in Louisville."

I just hated being patronized that way. But I made myself smile and say quietly: "Jim, I want to ask you to trust me on this. I've seen it work before." I could tell that nobody in the room was quite buying it. Except for Jim Long, who looked discreetly amused.

Finally, Hurt looked around and suggested, "Why don't we vote on it?"

Long gave a little laugh and said, "Well, now, I don't know that this is a democracy."

I said, "Jim's right about that. We're all trying to work together, but if it comes down to it, on torch relay arrangements the buck has to stop somewhere. It stops with me."

Everybody sat back a little and took pains not to look at each other. I imagined they were thinking, okay, if the Olympics want to trust this kid from California with the event, let them. All I knew with any certainty as we left the meeting was that this was the first time in my life I had ever told a whole city that we were going to do something my way or we weren't going to do it at all.

In politics, the glove is on the other hand. Advance workers for a candidate need the local power brokers; they don't need you. They don't care if your candidate is shown. They can tell you to forget it. But the Olympic torch! The feelings around it were no longer vague, as on our first time through. The torch had touched people's pride. Now they understood it. They wanted a piece of it.

MAY 26

Saturday. Ruth Berry, one of the two trip directors with the caravan, called at one in the morning to say they had just stopped for the night outside Indianapolis. They had been delayed by lightning storms.

Ruth had a favor to ask. Her sister, Jody Meredith, and Jody's four children lived in Elizabethtown, south of Louisville, and were coming up to see Muhammad Ali. "Can you try to get them up to the front? I've told them what you look like. They'll spot you."

MAY 27

Sunday. Suzanne had the first assignment of the day. She got up at five to meet the torch caravan at Uniontown, forty miles north of us on Route 31 in Indiana, and bring it into Louisville. I would work ahead of it until it left the city, replacing her in the lead car for the run to the governor's mansion and Keeneland.

The arts center is on Main Street, a block from the Galt House at Fourth and River. Walking over to make sure everything was placed right, I knew I would have to keep moving to work off the tension. There was one detail over which I had no control: Ali's arrival. On the phone, Jeffrey Hutter said, "We've got a limo waiting for Ali right now. Everything's fine."

Up in Indiana, the torch runners had started. By eleven o'clock I was running back and forth, clutching my walkie-talkie, making sure the band was all there, saying hello to the disk jockey who was emceeing the event and broadcasting it live to his station. Now the weather looked ominous. All week it had been sunny; this morning it was heavily overcast, and the forecast was for rain. Just a few spectators had come by. Jim Long and I tried to laugh off the sparse turnout. Three-quarters of a hour later the number of people standing around had crept to about a thousand or twelve hundred at most. What if we gave this party and nobody came?

Noon. A limousine pulled up in front of the steps. I took a couple of steps toward it. Nothing happened; the car just parked there. One more step; then a door opened and there was Muhammad Ali. He had come early to work the crowd. That was really nice. He wore a light gray sport jacket over the torch uniform we had sent him: White nylon running shorts with the Olympic rings on the left side, tank-top running shirt with the runner-in-motion emblem rainbowing between a line of words above, "1984 Olympic Torch Relay," and one below, "Participant." This was the moment.

He looked fine to me. Not fat. In good shape. He did seem a little remote—not dazed, yet not as keen in the eye as the old Ali—sort of stoic. Still, I was pleased.

The crowd was swelling and warming up. White people, black people, they leaned over the ropes and reached out to him, calling out things like, "Ali! Welcome back, Champ! Lookin' good! Ali!" They weren't yelling the way you hear photographers shout when they want to get some prime minister's attention at an airport; they were calling to him with affection. They really love him.

He started going up and down the ropes, shaking hands. With him the whole time were the Sloans, Harvey and Kathy, thirteen-year-old Abigail, eight-year-old Patrick, and seven-year-old Curtis. After all the buildup, I suddenly felt a little reluctant to go up and introduce myself to Ali, but that wasn't going to make me miss the chance. Besides, it was my job. I walked over and touched his arm.

"Hi, Champ. My name is Steve Barr, I'm from the Olympic Committee, and . . . uh . . . I'll be with you until you get the torch. You look great. Here's what's going to happen. . . ." At every exchange point there is a Pioneer who turns on the fuel supply of your torch when the caravan gets within earshot. You light the torch yourself, from the previous runner's torch. At that point you can hold it up or do whatever you want. There will be a runner with you to escort you. You'll rejoin the caravan at curbside, and you'll be off. Just run behind the press truck.

"Sure," Ali said. "No problem. I can handle it."

"How you feeling?"

He smiled. "Old."

He went back to touching the hands that were reaching for him. People swarmed around him so eagerly that it was becoming hard to hold them back.

Jody Meredith and her children waved from the crowd across the street and I went over to say hello. The littlest boy, Mark, was about four; he was so shy that he wouldn't even look up. So that we could all be included in the conversation, I squatted down beside him, and I think he took a liking to me.

"Would you like to meet Muhammad Ali?" I asked. He nodded twice. Taking all four children up might have started some muttering about "Why are those people special?" Alone, Mark was no threat to anyone. He let me put him on my shoulders, and we went up to Ali. Silently, Mark held his arms out straight in front as the big man in the running uniform reached up and took him from me. I could barely hear, but I think Muhammad Ali whispered, "Hi." They smiled at each other. Ali gave him a big kiss and held him with such affection that Mark relaxed against his shoulder, looking completely at ease in the center of attention.

It is so easy on the road to lose perspective—to forget about kids and dogs and the way it feels to be in a house. Once in a while I would see one or the other and think, "When was the last time I held a child, or petted a dog?" As Ali put Mark back on my shoulders for the ride back to the other side of the street, I hoped he heard how deeply I meant the thanks I said to him.

A chant was starting to build from the crowd: "A-li, A-li, A-li." A ton of press people had come. The master of ceremonies introduced Muhammad Ali.

Every word the Champ said drew a cheer. "Hello." Cheer. "Good to see you." Cheer. The people were having a love affair with the man.

The Postal Service had produced a special-edition postcard, complete with thirteen-cent stamp, for each big city along the torch route. A representative of the Postal Workers in Louisville handed Ali the local postcard. Ali looked at it, feigning incredulity. Then he looked past the microphone with just a trace of a grin.

"You mean," he said, "I came all the way out from Los Angeles, California . . . for thirteen cents?" His timing was perfect. It provoked the biggest, most delighted laugh of the day.

"Awk." The crackle of the walky-talky broke in. "Barr, Lipps." That was Suzanne within transmitting range. The caravan was less than two miles away. Our radio language had developed a peculiar CB style quite unlike normal speech. There was great potential for a ridiculous amount of confusion in putting a bunch of novices on the airwaves along with the cops and Security people and God knows who else, so we used as much formality as we could stand to keep some order. The "Ten-four, I've got a Code Seven" vocabulary didn't fly far with torch rats, but we did stick with this way of breaking through on Channel Two, the frequency for transmissions about caravan movements—the name you're calling first, then your own.

"Barr, Lipps." Through the crackling, "The flame is almost at center span. How's the crowd?"

"Lipps, Barr. It's great. Here, listen to this." I held up the handset so she could hear the chant that had started again after the laughter: "A-li, A-li, A-li."

"Barr, Lipps. Boy, I can't wait till we get there. Flame is at the city limits. We're right on time." The first toots of the calliope started through her transmitter, and a few seconds later the same notes echoed up Main Street from the river.

Every few minutes one or the other of us felt a sprinkle. "Lipps, Barr. Do you have rain? Hope it holds off a few minutes longer."

Six minutes to go. Feeling the strength of a packed crowd that looked like a slice right out of the middle of America—black people pressed up against whites, little children held high by grownups, old ladies, old men on canes, men in work shirts or short-sleeved shirts and some, unbelievably, in jackets and ties, women in dresses and in pants, every one of them looking as if this was exactly where he or she wanted to be right then—it would be an understatement to say I felt satisfied. We had come a long way together since the day I first crossed the bridge.

From Second Street we could hear the rumble of motorcycles and short whoops from police sirens. As the torch bearer turned the last corner onto Main and came into view, the noise from our crowd swelled so that it drowned out everything else. All you could hear was cheering.

The runner approaching with the torch was Bryce Kurfees, who is white, and beside him was Stan Harris, one of the few black cadre runners. I trotted out to fall in beside them, and pointed to Muhammad Ali at the top of the steps.

Ali's torch ignited on the first try. He raised it to the full length of his right arm, high over his head. He stood straight up, at attention. There was no irony in his posture now, nothing held back. When he'd lost the first time he fought Joe Frazier, I felt as if I had lost. When he won the next time, I felt I had won. When he went back into the ring with Larry Holmes and got beat up, I felt as if I were being beat up. When he raised that Olympic torch, I felt we were all champions.

Everywhere, people stretched their arms up, mirroring Ali's stance, to wave their American flags. The balloons suddenly rushed upward as a cloud of red, white, and blue. Heads and flags bobbed up and down as people jumped to push themselves even higher. The noise was chaotic. All faces were turned toward Ali and the torch. People were beaming, singing, calling out encouragement. Some were doing all that and crying, too. The tears that shined everywhere along the route were there, whether for the flag, or the ideals that the torch represented, or seeing Ali after all he had endured, or because they were acting out, for a moment, a dream of unity that they had thought was lost.

Ali jogged down the steps and started on his way, behind the press truck. He kept the torch high, over his head. He wasn't walking it, he was running. His gait had a little hitch in it, but I barely noticed. Some people broke out of the crowd to run along.

David Halliburton had shown up. He had done the Indianapolis day, then leapfrogged ahead of the caravan to see how things turned out in Louisville before flying on to his next assignment. We embraced and pounded each other's backs like long-separated brothers. David looked around and started emitting exclamations like, "Steve, what a great job! Remember when this was nothing?"

I shouted, "Let's see if we can jump ahead and catch Ali at the end of his kilometer!" and we ran toward the rental car, another Volvo.

We had five minutes. David had borrowed the keys earlier for some errands, so he drove. Like a crazy man. This pious, cautious, conservative burgher I had gone out of my way to avoid four months before, this sweet and cheerful man with whom I was now partners and friends, screeched up one-way streets and roared through speed limits, with both of us gasping and whooping like kids on a midnight drag strip.

David slammed on the brakes a block from the next exchange point, left the car halfway up on a sidewalk, and we ran over, out of breath and unable to stop laughing.

Muhammad Ali came around the corner as we arrived. He had not slowed to a walk. He still held the torch high, like a beacon, and he was still running with it. The run was not the easy lope we had all watched for so many miles when he trained in the days of his glory. He was hobbling. His body appeared drained of its abilities. For an instant his broken gait shocked me; just for an instant, before I turned my mind away from it. For that moment, I wanted to exult in our achievement. We had made it. Muhammad Ali had returned, and I had helped to bring him back.

He passed the flame to the next runner, Melinda Warren, who had raised the $3,000 she paid for the right to carry the torch by baking cookies and selling them, endlessly, from door to door. The caravan left. The crowd swarmed Ali. I had never before seen such adulation up close. People wanted to touch him, to attract his glance, to get his name on any slip of paper they could find. They pulled out laundry lists, dollar bills, gas receipts, and he wrote on every one. He faked boxing jabs with boys, and honored requests for hugs and kisses for women and children. He was writing his name as we walked back to the Volvo, and was bent patiently over the scraps of paper and ballpoint pens as David steered us away and I stared back for a last look.

Our next destination was Cherokee Park and Jack Olinick's Marines.

Halfway there, we saw a familiar blue Buick and the gaudy WE ♥ U.S.A.'S TORCH RUN tailer of Fred the souvenir huckster. From the day Fred first showed up across the street from United Nations Plaza, his stocky figure had been pursuing us across America. He popped up with his wares in every town. He sure was persistent. We would eventually come to admire his stamina, if not his methods, but at this point he was just a pest. I had asked the cops to chase him away from the arts center in the morning; now here was another inning in the transcontinental game of "How do we foil Fred?"

One thing we didn't need was a wire-service reporter filing a story: LOS ANGELES OLYMPIC ORGANIZING COMMITTEE CASHES IN ON SAM THE EAGLE TORCH NIGHTLIGHTS. The Greeks were already upset about Americans commercializing their sacred flame. Good old Fred could go down in history as the first traveling salesman to provoke an international sports incident.

We pulled up next to a state trooper who happened to be parked there, and I showed him my LAOOC badge. He was very solemn, very serious. I explained about Fred passing himself off as a Telephone Pioneer and member of the Olympic Committee, getting free hotel rooms, probably breaking local licensing ordinances, giving us all a bad name, and ended with, "Can you do something about him?"

The trooper gave a nod. He eased into his unit, flicked the siren on, and blasted around the traffic ahead. David and I looked at each other, wondering, "Good grief, what's he going to do?" He gunned up ahead of Fred, cut off the blue Buick, and jammed it into the curb. By the time we got up there he was looming over the driver's window. We angled by and tossed Fred a cheery salute.

Driving into Cherokee Park was a reminder in miniature of our beautiful ride through the horse farms toward Lexington. This place was more populated, with families playing catch under oaks and maples and hickories, or folding up the last waxed paper from the day's picnics. But it had hills with the same easy swell, a gentle rise and fall that said it was old ground. Its grass was the same seamless green, with finer blades. Though there was no sun to make shadows, the greens deepened almost to black in pools of shade under dogwoods and magnolias, and we could see pets and sometimes children in sunsuit bottoms dodging behind the spots of color—pink, lavender, saffron, crimson—that glowed from rhododendrons and azaleas. The moist air seemed ripened by the scent of the juices crushed from the grass by today's feet.

The Marines had assembled at the next transfer point, near the foot of a hill. They were easy to identify—twenty-five crewcut warriors in what looked like parade-ground running uniforms, red shorts and yellow shirts with a Marine stripe across the front. On shiny poles they had a satin American flag and a platoon flag.

Jack Olinick spotted us and trotted over. He and I tried to look casual, as little as possible like conspirators. "Hey, Jack, you guys look good," I said. "Sharp. Let's try to keep it as inconspicuous as possible." Wink wink. "Okay, now, run on the edges of the road. There's a GMC Suburban that follows the runner; you'll see the Security people on its running boards, hanging off the sides of it. Stay behind it. They want to keep a clear plane ahead of the runner and to the sides. If you stay out of that plane, I don't think anybody's going to get nervous and everybody will be happy. How's it sound to you?"

"Outstanding. We can do that, Steve." Jack let himself flash one grin. This operation must have been turning out to be as much fun for him as it was for me.

He got half his troops lined up on one side of the road and half on the other—"Hut! Hut! Hut!" They stood out so vividly that David rolled his eyes and I muttered, "Boy, let's hope this works."

Flanking the road were several hundred civilians, many of them also carrying flags. "Go for it!" a young man yelled.

"Number One! America!" another called out, and the Marines grinned.

The homemade signs stuck up above the crowd, as they had every day:

LOUISVILLE WELCOMES THE TORCH.

U.S.A. ALL THE WAY.

It was time to break the news to the people in the caravan. "Lipps, Barr. Listen, Suzanne, tell Ruth and Security that there's a group of Marines who will be accompanying you up the hill here. Tell them not to panic. The Marines know they have to stay out of the way. It's fine."

Ruth Berry didn't like it. She went by the book, and her book did not include surprises. Take it easy, I said, I've worked it out with Wally, don't worry about it. Okay.

The caravan approached. The Marines started marching in place, then running in place, chanting:

My Marine color is blue! Shows the world we are true!
My Marine color is red! Shows the world the blood we've shed!

The torch bearer arrived to pass on the flame to Chris Buehner, the Marines' boy, a thrilled-looking blond with his mother off to one side looking even more thrilled. As Chris's torch flared up, someone in the back of the crowd of civilians lining the road began humming. Someone else picked it up, and in seconds the words became audible: "O beautiful for spacious skies . . ." Hats came off. A few people put their right hands over their hearts. Then just about everyone did. One middle-aged woman squeezed a handkerchief in the hand over her heart as she told Chris, "God bless you, son. I didn't know I'd ever feel like this again."

Off they went. The road was too full for us to skip ahead this time, so we got the rear view: Chris padding along holding the torch as high as he could, straight up, radiating pride—no kidding, you could see it in his back. Behind him, his honor guard ran like two red and gold centipedes, their flags curling and snapping as fifty legs rose and fell in perfect unison, their voices bouncing over the grass:

My Marine color is gold! Shows the world we are bold!
My Marine color is green! Shows the world we are mean!
My Marine color is black! Shows the world we'll be back!

"Barr, Lipps. This is the most sensational thing I've ever seen. These guys are *great*."

We crept the Volvo up behind the caravan for half a mile or so, then parked and jumped out and ran the last few yards over the crest of the hill to see what was happening. There were the Marines, embracing Chris, punching each other on the shoulder, completely jazzed, yelling things like, "Get all over it, hogs! Harooga harooga harooga harooga!"

We're from different worlds, these guys and I. But, except for the clothes, right then you would not have seen a flicker of difference between us.

*   *   *

David left for the airport. After the caravan passed the beautiful Old Kentucky homes in East Louisville, I took Suzanne's place in the lead car for the run along Route 60 to Frankfort and the Keeneland Race Track where the caravan would camp overnight. The rain started coming down hard. As we had seen so many times before, a little inconvenience like a drenching rain could not make the people give up. They stood their ground and waved their greetings to the torch, and each other, with flags that gave off sprays of water at every wave.

We pulled into Keeneland at half past eleven. The crew had its customary little victory party to wind down. Tonight there was some extra entertainment: Film footage of the first week of the torch run had just arrived. We all went over to the Keeneland Motel to see the movies. While David and I had been careening through Louisville earlier in the day, Billy Rappaport, a cameraman for Burson Marsteller, had been riding the truck in front of Muhammad Ali, positioned for the most intimate of all views of Ali's run. I found Billy and asked how he thought the afternoon had come off.

"That was the saddest thing I've ever seen in my life," he said.

I felt as if iced water were running down my spine. "What do you mean?"

"He limped along, he had that stoic look on his face. He only smiled once, and that was when somebody on the truck yelled, 'How's it going, Champ?' and he said, 'You're smiling because you're riding.' That's the only time we could get him to wave. He seemed like he was out of it, and it really bummed me."

Jody Meredith and her children had come over to visit with Ruth, and the next morning we all got together for breakfast. It was delightful to have Mark hang all over me as if he had found a new buddy. It was also intriguing to think about what it must be like to be a celebrity.

Ruth and I were still in our red, white, and blue Olympic warm-up suits from getting up early to help the reporters at the torch-lighting ceremony. As we opened the door to the restaurant, people stopped what they were doing and just looked. We found a table, and while we were looking at menus a child walked over to ask for an autograph. We had learned on the road that it was a waste of time to protest that we were nobody; people didn't care. Out there, where things like an Olympic torch had never happened before, if you were part of it you *were* somebody. Another child came and then another, and halfway through the meal the whole restaurant was asking for autographs.

We ended up sitting down with a table of children who lived outside Lexington. One was blind, and another, a heavy boy, seemed a little slow. They told us they had skipped school for the day so their mom could bring them to see the torch. Right now, though, the most fascinating thing to them was my being from Los Angeles. They couldn't ask enough questions:

"Do you know Christopher Reeve? Jane Fonda? What's the beach like? Do you see famous people all the time?" They couldn't wait to grow up and move out there.

Their yen for faraway places gave me an odd jolt. They sounded like me a few months ago. Yes. I had gone all-out to get this job because I, too, wanted to see what's below the horizon. It had started opening my eyes, though, in ways I'd never expected. Now I had an impulse to give the kids a soapbox speech.

"Don't spend your life thinking some other place is better than where you are. Be careful about believing all you see on TV. What you have here is as beautiful as it gets. . . ." I said none of it. Who was I to lecture them on what to dream about? I couldn't tell them not to want to see someplace else. If somebody had tried it on me five months before, it wouldn't have kept me at home.

We had a few hours before a flight to Memphis. Part of the price of being with Ali was missing the show tomorrow in Knoxville; Jan Williams and Mark would be there. I thought I'd use the time to catch up on some sleep, after a look at the newspapers. The *Lexington Herald-Leader* had a big picture of a solemn Ali above the crease on the front page, next to a story that began,

> Twenty-four years ago, when he was an Olympic gold-medal winner instead of a preliminary attraction, Muhammad Ali could have back-pedaled a kilometer through downtown streets, a-punchin' and a-jab-bin' and a-jabberin' all the way.
>
> But the bee sting now comes from the pain of leaden legs; the butterfly floats no more.

Looking more like the slightly flabby, middle-aged jogger he is than the world heavyweight boxing champion he was . . .

The article was not cruel. Its author, Andy Mead, showed real affection for Ali. "He'll always be the champ in his hometown," Mead wrote. He simply said Ali is older than he was, slower, seemingly off in his own world at times. Maybe seeing those regrets in print is what struck me. Whatever the reason, they brought me suddenly, with no warning at all in the midst of my triumph, to that tightening in the throat and heat around the face that come when you're holding back tears.

You know, that is true, I thought. It would have been a great treat to see him do it—in fact, right then I could imagine him backpedaling, jabbing, and orating all at the same time. The Muhammad Ali I grew up with and loved could do it. The man who ran in Louisville yesterday could not.

Heroes were more than just important to me when I was growing up. They were part of my life. At times, looking up to a hero almost offset knowing my father had left us. Heroes come so easily when you're young. You fasten your attention on their exploits, they look perfect from a distance, and admiration can slip into hero-worship. Whether you direct it at Muhammad Ali or Uncle Sam, you see what you want to see. You don't look at flaws. You shut off your doubts.

Lying on a motel bed staring at the newspaper, for the first time I felt sad and empty in the middle about what we had done. For the first time I admitted the doubts: Maybe I admired Ali so extravagantly that I was willing to exploit him. In seeing only a hero, I had forgotten the person. Maybe it would have been kinder to leave him his privacy.

Thoughts sloshed back and forth in my head. Face it. I had my own selfish reasons for wanting him to run: To meet my hero. To stage a great story for the torch run. To put my day in Louisville on the national map.

Okay, the man who ran in Louisville was not the same hero I had when I was ten, when even people who hated him loved what he could do. The quickness and brightness of that Ali were not entirely gone, but they were muffled.

Yet the event did succeed, in ways it would take a while for me

194

to see. When the press likes someone, they do what they did the day Muhammad Ali carried the flame. Of all the photographs they could have used, they chose the one of him smiling. By the time the torch would arrive in Los Angeles two months later, I would understand what the picture meant:

The real contrast is not between the Ali who could once move hands and words with dazzling speed and the Ali who has lost that edge. It is between a young fighter whose skills, whether they came easy or hard, had a brilliant flash; and an older fighter whose courage, which cannot have come easily, has an enduring depth. The flash can never last. The courage can never die.

So the hero is not merely a myth, or a collection of bygone glories. The hero is also one of us, a man or woman who comes upon a challenge and meets it—in this instance, a man with a body that no longer does much of what he asks it to, who chose to run when he could have walked.

(Do many people know how tough it was? After six sedentary months, *all* the aerobic conditioning you ever had is gone. For a middle-aged man, running three-fifths of a mile after that is the same as starting to run from scratch, with the extra difficulty of holding a three-pound object, the torch, above shoulder level the whole way. Try it sometime when you're feeling old, or just weary.)

Damaged as he is, Muhammad Ali put himself out there. He gave it all he had and ran the whole way, alone in front of all those eyes that might be looking with love, or scorn, or pity, or who knows what. He accepted his limitations as well as his strengths, and ran with both.

Understanding would come later. As I stood up to leave the motel room, all I had was a collection of shapeless impressions. Over the next few days, until other places and different people poured in to replace them, I felt a pang of dread whenever I would think, I hope it isn't going to go badly for him. But farther down the road, the last piece would click into place. Ali was the hero as much for what he had done in Louisville as for anything he had done before.

So that's what heroism is about, I would eventually learn to think. Heroism pulls together both tragedy and triumph. When people call him Champ, they are talking to a champion who is still great.

We moved on. That was the power of the torch run, and, I began to suspect, the power of the country we were moving into. The adrenalin flowed, you climbed the heights, reached the peak of something you had been building for months, and the next morning you were on the road, heading for Memphis, to make a new beginning.

For a moment, the Muhammad Ali of my childhood appeared. The AT&T
cadre runner with him is Stan Harris of Atlanta.

(Copyright © 1984, the Courier-Journal. *Reprinted by permission.)*

A seven-oar salute in the
Smoky Mountains
(Bill Mattman)

_____

Farm people seemed, somehow,
the closest to the message the
runners were carrying. And
who cares if a flag was
backward once in a while?
(Bill Mattman)

_____

Two weeks before his one-hundredth birthday, Ansel Stubbs held the flame high in downtown Kansas City. With the temperature approaching Ansel's age, Royals pitcher Larry Gura waited at his right to act as a sort of co-torch bearer.

(Boys Club of Kansas City)

A brave beer vendor with big-league reflexes stopped a blast off the bat of a Kansas City Royal just before it would have beaned one of us. Torch Rats Barr, Suzanne Lipps, Kelly Sarber, and Jeff Black raise a toast to him by the right-field foul pole.

(Suzanne Lipps)

It's what we all kept saying to
each other: "Thank you for
coming."
(Bill Mattman)

These prototype running shoes
worked fine for one kilometer.
(Bill Mattman)

A unique and original welcome to the flame
(Suzanne Lipps)

Somewhere in Kansas live these fans of Bob.
(Bill Mattman)

When else would you ever see so many people out of their cars on the Interstate, cramming overpasses like this one in Colorado, to say how proud they are?
(Bill Mattman)

Even the businesslike highway patrolmen who helped escort the relay, like this one in Utah, could get caught up in the celebration.
(Bill Mattman)

Kate Washburn, one of the cadre runners' managers, got stress fractures in both legs from the constant pounding of pavement, but the people in the heartland wouldn't let that end her voyage. A bicycle shop owner near Denver met the caravan and gave Kate a $600 ten-speed, which she's riding here to stay with her team on the road to Seattle.
(Jeff Black)

One of the most talked-about torch bearers was Hell's Angel
George Christie (right), getting ready to run past an honor guard
of three hundred of his mates and their motorcycles outside
Ventura, California.
(Jeff Black)

The crush and excitement of big crowds were always impressive, yet the more intimate welcomes, like the one from this little boy, touched us the most deeply.
(Bill Mattman)

Opening ceremonies, July 28: A beginning for the 1984 Olympic games, a conclusion for us as we wait for the last steps of the 9,100-mile relay. Left to right in row two: Jan Williams (waving), me, Mark Zangrando, Jeff Black, and Larry Sillman.
(Larry Silman)

26

Beyond the Blues

"Let's see now," the desk clerk said. "Oh, it's after five. I'm afraid you've missed the ducks."

Ducks?

"Over at the Peabody. It's a great tradition in Memphis, you know. From the days when more of us were landed gentry. At cocktail time a flock of ducks walks across the lobby. People come from all over the world to see the Peabody Ducks. They're quite a sight in that Grand Hotel setting."

Sometime in the next few days it would be fun to see the ducks. But the clerk had already made a gift of the real pleasure—his delight in his hometown's own incomparable habits and accent and face. The place was like a person. That was something I'd begun to love about this journey through America: people who don't sit still for anyone's expectations. They, and the places they've built, have their own definite angles of character. They don't defy your expectations; they just let you hang around until you've reshaped what you thought you knew about them.

Memphis could have embalmed itself in its traditions, lamenting forever the decline of its cotton market after the War Between the States and consoling itself forever as the birthplace of the blues. Right off, though, it felt like another of those communities that holds tradition both firmly and lightly; ducks in the lobby are a reference to the past, and an amused one at that, not a bondage to it.

There is something mysterious about this country, and once I'd started seeing it elsewhere I could pick it up in Memphis before I'd even picked up the key to my room. It is our well-worn gift for being diverse and unified at the same time. In some ways, we are so unlike one another that in other parts of the world we would be separate countries. How can the raw thrust and clang and rush of New York live with a Memphis that by comparison seems almost quaint? What do the humid green fertility and courtly manners of this community on its bluffs above the Mississippi have to do with the harsh desert glare and startling smog of Phoenix? Yet we are one country, with the Federalist Papers in our history. We follow (more or less) the same notions of law. A casual plane ride over distances that in other parts of the world would cross half a dozen borders does not end with you reaching for your passport. When you leave the airport you can notice—with satisfaction or regret, according to your nature—that a Holiday Inn room is the same no matter where it is, in Memphis or Albuquerque. So is the local shopping mall. So is the language. For all the diversity of tongues that enrich us, from Afghan to Yiddish, the nation conducts its business in English as a mother tongue, everywhere alike.

Well, not so fast there. Mother tongue, okay, but nowhere near as alike as the motel rooms. Compared to the flat Californish I speak, the conversation of Memphis is closer to singing. I would say, "The barbecue at Charlie Vergo's Rendezvous sure is good." The room clerk would say, "Oh, my Lord, I thought I'd died and gone to heaven. They opened up those ovens and brought me out some ribs that just lit up my mouth."

It would be a mistake to suppose that Memphis is in any way quaint. It is itself. It has its ducks, memorials to the blues, and Cotton Carnival (it got the cotton market back—and now trades more than a third of the U.S. crop). It has its skyscrapers, expressways, suburbs, and visits from the Metropolitan Opera, its port and its research hospitals and universities, and its motels and malls that make it also part of the rest of us.

Now I wanted to get my bags up to the room. The elevator door was about to close, but a pale young passenger held it. "What floor, mate?" he asked. The words had a strong British Isles tang, Liverpool or London or Manchester—I don't know enough to say where from exactly, but working class for sure. His hair was jet black, dyed, I'd say from the stark white of his face and hands, and he had it slicked back in a sort of New Wave version of the fifties: a curl in front and a little duck tail in back. A rocker, in his oversize suit jacket, skinny tie, tight jeans, and pointed black dress shoes. Friendly, too. "What you in town for?" he said while we ascended.

"Oh, business. How about you?"

"Came over with some mates for a week in New York, and we thought since we'd got that far we should motor down for a go at Graceland." The Elvis Presley shrine. Why not? It was just another seven miles from here.

From the room I called to touch base with Kelly Sarber, the other torch rat handling Memphis this week. Then I noticed I was hungry. The coffee shop downstairs was nearly empty. The waitress smiled a welcome when I said "Hi" instead of "Hey."

"You here for the Cotton Carnival or the International Festival?"

"No." Frankly, I wanted a night off from the torch. "Thought I'd take a look at Graceland."

She nodded. "Yeah, a lot of folks come for that. And Beale Street."

"All fixed up, is it, Beale Street?"

"Oh, my, yes, has been for a long time, restored and full of fancy restaurants and hot spots."

A neat pair of parentheses, Beale Street and Graceland. When W. C. Handy blew the first lonesome, heartful notes of what he would call the blues in PeeWee's Saloon, Beale Street was down and dirty and he was telling what life was like when you were black. By the time Elvis picked it up, the music had bridged a gap, somehow; it told about the life so that even people who hadn't been born black could feel it, or some of it. Now people could come to the old shrine and the new one, and the wonderful thing was that the music isn't trapped in either one. It's still floating around the world, alive.

I wanted to know something else. "You know the motel where Martin Luther King was killed? The Lorraine? Where is it?"

"I don't know," she said, and went off for my burger.

Later, the same question got the same answer from the desk clerk. "Don't know."

Next day, a gas station attendant: "Couldn't tell you."

A waiter bringing a plate of the famous ribs: Shrug. The ribs did light up my mouth, sure enough. I liked them so much that I got sauce all over my shirt. Couldn't walk around like that, so I headed back to the room for a clean one.

The maid's cart was parked outside the door, and I must have slipped around it quietly to get in; the maid jumped when she turned and saw me. Sorry, I said, I didn't mean to startle you.

Standing around a hotel room while a maid works on it is pretty awkward—it's one thing to be idle, but another to be idle and in the way—so I started helping her make the bed. The trouble was, that made *her* feel awkward. She kept glancing at the door as if a supervisor might come in. The situation was out of gear just enough to push my mind back to how odd it was that everybody in this town knew where Elvis Presley died of a drug overdose but made a mystery of where Martin Luther King, Jr., died as a martyr to a great revolution. I hadn't set out on a big project of tracking down the address; the question just occurred to me every now and then, and the non-answers seemed peculiar.

We were pulling the bedspread over the pillows when I decided to say, "I don't know why, but nobody around here seems to be able to tell me how to find the place where Martin Luther King died."

The maid looked up, but didn't answer.

"I've asked four or five people who work around here. It's got to be downtown here somewhere."

She glanced at the door again. "Were they all white folks, the people you asked?"

Let me see . . . "Yeah, I guess so."

"Don't expect any white folks be telling you where Dr. King got shot. Everybody around here know, and nobody going to say."

"I miss Dr. King very much. I'd like to see where he spent his last day. Would you say?"

She would. The Lorraine Motel was three blocks away from the lobby. She told me the turns to take. With the location finally in hand, I dashed down and starting walking.

I wasn't sure what drew me there. Even asking had started to seem morbid. It would be pretentious to claim too much for my sense of history. Something had happened that shocked the world, but I didn't really comprehend it when it happened. I was seven years old then. Now, I wanted to go to the spot and see whatever was left of what the people who made history had seen. It was more than prurient interest. The Lorraine Motel is where a hero had died. Who knows why people go to the birthplaces and death-places of their heroes? For some little remnant of contact?

The Lorraine looked as if it had been closed for years. It was much smaller than I had imagined it, and didn't look much cared for. The sight of it took me back sharply to another place—our front door in Missouri, at Fort Leonard Wood, opening to let me in from school, my mother telling me the news. My first impulse was to run over and see my best friend, but Mom wouldn't let me out of the house. One of the few things I remembered about Butchie's parents' house was the plate they displayed over the fireplace, with a picture of Martin Luther King, Jr., on it. Butchie talked about Dr. King the way others of us talked about sports stars. For a week, Mom wouldn't let me go anywhere but school, for fear that someone, somewhere, would lose control. Besides, she didn't think Butchie's parents would want to have to deal with both their own grief and their son's white friend. That week gave me a sudden seven-year-old's view of what it was to be without freedom. Because of my race and my friend's race, we were separated, segregated. The world split then, and never came completely back together.

There was no plaque at the Lorraine, no vase of flowers, no marker of any sort. But there was that iron railing on the second floor and the row of doors. I imagined which one Dr. King had opened when he stepped out for a breath of air. Free at last . . . I remembered the photograph of all those arms of his friends pointing up to where the shot had come from.

The people passing by walked so casually, as if they were on any ordinary sidewalk. It seemed strange, so strange, that they didn't pause in their errands or even glance up at the place. It was just another rundown building. I had forgotten to change my shirt; nobody noticed my barbecue sauce, either.

Placing runners and revising schedules with Kelly through the rest of the week, I couldn't help feeling, as pretty as Memphis was, a slight shadow hanging over me. But this was not a time to brood over murder. Memphis had been doing what it could to get out from under the shadow. The people had put a massive steel sculpture called "The Mountain Top" in Civic Center Plaza to honor Dr. King. Walking past it, or driving through the neighborhoods on our way out to Tupelo, we moved in a salt-and-pepper mix of Memphians almost evenly composed of white skins and dark skins and resolutely holding the significance of either to a minimum.

The shadow just about evaporated on Saturday evening. The

Memphis Symphony Orchestra draws at least a third of the population of the city to its annual outdoor concert on the bank of the Mississippi. Backlighted by a setting sun, sixteen years after a white thug killed a black Nobel Prize winner at the Lorraine Motel, the crowd was a sprinkle of black and white faces, some Asians and Latins, here and there even an American Indian, diverse like Memphis itself. Memphis is more alive than ever.

A singer joined the orchestra. The crowd stirred. From my place way in the back he looked old, but if he was, he could thank age for deepening the richness of the bass tones that only a black voice can produce. He started the song from *Show Boat* that every person there knew, and every single one of them sang with him. Every one.

> . . . Show me dat stream called de river Jordan,
> Dat's de ol' stream dat I long to cross. . . .

Two hundred and fifty thousand voices made a bottomless harmony, like the voice of an immense organ under the deepening sky in the heat of a Tennessee evening, pouring out their song over the great current that flows through the center of America.

> Ol' man river, dat ol' man river,
> He must know sumpin', but don't say nothin',
> He jus' keeps rollin',
> He keeps on rollin' along.

27

Thank You for Coming

"One thing really scares me about baseball—I'm always afraid I'm going to get hit by a foul ball," Suzanne said. We were walking along the outside ramp at Royals Stadium, looking for the number of our section in the right-field bleachers, and she had said it three times already. "Really, I mean I really *hate* foul balls."

We turned down the steps toward the field and Jeff laughed, not at all annoyed, just amused and affectionate. "You can quit whining, Suzanne. Look how far down the line we are. That foul pole is three hundred and thirty feet from home plate. Anybody who can't get out of the way of a ball coming from that far off deserves to get beaned."

That would probably be me. All day Sunday, Kelly Sarber and I had ridden with the torch from Mississippi into Memphis, both of us amazed by the energy of the runners and the crowds in ninety-percent humidity and 110-degree heat. Now it was Monday night and this was Kansas City and there were three days to get ready to do it all over again on Friday. A letdown always came with a thud the day after we accompanied the relay. But it did not come with time to rest, think, or write more than a few notes in a journal. "Time," such as it was, consisted of schedules: Three days to firm up another hundred-and-fifty-mile route, with its towns, highways, cities, and events; three days until that surge of adrenalin you didn't think would ever come back kicked in again.

There is a lot to be said in favor of fatigue. In many ways, it makes a happy basis for existence. I wouldn't call it a long-term key to contentment, but it does provide a serviceable shield against the small discontents that usually take up so much attention. A life of deadlines does not make you feel competent; but it numbs your critical faculties and postpones much of the self-absorption that you could do without anyway. Preoccupied with memories of yesterday's events and schemes for tomorrow's, you tend to stop worrying about life in general and yourself in particular. We were beat, but felt no particular need to lie down.

Besides, I had reasons to feel good. One was the prospect of taking a deep breath now—out of the old civilizations of the East, into the plains states and some wide-open spaces. Also, when I checked into the Westin in Kansas City, there were my best pals from the advance team: Mark, Suzanne, Jeff, Jan. Only David was missing. Even Kelly Sarber dropped by. Party time.

We were so far out in right field that our section had almost nobody else in it, hence almost no refreshment vendors. Around the second inning we volunteered Suzanne for a beer run. She was gone so long that we figured she was lost, so Jeff flagged down a vendor from the more populated stands. He was cheerful and friendly, and didn't mind waiting while we rummaged for change. We were standing with him next to the big orange foul pole, kidding around with our backs to the game, when he yelled, "Heads up!"

Everyone ducked in different directions, except Jan. Always the good sport, she was the designated non-drinking driver for the night and was paying no attention to the beer negotiations. The next thing I knew, the vendor whipped his tray up as a shield behind Jan's head. "BANG!" A baseball caromed off it like a cannonball. Blasted three hundred and thirty feet on a line by a brawny Royal, it would have hit her squarely in the back of the skull and most likely killed her. The ball rolled past her, she picked it up and held it aloft, and the Kansas City fans cheered. With reflexes like that, our vendor friend should have got himself a tryout for the team.

Suzanne appeared at the top of the steps with a carton of drinks. "Getcha beers here," she called. "What's so funny?" Oh, nothing. Nobody wanted to give her a chance to say, "I told you so."

JUNE 5

In the hotel, Mark and I watched Mariel Hemingway cleaning fish on Letterman's show while we read through the schedule for

Friday. So far, there was no media event in Kansas City, just a succession of runners with no high point. Not good under any circumstances, but especially bad here. We'd just heard that the trip director for the day was going to be Wally McGuire himself.

We still had the frustration of the Olympic Torch Relay being, for all practical purposes, a local event. It brought out unbelievable crowds with thousands of flags and a warmth that lifted us off our feet. People who had lived through World War II had been saying they hadn't seen patriotism like this since then. I certainly had never seen anything like it. I could remember only a handful of times when America stood as one people: The moon landing. The hostages coming home from Iran. And . . . when else? Usually we stand as one after a disaster, or a war. But the relay was neither. That was its beauty. It was purely positive. And the national press made it a minor story when they didn't ignore it entirely.

"Wait a minute," Mark and I said together. The YMCA was sponsoring a ninety-nine-year-old man named Ansel Stubbs. Another runner named Katie Johnston was four. Mark didn't think he'd had any runners older or younger. I knew I hadn't. This was it. We had a natural media hook—the oldest runner in the torch relay passing the flame to the youngest, from Father Time to Baby Future. The papers will have to pay attention.

"And here's the local CBS anchorwoman on the list." Mark pointed to a name. "Anne Peterson. I've seen her. She's a beauty queen. Put Anne Peterson right before that Stubbs guy and KCTV'll lap it up—and the other network affiliates will have to follow, or lose their ratings."

The relay would hit Country Club Plaza, the first shopping center in America, at one—a perfect place and time for a crowd to see Anne Peterson light Ansel Stubb's flame. And three-fifths of a mile down the street, the crowd could see Stubbs light Katie Johnston's torch.

But. . . . Ninety-nine years old. Could Ansel Stubbs even walk? Not a whole kilometer, apparently. The YMCA had arranged for Larry Gura, a popular veteran pitcher for the Royals, to take the torch when Stubbs could carry it no farther. But they hadn't known we were going to make a big event of the oldest passing the flame to the youngest. I had to find a way to get Stubbs up to Katie

Johnston with a torch in his hand. The exchange is where everyone took pictures.

The Kansas City police made that part easy. A couple of phone calls, and they promised an air-conditioned car to carry Stubbs in comfort through the middle part of his kilometer. With more calls and some struggle, our own Security team gave a grudging okay to insert the police car in front of their own vehicle in the core caravan. Within a day, we had our plan: Anne Peterson would light Stubbs's torch, he would take a few steps, we would pop him into the police car where he would ride while Larry Gura carried the torch to within a few yards of the Katie exchange, Stubbs would pop out of the police car, take the torch again, and light Katie's flame. Neat—if Stubbs could and would do it.

None of us had met him yet. And that worried me. What if he wasn't strong enough to endure the jostling and noise and stress and heat? Temperatures and humidity were high all week, both of them in the nineties and hundreds, and the wind never stopped. Somebody said that flags in Kansas City last an average of five months.

I got on the phone to do some checking. Stubbs had a friend at the retirement home who screened his calls and tried to fend me off. "He might not have time. He's doing all these interviews."

That part of it was going great. Thanks to Anne Peterson and the others, Ansel was becoming a media star. But I had to see what kind of shape he was in. During the conversation with the friend, it came out that Ansel used a cane. All the more reason, though I couldn't come out and say so, to check up.

"I just really would like to meet Ansel," I lied, "because we like to get acquainted with as many of the torch runners as possible. You know, this is a very personal thing."

The truth was, I worried that the run would be too much for him. He was four times my age. We might be asking an old man to step out in front of a lot of people and break down. More selfishly, I was getting scared about the prospect of being known for the rest of my life as the advance man who made the torch run famous as the event that killed a ninety-nine-year-old man.

Reluctantly, the friend said, "Okay. You can stop by around dinner time on Thursday."

That was a bit late, with the event at lunch time the next day.

And more than a bit squeezed; Wally wanted me to pick him up at the airport that evening. But it was the best we could do.

Wally called to say he'd been hearing more and more complaints about commercialization of the sacred flame, so "Whatever you do, don't let AT&T fly that balloon any more." A little-known fact was that AT&T, not the Olympic Committee, paid Wally's salary; his telling me to shoot down the big helium billboard they had been floating at many events was one indication of the integrity that made the whole enterprise work. Some AT&T people took me out to a fancy lunch and we had a nice time together, during which I passed along Wally's message about the complaints.

"We definitely do not want the balloon in sight on Friday," I said. "Agreed?" Sure, sure, they said, we understand, no balloon.

JUNE 7

Thursday evening. Wally was about to land, other arrangements were hanging fire, I was trying to get a reservation on a five o'clock flight for the next evening so I could leave right after the event for a friend's wedding rehearsal in San Francisco, we weren't really certain about the balloon, and that left just a few minutes with Ansel Stubbs.

He did look ninety-nine. He didn't get up. I sure wasn't going to ask him, "Say, do me a favor and go a couple of laps around the couch, will ya?" While I was trying to think of what I could say, he made it easy for me.

"I'm not going to be able to run a whole kilometer, you know," he said. "Or if I could, it would take so long that nobody'd wait to see the end of it." Then I told him what we'd like to do. He listened, then said, "That's fine with me."

"I might as well tell you this scares me a bit, Mr. Stubbs," I told him.

"Don't you worry," he said. "I'll be fine."

Next, Wally. All the contact between the two of us so far had been strictly business, so I looked forward to a couple of hours alone with him as we drove from the airport to Warrensburg, fifty miles east, where the caravan would bivouac. The airport was jammed. Tornado warnings—a lot of them—had flights backed up for hours, and it was close to ten when Wally's United flight from San Francisco landed. I waited as passenger after passenger filed by. Finally, Wally appeared. His suit looked as if he had slept in it, his eyes were bloodshot, and before I could start welcoming him he gave a hoarse, "Hi. How far do we have to drive?"

I put his suitcase in the back of our car and headed for what I hoped would be Warrensburg. Mark's instructions had sounded foolproof: "Get on Route 50 and stop at Warrensburg." But in the flurry of the week I had broken a cardinal rule of advance. I hadn't driven over the route, and in the dark there were unexpected turns and exits. Wally was not in a good mood. Like all of us, he was tired, apprehensive about tomorrow, stretched thin. The most he would give was monosyllables. Eventually he said, "What about tomorrow? What have you guys done for a crowd?"

I told him about Ansel and Katie and Anne Peterson and the posters we had put up along the route. He grunted and said, "How much leafleting did you do?" I knew he would get to that. "None," I said. "We just got here on Monday" (I didn't say, and we went right to the ballpark). "It takes several days to get leaflets done, and—"

"You didn't paper the place?" He stared at me in disgust. "You *know* you've got to poster a town to get a crowd out." Sure; I also knew that when you're on the ground in a city, you get a feel for what is working, and the media coverage in Kansas City was doing the job. But in the face of Wally's blast, I started having doubts. "I don't know, Steve," he said, "you've had time to do more than you did."

Between complaints, Wally kept falling asleep, thank God. The wind buffeted us something fierce. A couple of times it flung the car off the road. This was no little Alliance; it was a big, heavy Volvo, and it was on the verge of being blown to Munchkin land. Squinting for signs to the right and the left, I finally spotted a motel and pulled in. Wrong motel. Wally woke up while I was trying to figure out where to go next.

"Zthizzit?"

"No, I'm waiting for the wind to die down a little."

He dozed until we found the Skyhaven Motel at a little before two. Earlier arrivals from the caravan must have been very friendly with the manager; he didn't seem annoyed to be rousted out of a nap to let us in. I fell toward the bed, half asleep already, then heard what sounded like a knock at the door.

That's what it was. Wally. "Hey, Barr," he said. "Wake me up at four-thirty."

At five, the caravan and runners—all of them AT&T cadre runners for the open stretch between here and Kansas City—assembled in the Safeway parking lot on Maguire Boulevard. At six, the runner and the core caravan started. Those cadre runners were incredible athletes. They didn't do one kilometer at a time like the sponsored people. They did six, seven, nine, at speeds of eight to twelve miles an hour depending on how much time we had to make up and how frisky they felt. The wind had gone somewhere else and the sun was coming up bright and hot. This morning's run along Route 50 went through farmland. Pittsville and Lonejack were on the map, but we hardly saw them standing tiny and shy off the road to the right. Even so, people lined the highway, farm people who had driven up to a hundred miles in pickup trucks to be there when the flame went by.

"8:44 A.M.," the schedule said, "*Cadre runner arrives at the Jackson County Line and proceeds west on U.S. 50.*"

"9:25 A.M. *Cadre runner arrives at Buckner Tarsley Rd. and proceeds. . . .*" A man who looked about ninety stood alone with his head bare to the sun, saluting. A tear worked its way down his cheek and glistened in the sun for a second, like a spark. His hat was tucked under his left arm, and in his left hand he held a length of dowel with a worn American flag tied to the end. He looked as if he had stepped out of a Norman Rockwell painting. We all saluted back.

That was the beauty of those days. No matter how many public relations events we planned, the unexpected moments, like a Missouri farmer's eyes overflowing in pride, were the ones that made us feel lucky.

"What's happening, Wally?" I asked. "We're moving so fast, I can't figure out what's going on. But something is. That old man came out of nowhere—no house in sight, no pickup truck, just him and his flag. It feels like I'm seeing people like him every day."

"It's overwhelming for me, too," Wally said. "You know what we've been seeing. People are out at eleven o'clock at night in the rain, at six in the morning, waiting on the road to see us flash by a couple hours later. You know what I think? There's been something out here in America waiting for this to happen. Some spirit. You hear it called patriotism. That's too simple. It's more than that. It's got thankfulness in it—thanks for what we have. And the kind of look at each other that we don't take very often. And pride in something special—the quality of a particular piece of land, a town, a region, our accomplishments, our people.

"They thank us for coming. There's something in the land that needed to be unleashed. There's joy in those tears."

"10:34 A.M. Cadre runner arrives at the intersection of Blue Parkway and 3rd and proceeds west on Blue Parkway." Time for Mark to jump into the car so I could leapfrog ahead and coordinate with the Ansel Stubbs event.

"What about that goddamn balloon?" Wally suddenly asked.

"No balloon," I reassured him. "They promised."

All the schoolchildren in Kansas City seemed to be pouring out of buses, all of them wearing red, white, and blue, to join the adults who already packed the sidewalks. Many of the children had made paper-and-aluminum-foil torches. Even with no runner in sight, they were waving them and making more noise than I had heard in any city so far.

There, floating over them, was the damned balloon. I ran up to Linda McDougal of AT&T and panted, "What's the story? You guys said you wouldn't fly that thing."

"Well, it's up now and I'm not bringing it down," she said.

A couple more sentences and we were yelling at each other. I went over to the balloon handler AT&T had hired for the job. "Pull down the balloon, please. The Olympic Committee doesn't want it up there."

"Sorry," he said. "Can't do it without official authorization."

"I'm official," I said.

"In writing," he said. "On official stationery."

I ripped open my briefcase and found a piece of paper with the LAOOC letterhead, and scrawled on it, "Take that fucking balloon down."

"If you do, you don't get paid!" Linda shouted at the man. He hesitated. I spotted a sheath knife on his belt.

"Lend me your knife," I said to him, as quietly and un-maniacally as I could, under the circumstances. If I couldn't bring the balloon down, I could at least make it fly away.

Linda grabbed my arm. All of a sudden it was as if the din around us went silent and the commotion stopped for an instant, and I thought, "What am I doing, waving a knife around? This thing is not that important." The balloon handler took back his knife and sheathed it, looking relieved.

"Do what you want," I said to Linda. "It's not my responsibility."

The temperature by then was in the nineties and climbing. There had been no thunderstorms to break the heat and humidity, and you could sweat just standing still. It was time to get over to the Hilton to see how Ansel Stubbs was holding up. He was waiting comfortably in a nice cool room that the hotel had donated for him, but I wondered how his nerves were, and what would happen when we brought him out into the heat and uproar.

When I got there I was still furious, my heart was pounding, and all I could produce for conversation was to start telling Ansel about "those idiots from AT&T." He looked at me patiently while I carried on, and then the perspective hit me: The man's one hundredth birthday would be in two weeks. He had been alive for half as long as this nation has existed. Who cares about my little fit of temper?

"You're from California?" he said, serenely. "I went out there when I was a little younger than you, in my teens. Before they had that earthquake in San Francisco." That would have been before 1906. Ansel may not have had much left in his legs, but his mind was sharp. We started comparing travel stories. We talked about sports and politics.

"Grover Cleveland was president when I was born. The only one I ever met was Harry Truman," he said. "My favorite president. Liked that man a lot."

There were some interesting comparisons between Truman and Jimmy Carter, I said.

"Starting with both of them being stubborn, hah?" Ansel laughed.

"And down-home enough to not let the job turn them into someone they weren't. Speaking of presidents, you've lived through—what is it, eighteen of them out of the forty we've had. What do you think of the current one?"

"Reagan? Too old to be president." I started to laugh, and he held up a finger. "Not in years. In the way he thinks. Can't believe he thinks the world has all the cowboys on one side, and all the Indians on the other."

Ansel had the same dignity about his age that Muhammad Ali had about his. Here we were, with seventy-five years separating us, and it seemed like no gap at all. He had enjoyed the media attention so much that week, and had collected such a following through his appearances with Anne Peterson and her competitors, that I started having fun calling him "Mayor Stubbs." He smiled every time he heard it.

Presently Ansel said, "I better have a beer. I'm getting kind of nervous." We toasted the second century of his life. For a few more minutes we sat in the room, sipping beers together.

Then we went down through the heat and he got into the air-conditioned police car with his cane. My fear for him came back, that in the heat and crush of the crowd he might suffer. Country Club Plaza was so full of people that even the police car had trouble getting through. The city had done our job for us. This was one of the biggest and thickest and loudest crowds of the entire torch run so far. They made the advance team look good, especially those bus loads of school children.

"Now listen," I went around saying over and over to the children, "your torches are *great*. When the runner comes by, there's going to be a convertible in front of her, and some friends of mine are riding in the car. How about all of you throwing your torches into the car when it gets close enough? They'll love it."

I checked in one last time with Anne Peterson and went back to Ansel. We had to keep clearing back the crowd to make room for him. He could have been elected mayor that day with the votes of the well-wishers who pressed close to give him a touch and a smile.

Mark's voice on the walky-talky meant the torch was only minutes away. Ansel got out of the car. As the caravan approached, the screeching of thousands of children became almost deafening. The adults yelled too and some started to sing. I pulled away the hand I'd had on Ansel's back to steady him, and he stood by himself. We shook hands. He gave me a wink. Anne ran up and touched her torch to his. It caught on the first try. When Ansel held that flame up high in one hand, leaning on his cane with the other, the place went totally nuts with the loudest noise I had heard in my entire life.

It worked like a Swiss watch. Ansel took four steps with the torch and handed it to Larry Gura. Gura handed it back at Forty-second and Broadway, where Katie Johnston was waiting with her father. The instant Ansel's torch lighted Katie's, I put my arm around him and we walked slowly together toward the police car.

"Steve." I thought I heard him say something, but couldn't be sure in all the racket. I leaned down. "Steve," he was saying, "I've lived a century. I've never seen so much love for this great country as I'm seeing right now."

For a second time, I let go of him so he could duck into the car. He turned and our eyes met. His matter-of-factness was back in place, except for a light in his eye, a real twinkle. We looked at each other for a second or two. Without a word, Ansel put both arms around me. We didn't have to say a word. Ansel had made it.

28

They Find Us

CUPERTINO, CALIFORNIA, JUNE 8

I could have flown home without the airplane. After Ansel, the streets were a blur of exhilaration. The torch was passing the last stop on my shift, at the city hall of Kansas City, Kansas, when a friendly policeman offered a ride to the airport—a chance to make the flight that was about to leave without me. "Thanks, thanks," I said. "I'm ready, let's go."

Holding the door of the police car open, I looked back for a last impression of it all, and saw Wally gazing around with a huge grin. We would never be able to make any words carry across all those people, in all that tumult. He spotted me, though, held up his right thumb, and jabbed it forward, as strong as a high five.

Passengers up and down the aisles craned to see the hollow-eyed guy with the matted hair and the red-white-and-blue suit who had sprinted aboard, dead last, a couple of minutes after the plane was scheduled to leave, and was now leaning back with his eyes closed, licking sweat off his upper lip. The flight attendant gave me a pillow and blanket, but the adrenalin was still pumping and I just sat there thinking I'd better get some sleep if I wanted to get through the rehearsal dinner in Cupertino. Ten minutes . . . twenty . . . a doze was creeping over me.

Then a dream voice started saying, "Ladies and gentlemen, we're pleased to welcome aboard United Flight 729 Steve Barr of the Los Angeles Olympic Organizing Committee. . . ." No, not a dream; a real voice.

From then on, friendly people cruising by on their way to the magazine rack and the drinking water kept stopping by to chat. A traveling businesswoman had seen the torch that day in Kansas City: "It makes you proud, being an American, doesn't it? Think what those poor Russians are missing, not coming to our party."

A man in Calvin Klein jeans: "How'd you get that job?"

A young blond woman in braces: "Ooh, cool, how do they pick the runners?"

A flight attendant: "Is it going through San Francisco so my brother can see it?"

My white-shirted, red-tied neighbor in the window seat had been shooting me sympathetic glances between visits. Something in his face—a kind, comforting look, very different from the coldly focused look of the business travelers who take off their jackets and snap open a *Wall Street Journal*—made it clear that he didn't want to lay on another torch question. On the other hand, he didn't want to be unfriendly. When he spoke for the first time, it was not so much a crowbar to pry open a conversation as it was a way of saying he understood. "Going home?"

It hadn't occurred to me before, but I was. Running between appointments and dashing for planes, I hadn't stopped to think about what this trip meant. Going to a wedding, and more. Home, that evening, was not an apartment in Los Angeles, not my parents' house, but friends with whom I had grown up—a home I had left when I went to college.

"Yes," I said, "going to be co–best man in a friend's wedding." The man seemed more interested in me than in the torch questions. As we talked quietly it came out that his name was Dick, he worked for IBM, had a son at UCSB and a daughter working at a shelter for the homeless in Los Angeles. "I get the feeling that Alan could use a year or two of travel," he mused. "I don't think he quite knows what he wants."

I think it's a little frightening when someone eighteen years old does know exactly what he wants to do with the rest of his life, and said so. "Isn't that what college is for? Hope you aren't worried about Alan."

We were descending toward San Francisco when he said, "I've just heard dribs and drabs about your torch run. It sounds like an incredible experience."

I went into a ramble on it. "Started by seeing it as just a public relations job for AT&T and politics wrapped in sports . . . but somehow, now, the thing has really got to me . . . I'm sure you've gone through this sort of thing: I remember months of meetings with manipulative jerks and being one myself, being dazed with overwork, days and nights of loneliness on the road . . . But the payoff, the position I'm in to see people's reactions to it . . . I don't know if I'll ever figure out why people get so happy and so emotional . . . It's just so frustrating, I don't know how to explain it when people ask about it . . . I'm just babbling, I'm sorry."

Dick smiled and seemed to grasp whatever I had managed to say, which could not have been much. Just after the wheels touched down, he wrote a phone number on a scrap of paper and said, "I think you'd fit into the IBM management training program. Call me if you ever want to talk about it."

His gesture really touched me. He must have actually listened. Or maybe he was just impressed with my clothes.

Randy Lewis and Mike Swanson were walking toward the apartment building in Cupertino when I popped out of a taxi.

"What are you doing in the cab?" Randy asked, flashing a look from my running shoes all the way up the patriotic warm-up suit. "I thought you were flying into San Francisco."

"I did," I said, "but my license expired yesterday and Hertz wouldn't rent me a car."

"You took a cab here? That must've cost fifty bucks. Why didn't you just call us?"

For the same reason I hadn't noticed it was time to renew the license: Too frazzled. All I could think of to say was, "Ah, thanks, no problem."

One of the strangest feelings I've ever had came over me as I walked into the rec room where the rehearsal dinner was in full swing. It was like being in an episode of *Bewitched:* I'm in Kansas City, running through a screaming crowd to catch up to a ninety-nine-year-old man who's about to step out of a police car to carry a shining symbol with international significance. Then Samantha twitches her nose and—pop!—I'm transported back five years to high school. A girl is handing me a plate of food and telling me about her job at Lockheed and I'm watching my friend Larry across the room. Larry was the one friend in all of high school who felt the way I did, every time. You never knew when you'd get a call from him saying, "Let's go to Germany next summer," or, "Let's get a car and drive around the country." Larry was itching to cut the Cupertino cord. Now he's paler, his hair is shorter, he had an ulcer in college worrying about his grades in accounting, and he's getting *married*. Each face I focus on takes me back five years to an incident in high school. The faces haven't evolved. They're just a little older. Everybody's hair in here is shorter than it used to be, button-downs have replaced surfer shirts, conversations are about down payments on houses in Fremont, the price of a Honda Accord, did you hear the Lewises are having a baby? And I'm suddenly here in the warm-up suit and the sweat that belong in Kansas City.

"So, Steve, what exactly are you doing now?" It was great seeing my friends. We were having a good time being together again, and I did want to explain. I wished I had a short cocktail-party sentence to describe what an advance man does, but I didn't. There was no frame of reference. No movie about it that we had all seen, no civics test we'd all studied for, no common knowledge, no shared memories. It would be like trying to describe a quark to a ceramics major. But I tried anyway, with another of my earnest swipes at explaining what I did for a living.

"You get paid for that?"

Desperately, I slid into stories about some of the people and emotions and diversity that were springing out all around us on the torch run. Again, no frame of reference. No *CBS Evening News*, no *Today*, no *Time* cover story. Their eyes glazed.

It was like talking with someone about people in the inner cities and having him keep saying, "Well, why don't those people just get a job?" My friends had been doing what I had done until a few months before: Staying home. They were sheltered.

Who could reproach them? It wasn't their fault. While every town the torch went through burst into patriotic fire, the rest of the country had not caught on to the spirit it kindled. The torch, and the fervor it aroused, were no big thing to my friends in this part of the country. Since it hadn't come here yet, and they hadn't been there, how could I help them feel it? How could I get them excited about some particle in the universe, some quark, so recently discovered that it had not been ratified by the authorities?

Here we had the one part of it all that puzzled and frustrated me the most. The national press was ignoring or missing a powerful American phenomenon. As a result, we had a growing, but exclusive, fraternity of special Americans who worked or witnessed or participated in the relay. Everybody else was left out.

It wasn't just the fault of the press. How could I convey what I'd been discovering if I couldn't put it into words myself? Besides, this was Larry's party, not mine, and I wasn't going to distract attention from him by pushing my adventure stories too hard. So I gave up.

But . . . our parents. *They* had been around, hadn't they? At the wedding reception the next day somebody's father, a schoolteacher, holding a highball glass tilting toward a spill, found himself standing in front of me. He inspected what he saw and asked with a sort of offhand reproof, "Steve, just exactly what *do* you do for a living?"

WALNUT CREEK, CALIFORNIA, JUNE 10

We hadn't had a family reunion in four months, except for one hurried dinner at the Oakland Airport. I had been looking forward to seeing my mom and my stepfather, Pete. But when we did get together the next day, something unexpected happened. After the first good night's sleep I'd had in months, I should have enjoyed a quiet Sunday at their house. Instead, I caught myself leaning forward, drumming my fingers, itching to get back up to speed. They were so happy I was there, and my mind was eleven hundred miles away.

I was already thinking ahead. Albuquerque was next. Before that was a meeting tomorrow morning with a woman at the Transamerica Corporation in San Francisco. Transamerica was sponsoring a lot of kilometers and we were working together to place their favored people in the run.

SAN FRANCISCO, JUNE 11

A bright Monday morning in San Francisco was a good time to ride to the top of the Transamerica Pyramid. The woman took me up to the tip, into a James Bond–type sleek VIP conference room with a 360-degree view of all San Francisco, the Bay, and the Pacific Ocean.

"By the way," she said, "did you see the story in *The New York Times* yesterday?" and handed me a few pages of the Sunday paper.

I put them in my briefcase to read after we finished our business, then went down to street level and found a coffee shop on Washington Street—Something Special, it was called—to sit and read. The place was packed, but I edged in and found a little spot near the window where I could sit, and pulled out the clipping from the *Times*.

The article by Andrew H. Malcolm started with a big picture of the runner and core caravan and a headline, MORE THAN OLYMPIC FLAME CROSSES AMERICA. Malcolm had datelined it Loose Creek, Missouri, a town of a couple of hundred people the day before Kansas City. Andrew Malcolm had found us. He described for the first time the people who reached out and touched us as we plodded across America:

> . . . Night and day, there is always a crowd gathered in this front yard or at that rural intersection to watch the wordless roadside exchange of the flame. . . .
>
> . . . something unusual and unplanned is also happening as the Olympic torch makes its way slowly across the nation these days. For, unseen by most of the country, as the flame moves through places like rural Missouri, communities like Useful, Linn and Knob Noster, Union, Sedalia, and Festus, it seems to be igniting some special feelings tied less to the Olympics and more to patriotism.
>
> . . . Some people, freshly roused by the flashing lights of police escorts, emerge from where they have been sleeping, on blankets in the grass or in the back of a pickup truck. Others bring lawn chairs or stand for hours in the sun. This afternoon one farmer could be seen atop his distant tractor applauding silently in the middle of a giant soybean field.
>
> . . . it is in the countryside, out beyond the range and interest of the big-city television stations, that the runners find themselves the most touched by efforts to become involved somehow: The crowds of 1,000 people in a town of 300. The little communities that line their sidewalks with scores of candles, their own glowing echoes of the traveling torch. . . .
>
> As a runner enters town, church bells sound, fire sirens blare, trucks blast air horns. Some people throw roses, offer beers or run alongside to touch someone, anyone, involved with the torch. "Look at that runner, Honey," one mother urged her daughter, "Look at that runner and always remember him!"
>
> . . . In Gray Summit, Skip Haffley took the afternoon off from cleaning houses. She was standing in front of her home with her brother and her son holding up the United States flag that had adorned her father's coffin. "It's America, you see," she said, "And we love it!"

227

. . ."I'm not sure why I'm here," admitted Jerri Benson, whose employer emptied his plant to greet the runners. "But I know there's more to it than standing in the sun a long time to watch a guy run by in his underwear carrying a huge match."

. . . Sharon Miller, the mother of a 12-year-old who would like to be an Olympian some day, and 71-year-old Oscar Hagemeyer have lived on adjoining farms for eight years but never got around to meeting each other. Then they both drove to the windy corner of Highways 50 and K to see the caravan. And they both shed a tear at the sight. "You see what that torch did?" said Mrs. Miller. "It brought us together."

I couldn't get through it. I started bawling, shaking uncontrollably. People kept giving me looks of concern. I tried to hold back my sobs, but every time I read a little more the weeping started again. Finally, I gave up trying to stop crying. I didn't care who saw me.

When the tears stopped, many minutes later, I wondered, "What is going on? What is happening to me?"

29

Different Americas

ALBUQUERQUE, JUNE 17

Native Americans inhabited New Mexico before anyone else, so it seemed right that Mark wanted to include them in a media event for Albuquerque. He loved meetings, so he declined my invitation to the Dukes game and got together with a group of Indian dancers to discuss his plan.

They said, "Sure, we'll do a dance for you, and it'll cost a hundred dollars."

Mark said, "But there isn't any hundred dollars. We don't have a budget. Besides, this is a great chance for you to contribute something to the spirit of the torch run, the coming together of everybody."

The Native American leader said, "You don't understand. We are poor. We do the dance for a living."

During all that, I was at the ballpark. My section ran from Fort Sumner to Moriarty, thirty miles east of Albuquerque. Driving over it the day before convinced me that it called for nothing but waiting for the runners to arrive. The road is so straight that you can see forty miles each way and so far out in the desert that the caravan would be alone for most of the way.

Baseball in the minor leagues is so intimate and relaxed, played so much closer to you in its aged little ballparks than it is in the big city stadiums, that it takes you back to the golden years before the major-league business got so glossy. The Albuquerque stadium looked as if it might hold a couple of thousand fans. This afternoon it had a few hundred. There were plenty of good seats behind home plate. Soon after I settled into one, I noticed my nearest neighbors, two children who were poking their fingers through the netting, leaning up to it to call to someone on the field. They were dressed very carefully, not in the cutoffs and T-shirts that other children in

229

the place wore. The older of the two, a boy about eight, wore a white shirt, a tie, creased pants, and polished leather shoes; his sister, who looked four or five, wore a lacy dress with patent leather shoes.

"Papa! Papa!" they called out now and then to the playing field. When I smiled at them, they quickly looked away. The boy took his little sister's hand and drew her a little farther off, very much the protective older brother.

Soon a player came to the net and pushed a folded bill through it to them. It was Alex Tavares, a utility infielder who'd had some good games with the Dodgers, playing shortstop here today. That's baseball. You go to work one day in your Dodger blue in the big, sparkling expanse of a stadium that surrounds you with the roar of those great crowds, and the next in your orange Dukes suit in this little ballpark where you can hear every individual comment any customer cares to yell. And sometimes you have to keep an eye on your children while you're trying to make it back to the bigs.

During the game, Tavares kept glancing over at our section. Even from the on-deck circle, he looked. In the bottom of the fourth inning the kids looked up to where a group of Dukes wives were sitting together and waved to one who was arriving, evidently their mother. By then they had let me buy them a hot dog and decided it was okay to chat. We had been sharing peanuts, cheering together, and doing high fives when the Dukes did something good. Tavares had his game face on, so it was hard to tell what he thought when he looked our way. Did he see me as a child molester? Whatever, he was half playing ball, half baby-sitting.

The boy, Pepito, spoke English; his little sister didn't. He had a batch of baseball cards with him, all of Dominican players: Pedro Guerrero, Cesar Cedeño, Joaquin Andujar. We looked them over and talked, not so much about baseball as about where he'd been and what he'd seen in America. Very polite and responsive, he said the family lives in the Dominican Republic and had come up to visit his father. Tavares had played for four or five major league teams in different cities, and his boy had probably seen more of America than all my high-school friends in Cupertino.

Their mother beckoned. Pepito escorted his little sister up there, and I could hear them talking in rapid Spanish, looking back at me, pleading to let them finish the game behind home plate. Their company made me happy. Hoping she would let them stay, I took a chance and waved and nodded to promise I would keep an eye on them. She nodded, Okay.

At the end of the game, Tavares trotted straight over from his position and stuck some fingers through the net to tickle his daughter and shake Pepito's hand. He paused as I got up to leave and said, "Thanks for the baby-sitting."

FORT SUMNER, NEW MEXICO, JUNE 18

The owner of the restaurant was a woman with dark hair who looked as if she enjoyed her food often. "This is usually our night to be closed, but as you see, we stayed open for you." How did you know? one of the people from the LAOOC news office asked. "You booked every room in the motel. That's big news here. And we do read the Albuquerque paper."

The caravan arriving in Fort Sumner must have been the biggest event since Sheriff Pat Garrett shot Billy the Kid. Driving through gravelly desert dotted with creosote bush, mesquite, ocotillo, and other unkillable vegetation, you came to a startling strip of green along the Pecos valley. Then you saw a few stores, two gas stations, a movie theater that appeared closed for good, a lane or two leading to some trailers, and the motel. Even if its manager had not spread the word, its phoneless rooms would have turned the trick. The line of men in red, white, and blue Olympic outfits waiting a turn at the pay booth in front might have attracted some attention.

Seeing a rickety eating place in a little ranch town breeds all sorts of hope: "Ah, *here* is where the Mexican food is going to be great, real, and true." Well, the owner did go out of her way to make a bunch of strangers comfortable. Some people from the LAOOC news office and Burson Marsteller and I started ordering chile rellenos and chorizo and whatnot for a little reunion around one of her tables when we noticed some of the other customers just standing back looking at us. It must have felt like an invasion from outer space—all those huge white vehicles with antennas, technicians swarming around them tending to computers and engines and acting like priests around some little flickering lights. And us in the cantina in our space suits.

231

One of the onlookers edged up toward the other side of our table. Maybe he had been eating in the place, or he could have been a drifter who had just wandered in. He'd have been a perfect extra on *Gunsmoke*—medium height, blond hair turning gray, some age between forty-five and sixty, a face so tanned that it looked like leather and lean as the rest of him. His jeans, boots, and Levi's jacket all had dust on them. He kept his hands in his pockets, hunched a little to one side, and seemed so hesitant that it was a wonder he had worked up the nerve to come so close.

He started talking. I didn't know what he was saying. He mumbled the way you did as a kid when you had to confess something to a parent and were too tense and embarrassed to untangle the words. His eyes moved from the floor, to the side, to our faces, and off to the side again. The conversation around the table went on, the way you do when you're a grown-up brushing off an intruder. He hadn't prepared a speech. All he wanted to do was meet the Olympic people. I couldn't just leave him standing there. So I nodded and said the first thing that came to mind, "Hi. I didn't catch your name. What did you say it was?"

"Jesse," he said.

Now what? At a loss, I introduced him around the table. "Jesse, this is Billy from New York, Angie from Fresno, Bill from Sacramento, David from England and now New York, Eric from New York, and I'm Steve from Los Angeles." While I was saying all that he was circling to my side. The others went back to their conversation. I asked him where he lived.

"Got a ranch down past Evanola." He seemed to be getting over his shyness a little. "Where you heading tomorrow?"

"We're going into Albuquerque."

"Shoot, the last time I was in Albuquerque was just after the war," he said, "nineteen forty-five, I think, or maybe forty-six."

"Do you follow sports?" I asked. "The Olympics is what all of this is for."

"Not really. Don't have a TV. I go to the neighbors' for that. Got a radio, though."

Jesse was more remote from the rest of the United States than anyone else I could remember meeting, even more remote than the Oregon mountain man who didn't hang around Klamath Falls. The New Mexico desert was Jesse's world, and he had very little to do with the country beyond it. There may be no such thing as one "America," and maybe that's part of our strength. Variety keeps ecosystems alive: A forest with just one kind of tree can easily be wiped out by a single family of bugs, but a forest with hundreds of types of plants can resist all the bugs there are.

We talked until the check came. Jesse looked as tough as beef jerky, but he was gentle and diffident, a very nice guy.

"I don't have much to give you," he said when I stood up, "but I would like you to have this." He took his right hand out of his pocket and held out a foreign coin. That dark, rough hand, with its cracked skin and blunt fingernails broken in places, had seen a lot of work. Touching it, mine looked feminine by comparison. The coin was Mexican, some denomination of pesos. My first reaction was, He must not have many of those, I can't take it. But I was sure he would be insulted if I handed it back.

"Thanks, Jesse," I said. "I'll keep this to remember you." In my own pocket I had only one item to give him in return. "Mind if I put this on your coat?" I asked, and tacked a star-in-motion Olympic pin to the pocket flap of his dusty denim jacket. He lifted the flap to look at it, then looked up.

"I appreciate it." His shyness came back. We looked at one another for a moment. He mumbled something, went back to his slouch, and turned away.

NEW MEXICO DESERT, JUNE 19

The day's torch run was going to be so straightforward that I got out a copy of *Wired*, Bob Woodward's account of the life with drugs that killed John Belushi, to read in the car. The book fascinated me. Woodward takes you along as he discovers a world of entertainers and dope that he wouldn't have believed until he saw the evidence for himself. Part of the fascination was that it made me feel like such a bumpkin; I've gone to a lot of those restaurants and hotels and clubs in Los Angeles, never suspecting the frantic dealing and doping that was going on. My friends in Cupertino would be more than justified if they ever said, "So who's sheltered now?" Sophistication is certainly relative. You can know your own territory well, and be lost the minute you step out of it.

233

The Pioneer beside me in the lead Buick knew his region. "Did you know," he filled me in, "that Kit Carson forced more than seven thousand Navajos to make the 'Long Walk' across the Continental Divide to here from near Gallup to 'resettle' them—guess that's what folks called internment in those days—and they never forgave their old friend. Up that way, believe it or not, is a reservoir full of water. . . ."

We got ourselves the caravan's usual gourmet breakfast, and I was munching away when I happened to glance over at the Pioneer. He was turning a pastry over and over in his right hand, inspecting it from all sides, obviously more curious about it than ready to eat it. After ten seconds or so he turned to me and said, "What is this thing?"

"A croissant," I said.

"Spell that, would you?" Okay. "Well, what is it?"

"Shoot, I don't know. Sort of a fancy breakfast roll. Made with lots of butter. I don't know how they get it so flaky. Maybe they do the dough in layers or something."

Trying to explain a bun with a French name to a man who would last a lifetime longer out in that desert than I would if they put us both off the caravan, I felt as if the two of us were in fact from different planets. Just as John Belushi and Jesse were. Just as a lot of us who think saying "I'm an American" explains all anyone needs to know about us. Yes, we're linked by geography and varying amounts of history and lots of other things. Yes, we're all beneficiaries of the luck that set us down on a continent stocked with riches and insulated—until now—by huge oceans. And sometimes we know almost nothing about one another.

Albuquerque itself was Mark's and Joyce Tate's. I stuck around in case they needed any help; they didn't, so I hopped on the press truck to enjoy the sights.

Just inside the city limits, people had driven from wherever they lived to stand beside the road as it came out of the desert and entered the city. They gathered in clusters, and always raised a cheer as the runner approached. Just inside the city limits, the clusters started connecting into the honor guard of people that by now always greeted the torch, and their yells of encouragement started drowning out the sounds of engines and the sputter of the Security team's radios.

"Yeah, baby, go!" a bunch of guys in hardhats shouted, clapping as the runner—a woman holding the torch high in one hand, no "baby" feat with something that weighed upward of three pounds—passed by.

"Stay with it, honey!" The flags were everywhere, snapping back and forth in the brilliant sunshine.

"Hola, *faralito*"—that's what some New Mexicans called the torch—"bienvenido! Hooray for you! Hooray for all of us! Hooray for the U.S.A.!"

Out of the overall noise of the crowd, somehow, I heard one voice screaming something different.

"Don Wert! Don Wert!"

There was something just familiar enough about the sound of it to catch my attention. But still I didn't know what it meant. Was there anyone near the torch named Don Wert? I searched both sides of the street for a clue. And there it was.

Rich Green, the Security man from our ride toward Detroit, stood across the street, wigwagging both arms over his head. People all around him were waving their flags, calling out to the runner. He must have been off duty and decided to see what it felt like to be in the crowd. When we spotted each other, he cupped his hands and yelled again.

"Don Wert! Third base!" The 1968 Tigers. The player none of us could remember on that quiet night a month ago. We pointed at each other, laughing in delight, and I made a two-handed, palms-down "safe" sign, as big as I could without knocking someone off the bed of the truck. Rich clapped his hands overhead, and disappeared into the crowd. The Dueling Tigers team was complete.

We came up to a man who looked as if he had outlived a lot of horses, standing with his flag up and his straw hat off. Cowboy— he was it. A red bandanna around his neck, faded jeans as bowed as his legs, high-heeled boots with pointy toes, the same leather-textured face as Jesse. I'm sure he didn't expect to do it, but as the torch runner passed him, the old man jammed his hat back on his head and took off, running alongside. He ran with little steps, wobbling on those boots that were meant for stirrups, hands up around his chest and shoulders high, as far as he could go.

"Eeyaahoo!" we cheered him on, "Run it, cowboy! Way to go!" Winded, he stopped after half a block and people from the crowd

235

surged around him, patting him on the back as he grinned from ear to ear and waved his flag at us in a triumphant arc.

For my day as a spectator, I was completely out of relay uniform. Instead of the Levi's running suit, my costume was some red and white checked Bermuda shorts I'd picked up in Memphis, a gray "Property of New Jersey Devils" T-shirt, and my L.A. Dodgers cap (Dick Hamilton's hat was too sacred to wear with such a motley outfit). Near the University of New Mexico campus, the crowds got so big that they pushed up into the runner's lane. At one point I had jumped off the flatbed to run alongside and help clear the path when I heard the runner call out.

"Hey, can you help me out?" She had her free hand to one eye. "Got to fix a contact lens," she yelled. "Here, hold this," and she handed me the torch.

In ten or fifteen steps she re-positioned her lens and took back the torch. Those few yards, though, gave the students alongside time to go into full cry: "Hey, nice shorts, dude! Whoo, a real New Jersey Devil!" I could imagine a scene at dinner that night in the local Kentucky Fried Chicken:

"What was it like, babe?"

"Oh, it was pretty neat, but you know, they let just anybody step out of the crowd and carry the torch. There was this guy in some New Jersey uniform running with it. . . ."

30

Old Ways and a New Mood

Are people in Mormon country as faithful an echo of the past as I'd heard? Six months in Salt Lake City might get me started on an answer. The six days we had were barely enough to inhale an impression of contrast on a grand scale:

Hot pavement connecting the huge copper-covered state capital dome and the even more huge temples of the religion that built the state.

A hundred and seventy-five miles to the east, the Bank of Vernal building built of bricks mailed from Salt Lake City when parcel post was cheaper than rail freight.

Midsummer sun gleaming on snow fields at thirteen thousand feet on the High Uintas.

A cool, calm canyon where the Green River winds through Dinosaur National Monument.

Humming along toward Vernal one day on Route 40 through the Uintah and Ouray Indian Reservation, I was admiring some of the most gorgeous country in the world—mountains on the left shouldering their white streaks into deep blue sky, grassland on the right rolling up to the Tavaputs Plateau—when I had to wrench my eyes to the sight ahead: acres of brown-backed beasts flowing like a river, raising dust around horsemen in big hats. A cattle drive straight out of *Bonanza*, an image so fresh from a hundred years ago that it nearly hypnotized me. I stamped on the brake to avoid hitting a steer.

This was the same state from which a senator, Jake Garn, was getting ready to rocket into space aboard the shuttle *Discovery*.

I started wondering if Salt Lake was the City Without Teenagers. Couples out in public seemed to have just little kids or none.

The new mood emerged more clearly every time I called home. Now people knew what I was talking about; they had seen it on the seven o'clock news. Andrew Malcolm's article had not only been accurate and moving, it had been on page 1 of *The New York Times*. That not only legitimized the torrents of elation we had seen, it also brought out the networks and magazines who hesitate on a story until they've seen it in the *Times*. Mile after mile across America, we had seen that we were working on something larger than life, but we'd had moments of wondering if we were really seeing as much as we thought. Now Cupertino could see what Cleveland knew. The closed doors of the exclusive club had swung open.

The torch run had become the phenomenon we had imagined back in December. Salt Lake City turned out almost a million people to welcome it. The citizens who packed themselves solid for seven miles were not out there because it was comfortable; before I changed into running clothes, my new khaki Brooks Brothers suit was soaked as if I had stood in front of a hose. The temperature was 105 on the pavement. Choirs sang "God Bless America." The press truck was full. Television crews worked on specials. The patriotism that had been coming out all along, mile upon mile, in comparative privacy was now coming out in public.

Mayor Ted Wilson got ready to take the torch from Danny Searle, a nineteen-year-old Special Olympian from Payson, Utah. Danny's retarded bone growth gave his kilometer that extra quality of challenge that inspired so many of the people along the way; his mother had watched him practice for a month, jogging around the high school track at home. Wilson had been warming up the crowd at his exchange point, urging them, "When we see him, we want to start a chant that says, 'Go, Danny, go.'"

The young mayor looked so fit that I said he looked like a runner. "I do about a marathon a month," he said.

I was so surprised that I blurted, "No shit!" Then so embarrassed that I blurted, "Oh, I'm sorry. Please forget I said that. Are you a Mormon?"

The mayor laughed until the chant started down the street, "Go, Danny, go." At the end of his kilometer, Ted Wilson threw me his cap. For the rest of the relay, I would alternate it with my other prize cap from Dick Hamilton.

31

Keep an Eye on the People

We were cruising on such a high that we stayed more or less oblivious to everyday life. But once in a while a reminder would hit.

Mark was in Klamath Falls when I called down from Eugene to remind him of a good restaurant he shouldn't miss. Right off, the way he said, "How you doing?" sounded unlike him.

"What's up?" I asked. "You sound like you just lost your best friend."

"Pretty close." His voice tailed off. This was not one of his put-ons, from the sound of it. "I just found out Jeannie's going to marry somebody else." Uh oh. Jeannie and Mark had been together since college, and he was devoted to her. Behind his wisecracks, the tough frat boy was a deeply moral monogamist. As he told about her call—the man she'd met when Mark was out of sight for long stretches on the road, his pleas for some time, her sad refusal—his voice sounded close to breaking.

This was part of the payment for our adventures. Wally had said at the start that we would give up our personal lives. Probably the only reason it hadn't happened to me was that I'd had no girl to leave behind.

There isn't much to say that will really comfort a friend at a time like that. Go home for the day and try to talk it out, I urged him; the relay can live without you for a day. You're more important anyway. He'd think about it, he said. Suzanne had just called, and that helped. Kelly had been with him all day and was there now. It was good to have us to talk to.

That was one return you got on the payment: the firm friendships among partners who had gone through a lot with you and would stick with you through a lot more.

Oregon had come out of the snow and ice of January into beautiful summer greenery that made my Fourth of July job, checking the route between Eugene and Salem, a pleasant prospect.

The only rental car available was a big black Trans Am muscle car with a gold eagle painted across the hood. I tended to think, and sometimes to say, that people who buy all that unnecessary power are compensating for some insecurity. That's what I got for my self-righteousness, a chance to be seen in one of the things myself.

From Salem, Suzanne said the major entertainment that night was going to be a fireworks and demolition derby spectacular at the fairgrounds. "Oh, boy," I said. "Sounds like real fun. Explosions and car crashes, my favorite things. You sure that's all there is?"

That night we pulled the macho Trans Am into a dirt parking lot (to some admiring glances; hey, this car might not be so bad after all). Up in the pavilion at one side of the track, we found seats and started looking around.

"Uh, Steve," Suzanne said after a few minutes, "do you notice anything unusual about this crowd?"

The stands were filling with cheery, burly people you could not possibly have mistaken for residents of New York or L.A. or Kansas City. The public address system filled the air with country and western music. Everywhere we looked the men had beards or long sideburns, and the women had swept-away Farrah Fawcett hairdos. A lot of plaid Pendleton shirts, bell-bottom jeans, and out-loud good nature. People yelled hello to friends a few rows down, held coolers full of refreshment overhead, and laughed fit to bust if they had a bigger supply of six-packs than someone else. There wasn't a mean look in this crowd, and you couldn't even imagine one.

About dusk, as the lights took effect on the infield, the demolition derby started. Twenty or thirty cars milled around, roaring and spinning their tires, most of them junky enough that they weren't going to last long. Suddenly, one driver would spot an opening and cut across the field, aiming at part of the pack. The crowd would let out a shout that built to a crescendo as the attacker gained speed, and when he bashed into his target the cheers exploded for him—and for his prey if it could still move.

A mountain of a man in front of us, a huge guy with a bushy

beard and a hero-size carton of beer, leaped up at each collision, throwing his arms in the air, yelling "Yeah!" and sending geysers of brew flying over all of us. Nobody minded. The enthusiasm and the glory of destruction infected me. Soon I started rooting for a Rambler that was taking out one victim after another, having too much fun to think until much later that it's a bit frightening to get sucked into such naked displays of violence. It looked like good therapy for tensions that build up in the week. It's just football with cars. My Rambler got trashed near the end, and soon the rockets' red glare lit up the sky.

EUGENE, JULY 8

The track capital of the United States. Of all the places for the torch runners to have a terrorist scare.

The Sunday of the run through Eugene, I came in from my morning jog and found a message. Call police headquarters. It's probably just a question about where to post the most officers or some such detail, I thought.

The captain who took the call came straight to the point. "There's been a threat on the torch. Chief would like you to come down to discuss it."

Whoa. This was an advance person's nightmare. We all imagined from time to time what it must be like to live with the memory of having told Robert Kennedy to walk through the kitchen at the Ambassador Hotel. "I'll be right down. I'm on my way. Wait right there," I said, or something about that calm.

"It's just a precaution," he assured me. "There's a little radical group at the university that's usually around for events like this, and we'd like to fill you in on them." That was very decent of them. No doubt they had already called Bill Mattman and the Security team in Salem or wherever the caravan was, and were now including the only person from the relay who was on the scene.

To get into police headquarters on a Sunday, you walk down a ramp into a garage full of patrol cars. An officer there calls upstairs and you wait for someone to fetch you. The captain came down, smiled a cordial hello, and escorted me through a maze of halls. He opened a door into what I thought would be his office. Instead we walked into a room containing a dozen men and women, all a hundred percent serious, sitting around a long table. They looked settled in, and the number of cigarette butts in the ashtrays suggested they had been there a while.

The no-nonsense looks stayed on as the captain introduced me around to representatives of what sounded like every facet of police work in a big city—detectives, traffic, community relations, campus security, the intelligence division, the chief. Who'd have thought a city of 106,000 in the middle of timber land even had an intelligence division? This had the look of more than a little chat with the chief.

One of the women handed me a folder identical to the folders in front of the other people around the table and said with deliberate force, "Here is information on some of the potential terrorists." Inside were about twenty photocopied pages stapled together. The top sheet carried a photograph of what was apparently a hippie kid walking across an open courtyard somewhere, taken from above by someone in a nearby building. It looked like one of those pictures from a bank security camera. A second photograph on the same page was a mug shot of the boy facing the camera. Underneath were typed his name, description, last known address, arrest record, probable position in the group, and comments on his activities.

"We'll go through the dossiers one by one," the woman said crisply. The arrest records mentioned crimes like shoplifting, vagrancy, disturbing the peace, failure to disperse, resisting arrest. Toward the bottom, on several pages about people she described as the ringleaders, they included some firearms possessions. That spooked me.

The chief spoke calmly. "What we have here, basically, is a group that's never done anything major or serious. But we did get a call from one of them—or someone claiming he was one of them— saying they plan to do something to the torch. We've called the state police to convoy the caravan in, and I'm putting every available officer on the scene."

There was nothing for me to do about the threat. This part of their meeting was a briefing for me. It was nice of them to bring me in on it and I felt reassured by their thoroughness, though shocked by the extremes of surveillance on college students in a small, out-of-the-way city. On the one hand the seriousness here was reassuring. On the other, it made me nervous—this was being treated as if a Libyan hit squad were on the way—and the chief must have noticed. He cracked a grin, the first time in the meeting anyone had taken off his game face.

"Actually, I'm more concerned about what the crowd will do to these guys than I am about anything else."

I didn't understand.

"These guys are nothing new to events here in Eugene, and the people in this town don't like 'em. This town is . . ." He paused and I expected the next word to be something like redneck. ". . . patriotic. Don't you worry. If anything happens, somebody in the crowd'll more than likely take care of them."

Back at the Hilton, Joe Donohue from Burson Marsteller had arrived. We tried to settle down by watching a Cubs-Giants game on television. Then there was little to do but re-check arrangements and hold the nervousness at bay by enjoying the festivities outside. Celebrations that several months before we'd had to plan were now being handled in town after town by people along the route: Eugene put on a day-long festival leading up to the seven o'clock arrival of the torch, with a local disk jockey on a public address system giving bulletins on its progress and announcing bands and local events. By five, a thousand or so people had gathered around the Hilton and I had to get out and walk around.

On the edge of the crowd were a couple of people from the radical group. I recognized them from their pictures. Not that they were trying to hide: They held up a yellow banner proclaiming that the Olympics were Ronald Reagan's training camp for war. One was a young woman who couldn't have been more than nineteen or twenty, with a sweet, innocent, girl-next-door face: big brown eyes, pug nose, freckles, and long dark hair. Her loose-fitting blouse, long print skirt, and sandals were holdovers from a 1960s anti-war demonstration. She smiled and handed me a little newspaper they had put together to explain that the Olympics were part of the war machine, and I stayed to find out what she had to say.

One item had Los Angeles going to such lengths to clear the way for the Olympic invasion that its police storm troopers had even cleared break dancers off the streets of Westwood and locked them up. "You know," I said, "I live a mile from there, and the Olympics had nothing to do with the break dancers. It was the store owners who wanted them off the sidewalks in front of their shops. Customers couldn't get past the crowds watching the dancers."

"Oh, yeah, well . . ." The girl's smile faltered. "Sure, store owners. Like, of course they support the status quo; it's the same thing." If that was all she had to say, this protest didn't show much focus. Who could tell what the people behind her might do?

As if things weren't tense enough, lightning stopped the run for a couple of hours outside Corvallis. The crowd didn't mind, and the disk jockey kept things rolling with reports from "Our eye-in-the-sky helicopter above the torch." The Eugene torch bearers waited patiently in their shorts and tank tops. One of them, Travis Kizer, was a ten-year-old jock who had talked me into running the 5K Butte-to-Butte race with him the day before, and we whiled away some time chatting about that. Travis played it eleven-year-old cool, suppressing his excitement. I played it twenty-three-year-old cool, suppressing my anxiety. Finally, around half past eight, the walky-talky crackled and I heard Suzanne's peppy "Barr, Lipps."

"Suzanne," I said into the transmitter, "how's Security?"

"Got it covered," she said, cool as could be.

The torch came into view. The crowd started yelling its loudest. The flags got up and waved. The runner approached. Travis was still trying to act cool, but his face started letting cracks of excitement through. He took the flame. Joe and I jumped on the flatbed and started scanning the crowd like Secret Service men. Security was stacked heavier than we had ever seen it: Eight or ten blue-shorted, white-shirted agents from Bill Mattman's crew, plus four motorcycle cops, along with a heavy sprinkling of uniforms through the crowd. Three blocks into Travis's run we started to relax.

Then, out of the crowd popped an apparition. A skeleton—rather, a small person in a head-to-toe black body stocking with bones painted on—appeared on the street, carrying a mock torch. It got abreast of Travis and ran along. Security tensed. But people were always running along with the torch, and even if this one looked bizarre it was not an out and out attack, yet. The skeleton ran for about ten steps. Security men began to converge on her or him.

Then a huge arm jutted out from the crowd, a Paul Bunyan arm like a steel beam, directly in front of the skeleton at chest level. The skeleton hit the arm at full speed. Its head stopped instantly and its feet snapped forward. While the skeleton was horizontal in midair, the arm hauled her, or him, into the swarm of people on the sidewalk. The last I saw of the skeleton was two feet disappearing into the crowd, and the fake torch flying end over end before it, too, was swallowed.

By nine the next morning we had been on Route 58 two hours and a cadre runner had the torch as the caravan purred up the foothills of the Cascades. The lead Pioneer, entertaining the passengers in the convertible with a travelogue, remarked that *Animal House* had been filmed around the University of Oregon. He pointed to a little bar on the right. "That's the famous Dexter Lake Club." Where the frat boys blunder in with their dates and end up having to run for their lives; I'd thought every time I saw the movie they were saying "Death Delay Club." The cadre runner carrying the torch was close enough to hear in the silence of the forest road. He stopped in his tracks and crowed the frat boys' famous last (almost) words, "Wait till Otis sees us, he *loves* us." We all cracked up.

The runners weren't laughing a couple of hours later as we climbed more than a mile from Eugene's 422-foot elevation to 5,626 feet at Willamette Summit. Driving this road in January, I had seen little but banks of snow. Now the air temperature was in the eighties and the sky was clear, the hills around us were lush and green, the scent of pine resin mixed with the smell of hot blacktop. We were in a completely beautiful stretch of country.

Just after Kansas City, I had finally stepped over the line from watching the AT&T cadre runners to joining them. By now, even I was up to fifteen miles a day, in two- and three-mile intervals. Among the cadre people who ran for hours every day, I studied who was slowest; from the list of runners who had paid for their kilometers, I picked out those who looked as if they might be slow; and I ran with them. There was a huge difference between running three-fifths of a mile on the flat with thousands of people cheering you on and running pretty much alone for four miles and

245

more, up hills that never seem to stop. Those cadre runners were really something.

Months before, taking the climb into account, we had scheduled this day to end at seven instead of eleven. The prospect of what amounted to an evening off, combined with the turn we had made toward the finish line in California, contributed to a festive atmosphere in the caravan as it pulled in at Crescent Lake. The resort area there has a couple of lodges, a restaurant, a general store, boats to rent and a ramp to launch them. We figured the caravan people would outnumber the regular residents there by at least four to one.

We pulled in to a crowd of at least six hundred people. I don't know where they came from. Doubtless, some were vacationers, and others seemed to have come down from the mountains. Just over a few more hills was the Home Made Soup restaurant from January; some of the soup guys might even be here. Shaking hands, patting backs, asking for autographs, they gave us another taste of undeserved celebrity. Dick Boehner, one of the cadre relay managers, had said it somewhere back in Missouri: "They're making heroes out of everyday people. But out here on the road, with the crowds cheering, it's hard to separate the torch bearer from the torch." And it didn't stop at torch bearers. As on our first day at the New York–New Jersey line, anyone in running clothes was surrounded.

Several times I tried explaining to the kids swarming me, "Look, I'm nobody. I'm not a runner. I'm not a celebrity." That didn't faze them. So, along with everyone else, I started signing. I still felt like a fraud, and I still knew it would have been worse not to give an autograph than to go ahead and play the part. Innocent, modest people wanted a piece of the moment's history. They seemed starved for heroes. Maybe they were giving us a lesson, in miniature, of what had been happening across all of America.

We signed fishing licenses, scraps of paper, hats—one kid wanted me to sign his arm. Looking over at one of the Pioneers, I noticed he was adding where he was from, so I started writing greetings.

"Thank you for showing us your part of the country. Steve Barr, Los Angeles," I wrote over and over. We wanted to leave behind something to keep the connection alive.

32

Cynics Don't Cry

The room had a big round bed on a platform, a red velvet spread, a mirror on the ceiling, even a curtain you could pull around it to close yourself in—somebody's idea of romance, I guess, that turned out seeming whorish.

Reno was going to be a simple job and Joyce Tate hadn't set up any meetings for that evening, so I called my mom in California. She loves to gamble. We could spend some time together if she and Pete, my stepfather, would come up for a day or two. They did come—only she put off one dinner invitation after another to spend time in the casinos. As I realized I was barely seeing them, I got more and more upset. We argued several times. On the morning of the third day, mom and I tried to have breakfast together and started squabbling instead, and I headed for the door.

"Forget it, Mom, to hell with it! I'll call you someday and maybe we can talk, okay?"

I had my hand on the doorknob when the game show on the television set in the corner cut away to a shot of Walter Mondale in Minnesota. Standing next to him was Geraldine Ferraro. That could mean only one thing. They were about to announce that she was going to be the first woman ever nominated by a major political party to run for vice president.

My mother and I turned, stopped, and sat down. Geraldine Ferraro standing there altered history at that moment, no matter how the election would turn out. I found myself thinking about some of the ways that people all over America had altered me in this half year.

We hadn't been outcasts when I was a child, but we were different. A child thinks he's got all the trouble, but part of growing

247

up was realizing how hard it had been for my mom. She was divorced, a single parent, a woman who worked all the time. She had a humble job. We would often be the people who weren't invited to the party. Yet she kept hanging in there. Watching how little credit she got for all she did, noticing the "respectable" people in town looking down their noses at her, had disenchanted me pretty early. A lot of our neighbors seemed less than wide open to the American Dream they liked to think they were part of. As we listened to a woman who could be vice president, the picture blurred and I found myself weeping, with my mom weeping beside me. She had come a long way, after all.

As the torch went through Reno, I skipped ahead a few hours to firm up some arrangements in Carson City, then headed for a sign that said ADELE'S RESTAURANT AND BAR for a quick lunch. The place had at least fifty people inside, slaking their thirst and waiting for the torch to arrive. I had left the Olympic jacket in the car, hoping for an anonymous burger in peace and quiet, but when the waitress said, "We don't see you in here much; where you from?" I said "Los Angeles," one thing led to another, and soon it came out. Heads turned, people nudged each other, they tried not to stare and gave me plenty of room to chew my food without butting in with conversation. It's a strange feeling to know you're being talked about and not know whether to nod or wave or pretend you're oblivious.

When I asked for the check, the waitress said, "It's been taken care of. You've got a room full of friends here." I looked around at my benefactors, and fifty people raised their glasses in a salute. I stood up to say thanks. Before I could get any sort of maudlin speech started, the bartender called out, "We got something else for you," and tossed a rolled-up handful of cloth. Unrolled, it was a T-shirt—maroon, with "Adele's Restaurant & Bar" in yellow print across the front.

"Thank you." That was my speech. "Thank you."

33

Comebacks

An endless carpet of little roofs baking under the sun; a speck of runway getting bigger and bigger; Los Angeles. We were almost home. The torch was finally in California, heading this way. "It's almost over," I caught myself thinking.

First, though, we had a few days to get a stretch along the Pacific Coast Highway ready, then several more with the runners before it all ended in Southern California.

Driving north from Santa Barbara to San Luis Obispo, checking the route and listening to the Democratic convention on the radio, I reached Pismo Beach just as Gary Hart was about to speak. Gotta see him. I swerved into the parking lot of the first hotel by the road and ran in. The place looked bare of guests, but a clerk had control of the desk.

"Quick!" I asked her. "Is there a television set in the bar?"

"We have no bar," she said. There was no sign of television in the lobby either.

"Then I'd like to rent a room, any room."

"How long will you be staying?"

"An hour."

She raised her head and fixed me with a turtle glare. "We don't do that sort of thing," she said.

"No, no, I just want to watch a speech on television. No funny business."

"No. We don't do that sort of thing."

Whatever she imagined my sort of thing was, they didn't do it. I listened to Hart on the car radio.

249

Back in Ohio one day, Jim Suennen had looked back at Kate
Washburn from the lead car and said, "Who's going to tell her?
She's not going to make it."

Kate, as one of the three AT&T relay managers along with Dick
Boehner and Lou Putnam, was an experienced runner. That day
outside Sandusky, though, her face was gray and she was faltering
like a marathon burnout. Stress fractures in both legs were about
to knock her off the road. Poor Kate. Riding the rest of the way
while her teammates did what she had trained for was a wretched
fate.

Then in Albuquerque, she showed up riding alongside on a
snazzy ten-speed bike.

"Yo, Kate," I'd yelled. "Where'd you get that?"

She called back, "A great guy near Denver—heard about my legs
and gave it to me. Said he hoped it would help me stay on the
road."

We had all been on the road to the point of exhaustion. Nearly
nine thousand miles of running-shoe soles slapping pavement
came close to doing in other cadre runners besides Kate. Like Kate,
none complained, none quit. Those people were just plain inspiring. And the near hysteria that had become constant around
the torch kept us drawing on reserves most of us hadn't known
we had.

Thanks to the bike, Kate had recovered enough to run again. Despite her injuries, she was definitely not one of the slow ones. Running beside Kate was such a pleasure, though, that I tried as hard as
I could to keep up with her. Near Refugio Beach on the way to
Santa Barbara, we were padding along in the dark on a quiet stretch
where we could do a little talking. I was puffing along, doing my
best to match Kate's pace. We had our heads down to check where
our feet were going.

At first I didn't notice the limousine that passed us on the left
and stopped. A few yards farther on, I did see a pair of bare feet, and
above them a pair of shorts and a tank top. I looked up to say,
"Careful, there, watch your feet"—and who was it, waving the little American flag that so many people brought to the torch route
and looking happy, but John Travolta.

Seeing a movie star was a sure sign that we were almost to L.A.

We passed him with a wave and a smile, as if we were old buddies. Soon the limo passed us again, and soon again there was Travolta, waving and beaming a smile that made him look like a little boy. And again, and again. About four times we passed him being a torch groupie, as giddy and as taken with the spirit of the thing as all those other people nobody ever heard of.

The Los Angeles we had left at the beginning of the year was a place that didn't really want the Olympics, where assemblymen said it would be too expensive, too much trouble, and nobody except a few early birds gave a damn.

We had been on the road as the long, long fuse of people's love for each other and our country caught fire from the torch. We had seen it set off an explosion of feelings people had bottled up— through the establishment East, into the reborn South, across the Midwest heartland and the sunburned desert states, down the flourishing Pacific rim. People who must have been longing to say, "This is the way I always wanted it to be," let go with all that yearning. They just plain wanted so much to tell each other that we're doing okay, it burst out on city streets and town squares and country roads, everywhere. From the road, we had not seen the fuse burning in California. As we approached Los Angeles, I was shocked.

People came out and went delirious. We plunged into wave after wave of people so excited that they could not stand still. The crowds grew so thick that the runner often couldn't push through until a wedge of security and advance people and a vehicle cleared a path. Almost every one of Bill Mattman's ex–Secret Service men had Ace bandages wrapped around his legs to ease the soreness from jumping on and off the vehicles.

The torch was going to enter Los Angeles through Santa Monica. At the top of the California Grade that connects the Pacific Coast Highway to Ocean Boulevard, thousands of onlookers pressed up to a platform built for celebrities—assorted mayors, movie stars, and politicos. Another platform for the press was crowded with television cameras, movie cameras, and long lenses from all over the world. You'd have thought this was a presidential appearance. At ground level, we waited for O.J. Simpson, who had been a world-class sprinter at USC before making the pro football Hall of Fame, to bring the torch up the grade.

O.J. put on a burst of speed up the grade and, exactly on time, lighted the torch of Michael Bailey, a seven-year-old with cerebral palsy. Michael ran with the aid of a wheeled carriage—and an assist from the great athlete, who ran along for an extra kilometer when he saw that Michael was having trouble holding the torch.

Michael and O.J. started their run together three blocks from an apartment I had left a lifetime, seven months, before.

OCEANSIDE, JULY 21

Dan Triest was already down the coast, setting up the last operation we would run together. Wally had given us the assignment with a merry laugh for me: "Gee, I'm sorry, but that's as close as I can get you to your old AT&T friend in San Diego." By now, those first-day troubles seemed like someone else's story. I was in bliss.

Checking into the hotel in Oceanside, I realized I hadn't called my mom since Reno. When she said hello, her usual upbeat tone wasn't there. She sounded weak.

"Where have you been?" she asked. "We've been trying to get in touch with you since yesterday."

"Mom, has something happened?"

"Mike was in an accident yesterday afternoon, a really bad one." Her voice wavered. "On his motorbike. A truck ran a red light and hit him and cut his foot almost off. It happened in front of John Muir Hospital, thank God. If they hadn't gotten him in there so fast, he'd have bled to death."

"But he didn't? He's gonna be all right?" It was impossible to think of my brother not being alive.

"He's alive. I don't know if he knows what happened to him yet. He looks awful, Steven. Oh . . ."

"I'll be there this afternoon. Are *you* okay? I'll meet you at the hospital."

"What about the torch run?" she asked. "What about your job?"

"I'll get the next plane out. You take care of yourself and we'll get together at the hospital, okay?"

I grabbed my unopened bag, slammed the door, and went looking for Dan. He was still in his room.

"Oh, man," he said. "Take off. I'll handle everything." Within minutes he had my notes and list of runners and contacts. I called for a plane reservation. I was on the freeway to the San Diego airport, still in my running clothes.

My younger brother and I had never been close. We were two years apart, opposites in almost every way. Growing up, I was a jock, he was a head. I was student body president, he dropped out. I went to college, he joined the navy. I drove big, safe cruisers like Volvos, he tore around on motorcycles. I took on a rumpled Joe College look, he flaunted the hoody look of the kid with the bugle back in New Jersey.

He wasn't what I wanted and I wasn't what he wanted. Or so we might have thought until now. Here I was, jittering my leg and clenching the arm rest, surprised at myself for the reflex that put me straight aboard a PSA flight to him without a flicker of hesitation or complaint. Until then, my love for him had not been tested.

From the San Francisco airport I drove like crazy up the east shore of the bay and inland to John Muir Hospital, a couple of blocks from the house in Walnut Creek where my folks now lived; paced around an elevator as it rose slowly to the fourth floor; hurried down the corridor to Mike's room. Mom was there, and the rest of the room was filled with Mike's biker friends. A talk show was gabbing away on the television screen. Nobody in the room was saying much.

Mike lay on the bed. His eyes were half open and he was rolling his head back and forth, fading in and out, obviously full of pain killers. The covers bulged over something big on his left leg. I circled around and leaned over the right side of the bed.

"They operated for five hours to re-attach his foot," Mom said.

Mike kept moving his head from side to side on the pillow. There were tear stains in the corners of both eyes. He mumbled as if he were having a nightmare. I couldn't think of anything to do but stand there, speechless. He didn't give any sign of noticing who was in the room.

His head swung to the right and stopped. He murmured, "What a cool hat."

I took it off to see which hat. It was Dick Hamilton's. Mike loves to wear baseball caps. What he was saying was, "I want that hat." So he was okay enough to sense that I was a soft touch. I loved that hat. All the way across the country it had been a precious symbol of closeness with a hard-working Pioneer. I didn't want to give it up. And Mike knew there was no way in hell I'd say no to him on his bed of pain. I slipped a hand under the back of his neck to raise him a bit and put the hat on his head. He grinned.

Visiting hours ended and the bikers started leaving. The nurse let Mom and me stay on for a while. Nobody had turned the television set off, and in a network news break between prime-time shows, Connie Chung's voice drew our attention to the screen: "After a nine-thousand mile journey across the United States, the Olympic flame finally made it to Los Angeles today." There on the screen was O.J. Simpson running, there was the crowd, there was a big public event like the ones you see on television every night, "real" but not really distinguishable from the scripted dramas it had interrupted, miles and miles away from us. A world away.

The picture on the screen had been my whole world that morning. In another world, my brother had almost died and now had a fifty-fifty chance, at best, of keeping his leg. When things are going great, you can lose perspective on everything else, including how lucky you are.

I wondered: Why am I so lucky? As we had hugged hello a few hours before, Mom had mentioned how tan and healthy I looked, and how happy I seemed to be with my work. On the flight back, I pulled out my Walkman and let a Talking Heads song haunt me:

> You may find yourself
> Living in a shotgun shack.
> You may find yourself
> In another part of the world.
> You may find yourself
> Behind the wheel of a large automobile.
> You may find yourself
> In a beautiful house
> With a beautiful wife.
> You may ask yourself,
> How did I get here?

34

Last Legs

My first and only time to see the torch as a spectator. The people were lined up five deep by the side of the road, yelling and singing encouragement. The runner approached, and for a few seconds you could see him holding up the torch. Then as fast as a man runs, he was gone. It was over. I caught myself thinking, "That's it? That's all there is?" All the emotion must be coming from something bigger than the torch itself.

CAMP PENDLETON, JULY 27

Marines in green battle fatigues stood by the road approaching their base and applauded the torch bearer. When Sgt. Maj. Dominic Irrera carried the flame through the camp, a hundred of his fellow Marines in shorts and T-shirts double-timed behind him, chanting and carrying their banner. They looked great. As far as I had heard, nobody fretted over this escort the way we had over the Marines in Louisville.

REDONDO BEACH, JULY 27

Almost in Los Angeles again. The five days since we first hit L.A. have all run together. I've run twenty miles a day, at least. Not all at once—five miles here, three miles there. The crowds keep us charged up. If you took a thousand slightly crazed people and got them all to scream as loud as they can—that's something like the sound we hear from seven in the morning when the torch starts until one or two the next morning when it stops. It's a beach party all the way now—temperatures of eight-five to a hundred degrees, sunny, half the people in bikinis, drinking beer and God knows what else.

The crowds surge into the street from both sides, trying to get a peek. We put three or four advance and security people a few hundred yards ahead of the torch runner. They keep asking the crowds to move back to the curbs, and sometimes push them back to make room for the caravan so it can stay on time. When you're on the point ahead of the runner, a lot of the time all you can see in front of you is a sea of bodies.

About one in the afternoon, the caravan is just entering Pacific Coast Highway in Redondo Beach. My LAOOC STAFF shirt has soaked up so much sweat that it's dripping from the bottom. We've just come out of the Palos Verdes hills and I'm almost spent. Just about every joint and muscle screams out to me to stop. I think of Kate Washburn. . . . But we're in the last full day of the relay and I keep pushing. The torch is due at the Coliseum tomorrow. Like an addict who doesn't know when to stop, I can't push away from this thing. My ankles burn with pain. My knees buckle every so often from the constant pounding on the hot pavement. Blisters have turned the soles of my feet into hamburger, raw but fairly numb. I'm running bowlegged. The insides of my thighs are scarlet from miles and miles of rubbing together, and the insides of the ankles are raw from the nicks they get every so often from the tread of my own shoes. And I'm running in a stoop, to lessen the pain in my lower back. Usually when I run I have the long stride of anyone six feet, two inches tall, but this day I'm taking short, energy-consuming, hunched-over steps. I must be such a sight, I can't understand why there aren't waves of laughter as I come along. From somewhere I keep dredging up a voice—"Move back, please! Let the runner through! Back! Back!"

Just as we parallel the ocean, I hear a familiar voice screaming above the crowd noise: "Steve!" I turn to my right and spot a good friend from UCSB, Zach Nadel. Like almost all the people along here, Zach is in beach attire. Wearing nothing but shorts, he jumps out of the crowd and starts running alongside. I reach out to shake my old buddy's hand, and cringe in pain. My hand is reddish-purple from high-fiving people along the curb. Seeing Zach takes my mind off the full-body pain. He is always in shape and is one of those guys who lets you know if you've put on a few pounds.

"You look great, man," he yells.

Actually, I feel I'm going to collapse. "Thanks," I say in a hoarse whisper, and he disappears back into the crowd.

A couple of miles later I'm still hobbling along with my mind cut off from my body's pleas for help. My eyes are lost in the miles of sunburned skin and bikinis and flags and beer cans of the immense party along the route.

Somewhere in there, I start to slow. Black spots start blotching the California dream. My jog slips to a walk. From the corner of one eye, I see a van from the caravan with its sliding door open. If I miss, I'll be left behind, probably on my face in the street. I lunge for it. A bump, a scrape of sweaty back on the edge of the opening, and I'm in.

I land at the feet of Joel Fishman, the Torch Foundation chairman. Joel gives me a concerned look, then dips a towel into a cooler full of sodas and ice cubes and drapes it over my head. I collapse in the back of the van. An hour later I can see clearly again; on the other hand, my head is pounding and the pain through the rest of me is getting sharper as the adrenaline drains off.

"We're almost at the office," Joel says. "You want to get out?"

I sit up in time to see we're close to the Olympic Committee on Washington and Venice. "Yes, thanks," I croak. This is my last chance to get photographed for my credential.

Our contracts expire on July 28, so the torch rats have no job after tomorrow—and for a while it seemed we'd have no tickets to the Olympic Games, either. Wally has pulled some strings and got us into the opening ceremony and all events. To get through security, though, we need proper credentials, including identification badges with our photographs.

The exchange point nearest the old helicopter factory on Washington is surrounded by thousands of LAOOC employees and volunteers who have been working for months, even years, and now have their one chance to taste this spectacle. I hobble through them. The building is cool, and the people still inside have neatly combed hair and neatly buttoned uniforms. My hair is soaked with sweat and sticking up all over the place, and I have the wet towel from Joel Fishman tied around my neck. Security gives me a startled look, passes me, and I get my picture taken.

I walk through the nearly deserted headquarters the same way I did on the way to Wally's office eight months before. The Torch Relay office is empty. I hope someone shows up so I can catch a ride back to the Sheraton. In a corner I spot a box of the socks that Levi Strauss gave us and the runners. I sit down to get a fresh pair. My gray running shoes come off, and inside them my socks are bright red with blood. I pull on a new white pair, drop the bloody veterans in a wastebasket, and cover them with scrap paper.

Just then Peggy Hicks, one of the office people who has been keeping our schedules through thick and thin all year, walks in. "Going to the party at the Sheraton?" she asks.

It was a nice party. My plan was to stop by, say hi to Wally, then shower off and catch up with the relay for its last night. There were a lot of Burson Marsteller people to say hello to. Then I spotted Wally sitting on a couch and went over to sit next to him. Somebody handed me a beer. I began to notice I couldn't move. Every muscle and bone in my body seemed to join in the general ache. Even my hair hurt. It took real effort to lift my arm and take a sip.

Billy Rappaport, the cameraman who had shot torch footage across the country, turned on a television set. ABC's preview of the Olympics had started to roll. Jim McKay was saying,

The picture is live, the moment is now, 6:00 P.M. on a summer Friday evening in Los Angeles, but a Friday like none other in the history of Southern California, because the picture is of the Olympic torch being carried through the streets on West Pico Boulevard. . . . Tomorrow a runner, yet to be named, will climb the final steps in the Memorial Coliseum and touch off the flame that will burn throughout the Games. But right now, this moment, this is a chance for many thousands who won't be at the opening ceremony to see the torch outshining the rays of the early evening sun. . . . It started in controversy . . . but the relay will end tomorrow as a moving, dramatic story, one that has involved great athletes and handicapped people, the strong, fleet, and handsome, the lame and the blind. In the story of the flame, there is a story of America in the year 1984.

Between profiles of Olympic athletes and other sections of the preview, ABC showed flashes of the torch coming across the country: Muhammad Ali in Louisville. Ansel Stubbs in Kansas City. West Point, Philadelphia, Knoxville, Memphis, Salt Lake City . . . I stared at the screen, spellbound. So did Wally. Around us people were talking, joking, and laughing. We sat there together. A bomb could have gone off and we wouldn't have moved.

I took a breath. We had come so far and seen so much, and now I'd had my fill.

35

Home

I thought I'd had my fill. But I hadn't counted on what was waiting for us.

The grand opening ceremonies at the Coliseum were scheduled for four o'clock. Wally gathered his torch rats at Olympic Committee headquarters a couple of hours before. He had arranged for some vans to take us all together to the Coliseum, where, even though the place had long been sold out, he had somehow cleared a block of seats for us. Some of us dragged ourselves in so exhausted that we could hardly talk, but excitement soon replaced fatigue. This was the first time we had all been together since the countdown meeting in April. The spirit of reunion pumped us up to something close to delirium.

We got out of the vans in the Coliseum parking lot and walked toward the gate. Pushed our way to the gate is more like it; thousands and thousands of people were streaming toward the opening, the lucky ones who had tickets to the ceremonies all funneling into the stadium under a bright sun and a light blue sky. David Wolper, the television producer in charge of the day's show, couldn't have ordered better weather.

The seats Wally had saved for us were about where the thirty-yard line would be in football season, midway up in the stands. Everywhere you looked, there was a feast of colors—pastel blues, oranges, lavenders, the whole Olympic rainbow; the brilliant green grass of the infield; a huge oval of shirts and pants and hats of every hue, more than ninety-two thousand faces of every human color. The number of people surrounding that playing field was three times the population of the town I grew up in.

To our left, the peristyle end of the Coliseum showed the five interlocked rings of the Olympic symbol, and atop the rim, the big torch that had been there since the Summer Games of 1932. It just stood there, quiet. The flame that would bring it to life was on its way.

"Ladies and gentlemen," a voice boomed out, "welcome to the Games of the Twenty-third Olympiad."

Shiny banners fluttered from the silver trumpets that sounded a fanfare. Marchers stepped smartly across the bright green grass, forming themselves into the Olympic rings, then into the word, "Welcome." A man flew in like someone from the next century, with a jet pack strapped to his back. White and gold balloons soared like wishes into the blue sky, and even up there, "Welcome" appeared in smoke. The marching bands kept forming and re-forming designs on the field. Covered wagons appeared; the history of the nation unrolled in a "Music of America" production. "Five, four, three, two, one," the announcer counted down, and all ninety-some thousand of us held up colored cards; across the field in the opposite stands we could see that we were making the flags of a hundred and forty nations—lots of blues and reds and greens and golds, dazzling and big, big in the sunshine. Eighty-four white baby grand pianos rolled out, and the peristyle end was filled with pianists wearing blue, for the George Gershwin "Rhapsody in Blue" that they played.

Spectacle followed spectacle for what seemed like hours, and through it all the fifteen of us simply couldn't make ourselves stay in our seats. The people behind us began to show increasing signs of irritation. They had paid—who knows? hundreds of dollars, probably—to come and enjoy themselves, and now a bunch of rowdies was blocking their view. Once in a while, the fatigue almost felled me. If I had allowed myself to close one eye, I'd have gone down. But elation kept us flying, yelling down the line to each other.

"Hey, David! How ya holdin' up?"

"Yo! Mark! Nice of you to get dressed up!" Mark had come in a T-shirt, the one clean garment he had left.

"Suzanne! Suzanne, can you believe this? We're here! This is *it*!"

We kept jumping up, running down the row to trade seats with friends, then jumping up again to climb over more people. This was our reunion. Our Christmas morning. Birthday party. Graduation. Every big day in one, and we couldn't get enough of each other as the festivities all around us rolled toward the one thing we had all come to see. We knew what we were waiting for: the parade of the athletes, country by country with their flags, and finally, the flame.

Who was the final torch bearer going to be? For seven months we had known everything in advance about the torch, but we didn't know this. Rumors had flown. It was going to be Nadia Comaneci, the darling of the Montreal Olympics. No, it would be a child, for the future. Yes, it should be a child. . . . We had all speculated, on and on. Now we'd see.

Our carrying on got to be too much for the suffering people behind us. They were too polite to complain, or just too surprised by all our commotion, but they were getting more and more aggravated, sighing heavily, clearing their throats, leaning around and craning their heads in exaggerated ways to see past us. At last a voice behind my end of the line burst out, "Come on, come on, will you?"

Mark and I turned. The face of the man who spoke was clouded, dark, stern, but the man was looking away, as if he didn't want an argument but had to do something to keep his afternoon from being spoiled.

"I'm really sorry," Mark said. "We'll try to hold it down. Please excuse us for getting carried away."

Now the man was looking at him.

"I know we're out of line," Mark said, "but most of us haven't seen each other for several months. We've been on the road for the last half year, helping the torch relay across the country, and we're pretty excited to be here."

"You *did*?" the man said. "The Olympic torch?" His scolding look was gone. "I saw it in Toledo!"

A woman near him overheard. She exclaimed, "I saw it in St. Louis!" People who had been looking on apprehensively a few seconds before clustered toward us, saying, "Hello, hello," and calling out the names of their home towns. Our line turned to them in a flurry of greetings, smiles, shy touches on the shoulder, even some formal handshakes, joining their party. From the corner of my eye, I saw one of the sternest-looking men walk off, and thought the reconciliation had come too late; he was probably getting Security to come and throw us out. Then he came back, balancing two full trays of beers.

"Here," he said as his neighbors helped pass the drink cartons down the line. "Have a drink on us. Well done."

The parade of athletes started from the tunnel at the end opposite the peristyle. Led by two high-stepping standard bearers, the Greeks came first in their traditional place of honor, behind their blue-and-white flag. Country by country, with fanfares and a steady, building roll of ceremonial music, the flags fluttered out of the dark tunnel and the athletes walked with their heads up, proud and glowing in the late-day sun. The People's Republic of China got a long, loud greeting. Exotic costumes swirled around the track: Morocco, Nigeria . . . Here came Romania. The crowd got on tiptoes to applaud the little country that had braved the Soviet-bloc boycott to join the Games.

Our row quieted down. In our seats now, too tired to stand any more, we talked among ourselves, turning our eyes every few minutes to the parade streaming by. We couldn't help glancing again and again at the tunnel from which the athletes were emerging; that is where we assumed the torch would appear. As the light softened towards evening, we knew the torch was almost there.

The last team to appear was the United States. They bounced out of the tunnel, carrying the little American flags we had seen every day for nine thousand miles, giving them a friendly little wave at every proud, bouncy step around the track. With everyone else in the stands, we came to our feet again, surrounded now by the stars and stripes. Everyone in the place seemed to have produced a flag.

The athletes filled the infield, and dignitaries made speeches. When Peter Ueberroth mentioned the torch relay, applause broke out. Of the millions of people who had stood along roadsides to cheer the runners, he said, "These Americans had two messages to give to the world. The first was an enormous rekindling of pride in our own country, the United States of America. And more important, these millions and millions and millions of people turned out along the way to express a friendship and a love and a caring for all nations of the world."

Then, a hush, like the hush of some of the crowds in the months before, along country roads in the South, on the plains—not silence, but a quiet buzz from almost a hundred thousand people who felt that something was about to happen. A thought floated into my mind: I bet at least half the people in the stands here saw the torch as it passed through their towns.

The anticipation stretched so taut that it almost cracked. I felt myself tremble. A flock of homing pigeons, released in the tunnel, wheeled out, turned, then turned again and headed for the sky.

In the dark of the tunnel, a little flame appeared. All fifteen of us leaped to our feet. A second or two later, we saw the person carrying it. A black woman—Gina Hemphill!—with a smile we could see all the way across the Coliseum. Jesse Owens's granddaughter held the familiar torch high and smiled and smiled, and the scene we had been part of so many times in the last few months repeated itself, one last time. Like people on roadsides everywhere, some of the finest athletes in the world crowded toward the torch. They reached for the runner, to pat her, to be part of the moment, to send her along with a touch. Many had little cameras, and leaned out to get an angle for a picture. Several times Hemphill had to stop until the crush of athletes made way for her.

A huge burst of cheering, from the stands and from the athletes in the infield, had greeted her when she first appeared. Applause rolled around the track with her as she ran her lap. But there was more than just cheering and applause. The sound had an undertone you almost never hear in a stadium—a murmur, a kind of throaty hum, that followed the flame. The moment was so big, so profound, that simple cheers were not enough. Applause was not enough. You had to turn to the person next to you and beam, and nod, and trade looks. You overflowed.

Suddenly, there was another runner beside Gina Hemphill. She handed the torch to him. His easy stride said he was an athlete. We saw who it was, and knew he was the final runner. Rafer Johnson, the hero of the decathlon at Rome in 1960. He had started the flame on its way on a rainy May day in New York, and he was here to take it to its new home.

He ran to the permanent steps, carpeted in Los Angeles Olympics pastels, that led to the arch supporting the five linked rings. Above them, the great torch of the Coliseum gleamed copper in the setting sun. A rising thrill of music built the suspense until once again it seemed so taut it might crack. How was he going to

264

get the flame to the top? The big cauldron on the Coliseum rim was way beyond anyone's reach. As his foot touched the bottom step, a monolith from science fiction began appearing at the top, smoothly, like magic: A long, slender ramp of steps, projecting hydraulically before him all the way to the peak of the arch, high and steep, with no guard rails—the final challenge before the flame got to where it had been journeying all these days and nights.

At last, it was all too much. All around, people were cheering, but there were fifteen of us who could not speak. We could only hold one another: A row of exhausted torch rats, clutching each other's hands, some clinging with an arm around the next person's waist, staring upward, with tears streaming down our faces. We couldn't hold it in any more. The first tears turned to sobs. I couldn't catch my breath. I just stood and held the person who was holding me, and we couldn't stop hugging, crying, blinking away the tears as we tried to see the man working his way upward with his arm held high. That was *us* in his hand.

Rafer Johnson reached the top. He stood more than a hundred feet above the ground. He turned and presented the torch to the people watching him, first to his right, then his left, then the center. The crowd sent him a roar of emotion. He reached to his full arm's length overhead, to touch his flame to a stem below the five rings. It leaped upward, curled around in rings of fire, and then, for an instant, it seemed to disappear.

You could hear (or imagine) a gasp of dismay from the city of people below. I really did stop breathing. Then the flame was back, bigger than we had ever seen it before, floating clear and calm from the torch above us all.

Vicki McClure, a young supermarket checker with a voice that was perfect for the moment, sang,

> Reach out and touch somebody's hand
> Make this world a better place if you can. . . .

Everyone in the place stood, held hands, and swayed to the music. There were smiles all around, and tears—many tears to join ours.

If you had looked, you would have seen fifteen faces turned toward the big flame. We couldn't take our eyes off it. To us, it was still the little spark in the lamp we had helped to carry across America.

36

We'll See

NEW YORK, FALL 1984

Moments after the Ray's Pizza guy dropped off a pepperoni and extra cheese medium, I turned on the TV. I was alone at Billy Rappaport's East Sixty-fifth Street apartment with a night off from the Mondale campaign, waiting for a call about my next assignment. Any realist knew that Mondale couldn't win even if Reagan got caught naked with a sheep, but I justified my involvement as an advance person for Geraldine Ferraro by reminding myself how important it is for a woman to run for national office. That's a part of it, but to tell the complete truth, I didn't want to say good-bye to the road.

The Republican convention was on every station. I hoped at least it wouldn't go long and bump Letterman off. Half listening, slurping pizza, and skimming a magazine, I noticed the president, about to accept his nomination. My eyes shot to the screen. Ronald Reagan was using the relay as the skeleton of his whole speech about how patriotic and proud our country is. He didn't miss a beat:

> . . . All along the way that torch became a celebration of America. And we all became participants in the celebration. . . . There was Ansel Stubbs, a youngster of ninety-nine, who passed the torch in Kansas to four-year-old Katie Johnston. . . . In West Virginia, the runner came across a line of deaf children and let each one pass the torch for a few feet, and at the end, those youngsters' hands talked excitedly in their sign language. Crowds spontaneously began singing "The Battle Hymn of the Republic."
>
> And then in San Francisco, a Vietnamese immigrant—his little son held up on his shoulders—dodged photographers and police motorcy-

cles to cheer a nineteen-year-old black man pushing an eighty-eight-year-old white woman in a wheelchair as she carried the torch.

My friends, that's America.

I put down the slice of pizza and sat in stunned silence.

Of course the politicians, corporations, and mass media got hold of what we had all felt. I could only smile, though. All of us along the route of the torch—everyone who saw it and took inspiration from it—shared a moment that, no matter what uses it might be put to, we will always have.

People don't have to be told about what to love. Mile after mile, we saw people who love this country. Not because any of us thinks it's perfect. Maybe because we're so keenly aware that it isn't. People have their own kindness, and basic goodness, and tenacity. Mile after mile, behind the applause and the tears, we saw people who spend most of their lives being completely willing to work. They do what they can to make life better, not just for themselves but for other people they don't even know. People might not have fancy words for what they're doing. I never heard one person call himself or herself an idealist or a patriot out there on the road. They just get down and slog through the work it takes to make themselves move. It doesn't take much to keep people going—just a little glimmer of motion every once in a while, a little sign that they're getting somewhere.

During the Olympics, I'd gone to events at the Coliseum, where the flame burned high over the crowds. I'd almost go into a trance, staring at it. I still didn't know exactly what I had seen and felt in that summer of '84, and I stared at the flame as if some answers might appear in it.

Not everybody is getting where he or she wants to get. I saw sad things that need fixing, and knew even at the time that I was passing them by. More than likely, most of my view of America was buffered by my job and expense account. But what I did see was the people of a diverse and sometimes divided country, lining up for nine thousand miles along the parade route of the torch to celebrate their freedom and hope. The hope was celebrated not only by those who have benefited the most from the American Dream, but just as openly by those who are not as fortunate. Sometimes I wonder, now that we have shed our tears together, if we will go back and forget why we were so moved.

When I was growing up, I would go to baseball games and think it was a nuisance to have to wait through "The Star-Spangled Banner." Last week I went to a game and when we all stood up for the national anthem I felt my eyes sting and without thinking I started to sing along.

The Route Taken by the Olympic Torch

New York, NY
New Haven, CT
Mystic, CT
Providence, RI
Boston, MA
Hartford, CT
Waterbury, CT
West Point, NY
Princeton, NJ
Lawrenceville, NJ
Trenton, NJ
Philadelphia, PA
Wilmington, DE
Baltimore, MD
Annapolis, MD
Washington, DC
Fairfax, VA
Romney, WV
Morgantown, WV
Pittsburgh, PA
Youngstown, OH
Cleveland, OH
Vermilion, OH
Toledo, OH
Detroit, MI
Flint, MI
Battle Creek, MI
Lansing, MI
Chicago, IL
Lake Village, IN

Indianapolis, IN
Louisville, KY
Lexington, KY
Frankfort, KY
Knoxville, TN
Cherokee, NC
Murphy, NC
Blairsville, GA
Atlanta, GA
Irondale, AL
Birmingham, AL
Fulton, MS
Memphis, TN
Turrell, AR
Apple Creek, MO
St. Louis, MO
Jefferson City, MO
Warrensburg, MO
Kansas City, MO and KS
Topeka, KS
Tulsa, OK
Oklahoma City, OK
Dixon, OK
Dallas, TX
Forth Worth, TX
Benjamin, TX
Guthrie, TX
Lubbock, TX
Melrose, NM
Fort Sumner, NM

Albuquerque, NM

Santa Fe, NM

Nathrop, CO

Colorado Springs, CO

Denver, CO

Golden, CO

Steamboat Springs, CO

Vernal, UT

Roosevelt, UT

Salt Lake City, UT

Tremonton, UT

Twin Falls, ID

Boise, ID

Pendleton, OR

Kennewick, WA

Moses Lake, WA

Seattle, WA

Olympia, WA

Portland, OR

Salem, OR

Eugene, OR

Springfield, OR

Cascade Summit, OR

Tulelake, CA

Susanville, CA

Reno, NV

Carson City, NV

South Lake Tahoe, CA

Placerville, CA

Sacramento, CA

Oakland, CA

San Francisco, CA

San Jose, CA

Pacific Grove, CA

San Luis Obispo, CA

Santa Barbara, CA

Malibu, CA

Los Angeles, CA

San Bernardino, CA

San Diego, CA

Camp Pendleton, CA

San Clemente, CA

Garden Grove, CA

Long Beach, CA

Los Angeles, CA